ADAPTIVE STREAM MINING: PATTERN LEARNING AND MINING FROM EVOLVING DATA STREAMS

Frontiers in Artificial Intelligence and Applications

FAIA covers all aspects of theoretical and applied artificial intelligence research in the form of monographs, doctoral dissertations, textbooks, handbooks and proceedings volumes. The FAIA series contains several sub-series, including "Information Modelling and Knowledge Bases" and "Knowledge-Based Intelligent Engineering Systems". It also includes the biennial ECAI, the European Conference on Artificial Intelligence, proceedings volumes, and other ECCAI – the European Coordinating Committee on Artificial Intelligence – sponsored publications. An editorial panel of internationally well-known scholars is appointed to provide a high quality selection.

Series Editors:
J. Breuker, R. Dieng-Kuntz, N. Guarino, J.N. Kok, J. Liu, R. López de Mántaras,
R. Mizoguchi, M. Musen, S.K. Pal and N. Zhong

Volume 207

Recently published in this series

Vol. 206. T. Welzer Družovec et al. (Eds.), Information Modelling and Knowledge Bases XXI
Vol. 205. G. Governatori (Ed.), Legal Knowledge and Information Systems – JURIX 2009: The Twenty-Second Annual Conference
Vol. 204. B. Apolloni, S. Bassis and C.F. Morabito (Eds.), Neural Nets WIRN09 – Proceedings of the 19th Italian Workshop on Neural Nets
Vol. 203. M. Džbor, Design Problems, Frames and Innovative Solutions
Vol. 202. S. Sandri, M. Sànchez-Marrè and U. Cortés (Eds.), Artificial Intelligence Research and Development – Proceedings of the 12th International Conference of the Catalan Association for Artificial Intelligence
Vol. 201. J.E. Agudo et al. (Eds.), Techniques and Applications for Mobile Commerce – Proceedings of TAMoCo 2009
Vol. 200. V. Dimitrova et al. (Eds.), Artificial Intelligence in Education – Building Learning Systems that Care: From Knowledge Representation to Affective Modelling
Vol. 199. H. Fujita and V. Mařík (Eds.), New Trends in Software Methodologies, Tools and Techniques – Proceedings of the Eighth SoMeT_09
Vol. 198. R. Ferrario and A. Oltramari (Eds.), Formal Ontologies Meet Industry
Vol. 197. R. Hoekstra, Ontology Representation – Design Patterns and Ontologies that Make Sense
Vol. 196. F. Masulli et al. (Eds.), Computational Intelligence and Bioengineering – Essays in Memory of Antonina Starita
Vol. 195. A. Boer, Legal Theory, Sources of Law and the Semantic Web
Vol. 194. A. Petcu, A Class of Algorithms for Distributed Constraint Optimization

ISSN 0922-6389

Adaptive Stream Mining: Pattern Learning and Mining from Evolving Data Streams

Albert Bifet

Computer Science Department, University of Waikato, Hamilton, New Zealand

Amsterdam • Berlin • Tokyo • Washington, DC

© 2010 The author and IOS Press.

All rights reserved. No part of this book may be reproduced, stored in a retrieval system, or transmitted, in any form or by any means, without prior written permission from the publisher.

ISBN 978-1-60750-090-2 (print)
ISBN 978-1-60750-472-6 (online)
Library of Congress Control Number: 2009942750
doi: 10.3233/978-1-60750-472-6-i

Publisher
IOS Press BV
Nieuwe Hemweg 6B
1013 BG Amsterdam
Netherlands
fax: +31 20 687 0019
e-mail: order@iospress.nl

Distributor in the USA and Canada
IOS Press, Inc.
4502 Rachael Manor Drive
Fairfax, VA 22032
USA
fax: +1 703 323 3668
e-mail: iosbooks@iospress.com

LEGAL NOTICE

The publisher is not responsible for the use which might be made of the following information.

PRINTED IN THE NETHERLANDS

Foreword

Knowledge Discovery from data streams is one of the most relevant challenges that we face today. Data mining algorithms for analyzing static data sets, assuming stationary distributions, unlimited memory, and generating static models are almost obsolete for the real challenging problems we are faced nowadays.

Albert's research is not in the established data mining. He does steps ahead, focusing his research in cutting-the-edge topics, methods and algorithms. His work focuses on evolving data, going far way from iid assumption. Models are not static, training sets are not fixed. Albert's approach tries to capture the dynamics of patterns in the problem under study: how patterns evolve, grow, decrease and die.

The book focus on the design of learning algorithms for evolving and time-changing data streams. The basic building block is the adaptive sliding window algorithm, `ADWIN`, for change detection and value estimation with strong theoretical guarantees. The book presents evidence of the advantages of the framework in predictive learning, clustering, and closed frequent tree mining from time-changing data streams. The work opens new research opportunities and a large space for applications. The work presents an in-depth study in streaming mining. The author carefully presents theoretical analysis of the proposed methods and algorithms. It introduces new contributions on several different aspects of the problem. Overall this is an interesting dissertation that makes significant contributions to mining time-changing streams.

It is not a surprise, the author's good record of publications in top-level conferences. The ideas come from and reflect a world in movement: a pleasure to read. I'm sure you will enjoy it.

Porto, 21 November, 2009
João Gama

Preface

Green computing is the study and practice of using computing resources efficiently. A main approach to green computing is based on algorithmic efficiency. In the data stream model, data arrive at high speed, and the algorithms that must process them have very strict constraints of space and time. The first part of this book introduces a framework for developing algorithms that can adaptively learn from data streams that change over time. These methods are based on using change detectors and estimator modules at the right places. It presents an adaptive sliding window algorithm ADWIN for detecting change and keeping updated statistics from a data stream, and use it as a black-box in place or counters or accumulators in algorithms initially not designed for drifting data. Since ADWIN has rigorous performance guarantees, this opens the possibility of extending such guarantees to learning and mining algorithms. This methodology is tested with several learning methods as Naïve Bayes, clustering, decision trees and ensemble methods. An experimental framework for data stream mining with concept drift is built, based on the MOA framework, similar to WEKA, so that it will be easy for researchers to run experimental data stream benchmarks.

Trees are connected acyclic graphs and they are studied as link-based structures in many cases. The second part of this book describes a rather formal study of trees from the point of view of closure-based mining. Moreover, it presents efficient algorithms for subtree testing and for mining ordered and unordered frequent closed trees. An analysis of the extraction of association rules of full confidence out of the closed sets of trees is included, and it is found there an interesting phenomenon: rules whose propositional counterpart is nontrivial are, however, always implicitly true in trees due to the peculiar combinatorics of the structures.

And finally, using these results on evolving data streams mining and closed frequent tree mining, the last part of the book presents high performance algorithms for mining closed unlabeled rooted trees adaptively from data streams that change over time. It introduces a general methodology to identify closed patterns in a data stream. Using this methodology, it then develops an incremental one, a sliding-window based one, and finally one that mines closed trees adaptively from data streams. It uses these methods to introduce classification methods for tree data streams.

Many people deserve my thanks. I am extremely grateful to my phD advisors, Ricard Gavaldà and José L. Balcázar. They have been great role models as researchers, mentors, and friends. Ricard provided me with the ideal environment to work, his valuable and enjoyable time, and his wisdom. I admire him deeply for his way to ask questions, and his silent sapience. I learnt from him that less may be more.

José L. has been always motivating me for going further and further. His enthusiasm, dedication, and impressive depth of knowledge has been of great inspiration to me. He is a man of genius and I learnt from him to focus and spend time on important things.

I would like to thank Antoni Lozano for his support and friendship. Without him, this book could not have been possible. Also, I would like to thank Víctor Dalmau, for introducing me to research, and Jorge Castro for showing me the beauty of high motivating objectives.

I am also greatly indebted with Geoff Holmes and Bernhard Pfahringer for the pleasure of collaborating with them and for encouraging me, the very promising work on MOA stream mining. And João Gama, for writing the Foreword of this book and for introducing and teaching me new and astonishing aspects of mining data streams.

I thank all my coauthors, Carlos Castillo, Paul Chirita, Ingmar Weber, Manuel Baena, José del Campo, Raúl Fidalgo, Rafael Morales, and Richard Kirkby for their help and collaboration. I want to thank Jesse Read, Eibe Frank, Ian Witten, Stefan Mutter, Robert Larkins, Edmond Zhang and my former officemates at LSI for their support: Marc Comas, Bernat Gel, Carlos Mérida, David Cabanillas, Carlos Arizmendi, Mario Fadda, Ignacio Barrio, Felix Castro, Ivan Olier, and Josep Pujol.

Most of all, I am grateful to my family.

Contents

I	Introduction and Preliminaries	1

1	Introduction	3
	1.1 Data Mining	3
	1.2 Data stream mining	4
	1.3 Frequent tree pattern mining	6
	1.4 Overview of the book	9

2	Preliminaries	13
	2.1 Classification and Clustering	13
	2.1.1 Naïve Bayes	14
	2.1.2 Decision Trees	14
	2.1.3 k-means clustering	15
	2.2 Change Detection and Value Estimation	15
	2.2.1 Change Detection	16
	2.2.2 Estimation	18
	2.3 Frequent Pattern Mining	21
	2.4 Mining data streams: state of the art	22
	2.4.1 Sliding Windows in data streams	23
	2.4.2 Classification in data streams	23
	2.4.3 Clustering in data streams	26
	2.5 Frequent pattern mining: state of the art	26
	2.5.1 CMTreeMiner	28
	2.5.2 DRYADEPARENT	29
	2.5.3 Streaming Pattern Mining	29

II	Evolving Data Stream Learning	31

3	Mining Evolving Data Streams	33
	3.1 Introduction	33
	3.1.1 Theoretical approaches	34
	3.2 Algorithms for mining with change	34
	3.2.1 FLORA: Widmer and Kubat	35
	3.2.2 Suport Vector Machines: Klinkenberg	35
	3.2.3 OLIN: Last	36
	3.2.4 CVFDT: Domingos	37

		3.2.5	UFFT: Gama	37
	3.3	A Methodology for Adaptive Stream Mining		39
		3.3.1	Time Change Detectors and Predictors: A General Framework	40
		3.3.2	Window Management Models	42
	3.4	Optimal Change Detector and Predictor		44
	3.5	Experimental Setting		45
		3.5.1	Concept Drift Framework	47
		3.5.2	Datasets for concept drift	49
		3.5.3	MOA Experimental Framework	52

4 Adaptive Sliding Windows — 53

	4.1	Introduction		53
	4.2	Maintaining Updated Windows of Varying Length		54
		4.2.1	Setting	54
		4.2.2	First algorithm: ADWIN0	54
		4.2.3	ADWIN0 for Poisson processes	59
		4.2.4	Improving time and memory requirements	60
	4.3	Experimental Validation of ADWIN		64
	4.4	Example 1: Incremental Naïve Bayes Predictor		72
		4.4.1	Experiments on Synthetic Data	74
		4.4.2	Real-world data experiments	75
	4.5	Example 2: Incremental k-means Clustering		78
		4.5.1	Experiments	79
	4.6	K-ADWIN = ADWIN + Kalman Filtering		79
		4.6.1	Experimental Validation of K-ADWIN	81
		4.6.2	Example 1: Naïve Bayes Predictor	83
		4.6.3	Example 2: k-means Clustering	83
		4.6.4	K-ADWIN Experimental Validation Conclusions	84
	4.7	Time and Memory Requirements		86

5 Decision Trees — 89

	5.1	Introduction		89
	5.2	Decision Trees on Sliding Windows		90
		5.2.1	HWT-ADWIN : Hoeffding Window Tree using ADWIN	90
		5.2.2	CVFDT	93
	5.3	Hoeffding Adaptive Trees		94
		5.3.1	Example of performance Guarantee	95
		5.3.2	Memory Complexity Analysis	96
	5.4	Experimental evaluation		96
	5.5	Time and memory		102

6 Ensemble Methods — 105
- 6.1 Bagging and Boosting — 105
- 6.2 New method of Bagging using trees of different size — 106
- 6.3 New method of Bagging using `ADWIN` — 109
- 6.4 Adaptive Hoeffding Option Trees — 109
- 6.5 Comparative Experimental Evaluation — 109

III Closed Frequent Tree Mining — 115

7 Mining Frequent Closed Rooted Trees — 117
- 7.1 Introduction — 117
- 7.2 Basic Algorithmics and Mathematical Properties — 118
  - 7.2.1 Number of subtrees — 119
  - 7.2.2 Finding the intersection of trees recursively — 120
  - 7.2.3 Finding the intersection by dynamic programming — 122
- 7.3 Closure Operator on Trees — 123
  - 7.3.1 Galois Connection — 125
- 7.4 Level Representations — 127
  - 7.4.1 Subtree Testing in Ordered Trees — 130
- 7.5 Mining Frequent Ordered Trees — 131
- 7.6 Unordered Subtrees — 132
  - 7.6.1 Subtree Testing in Unordered Trees — 133
  - 7.6.2 Mining frequent closed subtrees in the unordered case — 133
  - 7.6.3 Closure-based mining — 136
- 7.7 Induced subtrees and Labeled trees — 137
  - 7.7.1 Induced subtrees — 137
  - 7.7.2 Labeled trees — 138
- 7.8 Applications — 138
  - 7.8.1 Datasets for mining closed frequent trees — 138
  - 7.8.2 Intersection set cardinality — 140
  - 7.8.3 Unlabeled trees — 141
  - 7.8.4 Labeled trees — 145

8 Mining Implications from Lattices of Closed Trees — 153
- 8.1 Introduction — 153
- 8.2 Itemsets association rules — 155
  - 8.2.1 Classical Propositional Horn Logic — 156
- 8.3 Association Rules — 158
- 8.4 On Finding Implicit Rules for Subtrees — 160
- 8.5 Experimental Validation — 166

IV Evolving Tree Data Stream Mining — 169

9 Mining Adaptively Frequent Closed Rooted Trees — 171
9.1 Relaxed support — 171
9.2 Closure Operator on Patterns — 172
9.3 Closed Pattern Mining — 174
    9.3.1 Incremental Closed Pattern Mining — 174
    9.3.2 Closed pattern mining over a sliding window — 176
9.4 Adaptive closed pattern mining — 176
    9.4.1 Closed pattern mining in the presence of distribution change — 176
9.5 Closed Tree Mining Application — 177
    9.5.1 Incremental Closed Tree Mining — 177
9.6 Experimental Evaluation — 178
    9.6.1 Unlabeled Trees — 178
    9.6.2 Labeled Trees — 181

10 Adaptive XML Tree Classification — 187
10.1 Introduction — 187
10.2 Classification using Compressed Frequent Patterns — 189
    10.2.1 Closed Frequent Patterns — 191
    10.2.2 Maximal Frequent Patterns — 191
10.3 XML Tree Classification framework on data streams — 192
    10.3.1 Adaptive Tree Mining on evolving data streams — 193
10.4 Experimental evaluation — 194

Bibliography — 199

Part I

Introduction and Preliminaries

Introduction

In today's information society, extraction of knowledge is becoming a very important task for many people. We live in an age of knowledge revolution. Peter Drucker [Dru92], an influential management expert, writes "From now on, the key is knowledge. The world is not becoming labor intensive, not material intensive, not energy intensive, but knowledge intensive". This knowledge revolution is based in an economic change from adding value by producing things which is, ultimately limited, to adding value by creating and using knowledge which can grow indefinitely.

The digital universe in 2007 was estimated in [GRC$^+$08] to be 281 exabytes or 281 billion gigabytes, and by 2011, the digital universe will be 10 times the size it was 5 years before. The amount of information created, or captured exceeded available storage for the first time in 2007.

To deal with these huge amount of data in a responsible way, green computing is becoming a necessity. *Green computing* is the study and practice of using computing resources efficiently. A main approach to green computing is based on algorithmic efficiency. The amount of computer resources required for any given computing function depends on the efficiency of the algorithms used. As the cost of hardware has declined relative to the cost of energy, the energy efficiency and environmental impact of computing systems and programs are receiving increased attention.

1.1 Data Mining

Data mining (DM) [HK06, HMS01, WF05, MR05, BL99, BL04, LB01], also called Knowledge Discovery in Databases (KDD) has been defined as "the nontrivial extraction of implicit, previously unknown, and potentially useful information from data" and "the science of extracting useful information from large data sets or databases". Data mining is a complex topic and has links with multiple core fields such as statistics [HTF01], information retrieval [BYRN99, Cha02a, LB01], machine learning [Lan95, Mit97] and pattern recognition [DHS00, PM04].

Data mining uses tools such as classification, association rule mining, clustering, etc. Data is generated and collected from many sources: scientific data, financial data, marketing data, medical data, demographical data, etc. Nowadays, we are also overwhelmed by data generated by computers and machines: Internet routers, sensors, agents, webservers and the grid are some examples.

The most important challenges in data mining [Luc08] belong to one of the following:

Challenges due to the size of data Data is generated and collected permanently, so its volume is becoming very large. Traditional methods assume that we can store all data in memory and there is no time limitation. With massive data, we have space and time restrictions. An important fact is that data is evolving over time, so we need methods that adapt automatically, without the need to restart from scratch every time a change on the data is detected.

Challenges due to the complexity of data types Nowadays, we deal with complex types of data: XML trees, DNA sequences, GPS temporal and spatial information. New techniques are needed to manage such complex types of data.

Challenges due to user interaction The mining process is a complex task, and is not easily understandable by all kind of users. The user needs to interact with the mining process, asking queries, and understanding the results of these queries. Not all users have the same background knowledge of the data mining process, so the challenge is to guide people through most of this discovery process.

In this book, we deal with two problems of data mining that relate to the first and second challenges :

- Mining evolving massive data streams

- Mining closed frequent tree patterns

In the last part of this book, we focus on mining massive and evolving tree datasets, combining these two problems at the same time.

1.2 Data stream mining

Digital data in many organizations can grow without limit at a high rate of millions of data items per day. Every day WalMart records 20 million transactions, Google [BCCW05] handles 100 million searches, and AT&T produces 275 million call records. Several applications naturally generate data streams: financial tickers, performance measurements in network monitoring and traffic management, log records or click-streams in web tracking and personalization, manufacturing processes, data feeds from sensor applications, call detail records in telecommunications, email messages, and others.

The main challenge is that 'data-intensive' mining is constrained by limited resources of time, memory, and sample size. Data mining has traditionally been performed over static datasets, where data mining algorithms can afford to read the input data several times. When the source of data items is an open-ended data stream, not all data can be loaded into the memory and off-line mining with a fixed size dataset is no longer technically feasible due to the unique features of streaming data.

The following constraints apply in the Data Stream model:

1. The amount of data that has arrived and will arrive in the future is extremely large; in fact, the sequence is potentially infinite. Thus, it is impossible to store it all. Only a small summary can be computed and stored, and the rest of the information is thrown away. Even if the information could be all stored, it would be unfeasible to go over it for further processing.

2. The speed of arrival is large, so that each particular element has to be processed essentially in real time, and then discarded.

3. The distribution generating the items can change over time. Thus, data from the past may become irrelevant (or even harmful) for the current summary.

Constraints 1 and 2 limit the amount of memory and time-per-item that the streaming algorithm can use. Intense research on the algorithmics of Data Streams has produced a large body of techniques for computing fundamental functions with low memory and time-per-item, usually in combination with the sliding-window technique discussed next.

Constraint 3, the need to adapt to time changes, has been also intensely studied. A typical approach for dealing is based on the use of so-called sliding windows: The algorithm keeps a window of size W containing the last W data items that have arrived (say, in the last W time steps). When a new item arrives, the oldest element in the window is deleted to make place for it. The summary of the Data Stream is at every moment computed or rebuilt from the data in the window only. If W is of moderate size, this essentially takes care of the requirement to use low memory.

In most cases, the quantity W is assumed to be externally defined, and fixed through the execution of the algorithm. The underlying hypothesis is that the user can guess W so that the distribution of the data can be thought to be essentially constant in most intervals of size W; that is, the distribution changes smoothly at a rate that is small w.r.t. W, or it can change drastically from time to time, but the time between two drastic changes is often much greater than W.

Unfortunately, in most of the cases the user does not know in advance what the rate of change is going to be, so its choice of W is unlikely to be optimal. Not only that, the rate of change can itself vary over time, so the optimal W may itself vary over time.

1.3 Frequent tree pattern mining

Tree-structured representations are a main key idea pervading all of Computer Science; many link-based structures may be studied formally by means of trees. From the B+ indices that make our commercial Database Management Systems useful, through search-tree or heap data structures or Tree Automata, up to the decision tree structures in Artificial Intelligence and Decision Theory, or the parsing structures in Compiler Design, in Natural Language Processing, or in the now-ubiquitous XML, they often represent an optimal compromise between the conceptual simplicity and processing efficiency of strings and the harder but much richer knowledge representations based on graphs. Accordingly, a wealth of variations of the basic notions, both of the structures themselves (binary, bounded-rank, unranked, ordered, unordered) or of their relationships (like induced or embedded top-down or bottom-up subtree relations) have been proposed for study and motivated applications. In particular, mining frequent trees is becoming an important task, with broad applications including chemical informatics [HAKU$^+$08], computer vision [LG99], text retrieval [WIZD04], bioinformatics [SWZ04] [HJWZ95], and Web analysis [Cha02b] [Zak02]. Some applications of frequent tree mining are the following [CMNK01]:

- Gaining general information of data sources
- Directly using the discovered frequent substructures
- Constraint based mining
- Association rule mining
- Classification and clustering
- Helping standard database indexing and access methods design
- Tree mining as a step towards efficient graph mining

For example, association rules using web log data may give useful information [CMNK01]. An association rule that an online bookstore may find interesting is "According to the web logs, 90% visitors to the web page for book A visited the customer evaluation section, the book description section, and the table of contents of the book (which is a subsection of the book description section)." Such an association rule can provide the bookstore with insights that can help improve the web site design.

Closure-based mining on purely relational data, that is, itemset mining, is by now well-established, and there are interesting algorithmic developments. Sharing some of the attractive features of frequency-based summarization of subsets, it offers an alternative view with several advantages; among them, there are the facts that, first, by imposing closure, the number of frequent sets is heavily reduced and, second, the possibility appears of developing a mathematical foundation that connects closure-based mining with lattice-theoretic approaches such as Formal Concept Analysis. A downside, however, is that, at the time of influencing the practice of Data Mining, their conceptual sophistication is higher than that of frequent sets, which are, therefore, preferred often by non-experts. Thus, there have been subsequent efforts in moving towards closure-based mining on structured data.

Trees are connected acyclic graphs, *rooted trees* are trees with a vertex singled out as the root, n-*ary trees* are trees for which each node which is not a leaf has at most n children, and *unranked* trees are trees with unbounded arity.

We say that $t_1, \ldots, t_k$ are the *components* of tree t if t is made of a node (the root) joined to the roots of all the t_i's. We can distinguish betweeen the cases where the components at each node form a sequence (ordered trees) or just a multiset (*unordered trees*). For example, the following two trees are two different ordered trees, but they are the same unordered tree.

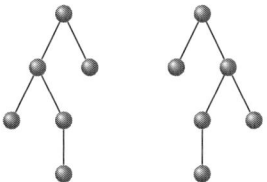

In this book, we will deal with rooted, unranked trees. Most of the time, we will not assume the presence of labels on the nodes, however in some sections we will deal with labeled trees. The contributions of this text mainly concern on unlabeled trees.

An *induced subtree* of a tree t is any connected subgraph rooted at some node v of t that its vertices and edges are subsets of those of t. An *embedded subtree* of a tree t is any connected subgraph rooted at some node v of t that does not break the ancestor-descendant relationship among the vertices of t. We are interested in induced subtrees. Formally, let s be a rooted tree with vertex set V' and edge set E', and t a rooted tree t with vertex set V and edge set E. Tree s is an *induced subtree* (or simply a *subtree*) of t (written $t' \preceq t$) if and only if 1) $V' \subseteq V$, 2) $E' \subseteq E$, and 3) the labeling of V' is preserved in t. This notation can be extended to sets of trees $A \preceq B$: for all t ∈ A, there is some t′ ∈ B for which t ≼ t′.

In order to compare link-based structures, we will also be interested in a notion of subtree where the root is preserved. In the unordered case, a tree t′ is a *top-down subtree* (or simply a *subtree*) of a tree t (written t′ ≼ t) if t′ is a connected subgraph of t which contains the root of t. Note that the ordering of the children is not relevant. In the ordered case, the order of the existing children of each node must be additionally preserved. All along this book, the main place where it is relevant whether we are using ordered or unordered trees is the choice of the implementation of the test for the subtree notion.

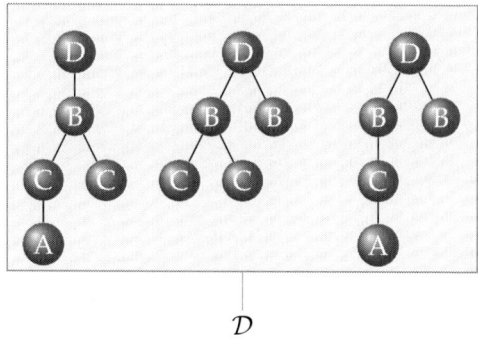

Figure 1.1: A dataset example

Given a finite dataset $\mathcal{D}$ of transactions, where each transaction $s \in \mathcal{D}$ is an unlabeled rooted tree, we say that a transaction s *supports* a tree t if the tree t is a subtree of the transaction s. Figure 1.1 shows a finite dataset example. The number of transactions in the dataset $\mathcal{D}$ that support t is called the *support* of the tree t. A tree t is called *frequent* if its support is greater than or equal to a given threshold min_sup. The frequent tree mining problem is to find all frequent trees in a given dataset. Any subtree of a frequent tree is also frequent and, therefore, any supertree of a nonfrequent tree is also nonfrequent.

We define a frequent tree t to be *closed* if none of its proper supertrees has the same support as it has. Generally, there are much fewer closed trees than frequent ones. In fact, we can obtain all frequent subtrees with their support from the set of closed frequent subtrees with their supports, as explained later on: whereas this is immediate for itemsets, in the case of trees we will need to organize appropriately the frequent closed trees; just the list of frequent trees with their supports does not suffice. However, organized as we will propose, the set of closed frequent subtrees maintains the same information as the set of all frequent subtrees

1.4 Overview of the book

The structure of the book is as follows:

- **Chapter 2.** We introduce some preliminaries on data mining, data streams and frequent closed trees. We review the classic change detector and estimator algorithms and we survey briefly the most important classification, clustering, and frequent pattern mining methods available in the literature.

- **Chapter 3.** We study the evolving data stream mining problem. We present a new general algorithm framework to deal with change detection and value estimation, and a new experimental framework for concept drift.

- **Chapter 4.** We propose our adaptive sliding window method ADWIN, using the general framework presented in the previous chapter. The algorithm automatically grows the window when no change is apparent, and shrinks it when data changes. We provide rigorous guarantees of its performance, in the form of bounds on the rates of false positives and false negatives. We perform some experimental evaluation on Naïve Bayes and k−means.

- **Chapter 5.** We propose adaptive decision tree methods. After presenting the Hoeffding Window Tree method, a Hoeffding Adaptive Tree is presented using the general framework presented in Chapter 3 and the ADWIN method presented in Chapter 4.

- **Chapter 6.** We propose two new bagging methods able to deal with evolving data streams: one that uses trees of different size, and one that uses using ADWIN. Using the experimental framework of Chapter 3, we carry our experimental comparison of several classification methods.

- **Chapter 7.** We propose methods for closed tree mining. First we present a new closure operator for trees and a powerful representation for unlabelled trees. We present some new mining methods for mining closed trees in a non incremental way.

- **Chapter 8.** We propose a way of extracting high-confidence association rules from datasets consisting of unlabeled trees. We discuss in more detail the case of rules that always hold, independently of the dataset.

- **Chapter 9.** We combine the methods of Chapters 3 and 4, and Chapters 7 and 8 to propose a general adaptive closed pattern mining method for data streams and, in particular, an adaptive closed tree mining algorithm. We design an incremental closed tree mining method, a sliding window mining method and finally, using `ADWIN` an adaptive closed tree mining algorithm.

- **Chapter 10.** We propose a new general method to classify patterns, using closed and maximal frequent patterns. We design a framework to classify XML trees, composed by a Tree XML Closed Frequent Miner, and a classifier algorithm.

The results in this book appeared in the following publications:

- Chapter 3 contains results from [BG06] and part of [BHP+09]

[BG06] Albert Bifet and Ricard Gavaldà. Kalman filters and adaptive windows for learning in data streams. In *Discovery Science*, pages 29–40, 2006.

[BHP+09] Albert Bifet, Geoff Holmes, Bernhard Pfahringer, Richard Kirkby, and Ricard Gavaldà. New ensemble methods for evolving data streams. In *15th ACM SIGKDD International Conference on Knowledge Discovery and Data Mining*, 2009.

- Chapter 4 contains results from [BG07c, BG06]

[BG07c] Albert Bifet and Ricard Gavaldà. Learning from time-changing data with adaptive windowing. In *SIAM International Conference on Data Mining*, 2007.

[BG06] Albert Bifet and Ricard Gavaldà. Kalman filters and adaptive windows for learning in data streams. In *Discovery Science*, pages 29–40, 2006.

- Chapter 5 is from [BG09a]

[BG09] Albert Bifet and Ricard Gavaldà. Adaptive parameter-free learning from evolving data streams. In *8th International Symposium on Intelligent Data Analysis*, 2009.

- Chapter 6 is from [BHP+09]

[BHP+09] Albert Bifet, Geoff Holmes, Bernhard Pfahringer, Richard Kirkby, and Ricard Gavaldà. New ensemble methods for evolving data streams. In *15th ACM SIGKDD International Conference on Knowledge Discovery and Data Mining*, 2009.

- Chapter 7 contains results from [BBL06, BBL07b, BBL07c, BBL07a, BBL09]

1.4. OVERVIEW OF THE BOOK

[BBL06] José L. Balcázar, Albert Bifet, and Antoni Lozano. Intersection algorithms and a closure operator on unordered trees. In *MLG 2006, 4th International Workshop on Mining and Learning with Graphs*, 2006.

[BBL07b] José L. Balcázar, Albert Bifet, and Antoni Lozano. Mining frequent closed unordered trees through natural representations. In *ICCS 2007, 15th International Conference on Conceptual Structures*, pages 347–359, 2007.

[BBL07c] José L. Balcázar, Albert Bifet, and Antoni Lozano. Subtree testing and closed tree mining through natural representations. In *DEXA Workshops*, pages 499–503, 2007.

[BBL07a] José L. Balcázar, Albert Bifet, and Antoni Lozano. Closed and maximal tree mining using natural representations. In *MLG 2007, 5th International Workshop on Mining and Learning with Graphs*, 2007.

[BBL09] José L. Balcázar, Albert Bifet, and Antoni Lozano. Mining Frequent Closed Rooted Trees. In *Machine Learning Journal*, 2009. Includes results from [BBL06, BBL07b, BBL07c, BBL07a].

- Chapter 8 contains results from [BBL08]

[BBL08] José L. Balcázar, Albert Bifet, and Antoni Lozano. Mining implications from lattices of closed trees. In *Extraction et gestion des connaissances (EGC'2008)*, pages 373–384, 2008.

- Chapter 9 contains results from [BG08]

[BG08] Albert Bifet and Ricard Gavaldà. Mining adaptively frequent closed unlabeled rooted trees in data streams. In *14th ACM SIGKDD International Conference on Knowledge Discovery and Data Mining*, 2008.

- Chapter 10 is from [BG09b]

[BG09] Albert Bifet and Ricard Gavaldà. Adaptive XML Tree Classification on evolving data streams In *Machine Learning and Knowledge Discovery in Databases, European Conference, ECML/PKDD*, 2009.

2
Preliminaries

In the first part of this book, the data mining techniques that we will use come essentially from Machine Learning. In particular, we will use the traditional distinction between supervised and unsupervised learning. In *supervised* methods data instances are labelled with a "correct answer" and in *unsupervised* methods they are unlabelled. Classifiers are typical examples of *supervised* methods, and clusterers of *unsupervised* methods.

In the second part of this book, we will focus on closed frequent pattern mining. Association rule learning is the task of discovering interesting relations between patterns in large datasets, and it is very closely related to pattern mining.

2.1 Classification and Clustering

Classification is the distribution of a set of instances of examples into groups or classes according to some common relations or affinities. Given n_C different classes, a classifier algorithm builds a model that predicts for every unlabelled instance I the class C to which it belongs with accuracy. A spam filter is an example of classifier, deciding every new incoming e-mail, if it is a valid message or not.

The discrete classification problem is generally defined as follows. A set of N training examples of the form (x, y) is given, where y is a discrete class label and x is a vector of d attributes, each of which may be symbolic or numeric. The goal is to produce from these examples a model f that will predict the class $y = f(x)$ of future examples x with high accuracy. For example, x could be a description of a costumer's recent purchases, and y the decision to send that customer a catalog or not; or x could be a record of a costumer cellphone call, and y the decision whether it is fraudulent or not.

The basic difference between a classifier and a clusterer is the labelling of data instances. In *supervised* methods data instances are labelled and in *unsupervised* methods they are unlabelled. A classifier is a *supervised* method, and a clusterer is a *unsupervised* method.

Literally hundreds of model kinds and model building methods have been proposed in the literature (see [WF05]). Here we will review only those that we will use in this book.

2.1.1 Naïve Bayes

Naïve Bayes is a classifier algorithm known for its simplicity and low computational cost. Given n_C different classes, the trained Naïve Bayes classifier predicts for every unlabelled instance I the class C to which it belongs with high accuracy.

The model works as follows: Let $x_1, \ldots, x_k$ be k discrete attributes, and assume that x_i can take n_i different values. Let C be the class attribute, which can take n_C different values. Upon receiving an unlabelled instance $I = (x_1 = v_1, \ldots, x_k = v_k)$, the Naïve Bayes classifier computes a "probability" of I being in class c as:

$$\Pr[C = c | I] \cong \prod_{i=1}^{k} \Pr[x_i = v_i | C = c]$$

$$= \Pr[C = c] \cdot \prod_{i=1}^{k} \frac{\Pr[x_i = v_i \wedge C = c]}{\Pr[C = c]}$$

The values $\Pr[x_i = v_j \wedge C = c]$ and $\Pr[C = c]$ are estimated from the training data. Thus, the summary of the training data is simply a 3-dimensional table that stores for each triple (x_i, v_j, c) a count $N_{i,j,c}$ of training instances with $x_i = v_j$, together with a 1-dimensional table for the counts of $C = c$. This algorithm is naturally incremental: upon receiving a new example (or a batch of new examples), simply increment the relevant counts. Predictions can be made at any time from the current counts.

2.1.2 Decision Trees

Decision trees are classifier algorithms [BFOS94, Qui93]. In its simplest versions, each internal node in the tree contains a test on an attribute, each branch from a node corresponds to a possible outcome of the test, and each leaf contains a class prediction. The label $y = DT(x)$ for an instance x is obtained by passing the instance down from the root to a leaf, testing the appropriate attribute at each node and following the branch corresponding to the attribute's value in the instance.

A decision tree is learned by recursively replacing leaves by test nodes, starting at the root. The attribute to test at a node is chosen by comparing all the available attributes and choosing the best one according to some heuristic measure.

2.1.3 k-means clustering

k-means clustering divides the input data instances into k clusters such that a metric relative to the centroids of the clusters is minimized. Total distance between all objects and their centroids is the most common metric used in k-means algorithms.

The k-means algorithm is as follows:

1. Place k points into the data space that is being clustered. These points represent initial group centroids.

2. Assign each input data instance to the group that has the closest centroid.

3. When all input instances have been assigned, recalculate the positions of each of the k centroids by taking the average of the points assigned to it.

4. Repeat Steps 2 and 3 until the metric to be minimized no longer decreases.

2.2 Change Detection and Value Estimation

The following different modes of change have been identified in the literature [Tsy04, Sta03, WK96]:

- concept change
    - concept drift
    - concept shift
- distribution or sampling change

Concept refers to the target variable, which the model is trying to predict. *Concept change* is the change of the underlying concept over time. Concept drift describes a gradual change of the concept and concept shift happens when a change between two concepts is more abrupt.

Distribution change, also known as sampling change or shift or virtual concept drift , refers to the change in the data distribution. Even if the concept remains the same, the change may often lead to revising the current model as the model's error rate may no longer be acceptable with the new data distribution.

Some authors, as Stanley [Sta03], have suggested that from the practical point of view, it is not essential to differentiate between concept change and sampling change since the current model needs to be changed in both cases. We agree to some extent, and our methods will not be targeted to one particular type of change.

2.2.1 Change Detection

Change detection is not an easy task, since a fundamental limitation exists [Gus00]: the design of a change detector is a compromise between detecting true changes and avoiding false alarms. See [Gus00, BN93] for more detailed surveys of change detection methods.

The CUSUM Test

The cumulative sum (CUSUM algorithm), first proposed in [Pag54], is a change detection algorithm that gives an alarm when the mean of the input data is significantly different from zero. The CUSUM input ϵ_t can be any filter residual, for instance the prediction error from a Kalman filter.

The CUSUM test is as follows:

$$g_0 = 0$$

$$g_t = \max(0, g_{t-1} + \epsilon_t - v)$$

if $g_t > h$ then alarm and $g_t = 0$

The CUSUM test is memoryless, and its accuracy depends on the choice of parameters v and h.

The Geometric Moving Average Test

The CUSUM test is a stopping rule. Other stopping rules exist. For example, the Geometric Moving Average (GMA) test, first proposed in [Rob00], is the following

$$g_0 = 0$$

$$g_t = \lambda g_{t-1} + (1-\lambda)\epsilon_t$$

if $g_t > h$ then alarm and $g_t = 0$

The forgetting factor λ is used to give more or less weight to the last data arrived. The treshold h is used to tune the sensitivity and false alarm rate of the detector.

Statistical Tests

CUSUM and GMA are methods for dealing with numeric sequences. For more complex populations, we need to use other methods. There exist some statistical tests that may be used to detect change. A statistical test is a procedure for deciding whether a hypothesis about a quantitative feature of a population is true or false. We test an hypothesis of this sort by drawing a random sample from the population in question and calculating an appropriate statistic on its items. If, in doing so, we obtain a value of

2.2. CHANGE DETECTION AND VALUE ESTIMATION

the statistic that would occur rarely when the hypothesis is true, we would have reason to reject the hypothesis.

To detect change, we need to compare two sources of data, and decide if the hypothesis H_0 that they come from the same distribution is true. Let's suppose we have two estimates, $\hat{\mu}_0$ and $\hat{\mu}_1$ with variances σ_0^2 and σ_1^2. If there is no change in the data, these estimates will be consistent. Otherwise, a hypothesis test will reject H_0 and a change is detected. There are several ways to construct such a hypothesis test. The simplest one is to study the difference

$$\hat{\mu}_0 - \hat{\mu}_1 \in N(0, \sigma_0^2 + \sigma_1^2), \text{ under } H_0$$

or, to make a χ^2 test

$$\frac{(\hat{\mu}_0 - \hat{\mu}_1)^2}{\sigma_0^2 + \sigma_1^2} \in \chi^2(1), \text{ under } H_0$$

from which a standard hypothesis test can be formulated.

For example, suppose we want to design a change detector using a statistical test with a probability of false alarm of 5%, that is,

$$\Pr\left(\frac{|\hat{\mu}_0 - \hat{\mu}_1|}{\sqrt{\sigma_0^2 + \sigma_1^2}} > h\right) = 0.05$$

A table of the Gaussian distribution shows that $P(X < 1.96) = 0.975$, so the test becomes

$$\frac{(\hat{\mu}_0 - \hat{\mu}_1)^2}{\sigma_0^2 + \sigma_1^2} > 1.96$$

Note that this test uses the normality hypothesis. In Chapter 4 we will propose a similar test with theoretical guarantees. However, we could have used this test on the methods of Chapter 4.

The Kolmogorov-Smirnov test [Kan06] is another statistical test used to compare two populations. Given samples from two populations, the cumulative distribution functions can be determined and plotted. Hence the maximum value of the difference between the plots can be found and compared with a critical value. If the observed value exceeds the critical value, H_0 is rejected and a change is detected. It is not obvious how to implement the Kolmogorov-Smirnov test dealing with data streams. Kifer et al. [KBDG04] propose a KS-structure to implement Kolmogorov-Smirnov and similar tests, on the data stream setting.

Drift Detection Method

The drift detection method (DDM) proposed by Gama et al. [GMCR04] controls the number of errors produced by the learning model during prediction. It compares the statistics of two windows: the first one contains all the data, and the second one contains only the data from the beginning until the number of errors increases. This method does not store these windows in memory. It keeps only statistics and a window of recent data.

The number of errors in a sample of n examples is modelized by a binomial distribution. For each point i in the sequence that is being sampled, the error rate is the probability of misclassifying (p_i), with standard deviation given by $s_i = \sqrt{p_i(1-p_i)/i}$. It assumes (as can be argued e.g. in the PAC learning model [Mit97]) that the error rate of the learning algorithm (p_i) will decrease while the number of examples increases if the distribution of the examples is stationary. A significant increase in the error of the algorithm, suggests that the class distribution is changing and, hence, the actual decision model is supposed to be inappropriate. Thus, it stores the values of p_i and s_i when $p_i + s_i$ reaches its minimum value during the process (obtaining p_{pmin} and s_{min}), and when the following conditions triggers:

- $p_i + s_i \geq p_{min} + 2 \cdot s_{min}$ for the warning level. Beyond this level, the examples are stored in anticipation of a possible change of context.

- $p_i + s_i \geq p_{min} + 3 \cdot s_{min}$ for the drift level. Beyond this level the concept drift is supposed to be true, the model induced by the learning method is reset and a new model is learnt using the examples stored since the warning level triggered. The values for p_{min} and s_{min} are reset too.

This approach has a good behaviour of detecting abrupt changes and gradual changes when the gradual change is not very slow, but it has difficulties when the change is slowly gradual. In that case, the examples will be stored for long time, the drift level can take too much time to trigger and the example memory can be exceeded.

Baena-García et al. proposed a new method EDDM in order to improve DDM. EDDM [BGdCÁF+06] is shown to be better than DDM for some data sets and worse for others. It is based on the estimated distribution of the distances between classification errors. The window resize procedure is governed by the same heuristics.

2.2.2 Estimation

An Estimator is an algorithm that estimates the desired statistics on the input data, which may change over time. The simplest Estimator algorithm for the expected is the *linear estimator*, which simply returns the average of the data items contained in the Memory. Other examples of run-time

2.2. CHANGE DETECTION AND VALUE ESTIMATION

efficient estimators are Auto-Regressive, Auto Regressive Moving Average, and Kalman filters.

Exponential Weighted Moving Average

An exponentially weighted moving average (EWMA) estimator is an algorithm that updates the estimation of a variable by combining the most recent measurement of the variable with the EWMA of all previous measurements:

$$X_t = \alpha z_t + (1-\alpha) X_{t-1} = X_{t-1} + \alpha(z_t - X_{t-1})$$

where X_t is the moving average, z_t is the latest measurement, and α is the weight given to the latest measurement (between 0 and 1). The idea is to produce an estimate that gives more weight to recent measurements, on the assumption that recent measurements are more likely to be relevant. Choosing an adequate α is a difficult problem, and it is not trivial.

The Kalman Filter

One of the most widely used Estimation algorithms is the Kalman filter. We give here a description of its essentials; see [WB95] for a complete introduction.

The Kalman filter addresses the general problem of trying to estimate the state $x \in \Re^n$ of a discrete-time controlled process that is governed by the linear stochastic difference equation

$$x_t = A x_{t-1} + B u_t + w_{t-1}$$

with a measurement $z \in \Re^m$ that is

$$Z_t = H x_t + v_t.$$

The random variables w_t and v_t represent the process and measurement noise (respectively). They are assumed to be independent (of each other), white, and with normal probability distributions

$$p(w) \sim N(0, Q)$$

$$p(v) \sim N(0, R).$$

In essence, the main function of the Kalman filter is to estimate the state vector using system sensors and measurement data corrupted by noise.

The Kalman filter estimates a process by using a form of feedback control: the filter estimates the process state at some time and then obtains feedback in the form of (noisy) measurements. As such, the equations for the Kalman filter fall into two groups: time update equations and measurement update equations. The time update equations are responsible for projecting forward (in time) the current state and error covariance estimates to obtain the a priori estimates for the next time step.

$$x_t^- = Ax_{t-1} + Bu_t$$
$$P_t^- = AP_{t-1}A^T + Q$$

The measurement update equations are responsible for the feedback, i.e. for incorporating a new measurement into the a priori estimate to obtain an improved a posteriori estimate.

$$K_t = P_t^- H^T (HP_t^- H^T + R)^{-1}$$
$$x_t = x_t^- + K_t(z_t - Hx_t^-)$$
$$P_t = (I - K_t H)P_t^-.$$

There are extensions of the Kalman filter (Extended Kalman Filters, or EKF) for the cases in which the process to be estimated or the measurement-to-process relation is nonlinear. We do not discuss them here.

In our case we consider the input data sequence of real values $z_1, z_2, \ldots, z_t, \ldots$ as the measurement data. The difference equation of our discrete-time controlled process is the simpler one, with $A = 1, H = 1, B = 0$. So the equations are simplified to:

$$K_t = P_{t-1}/(P_{t-1} + R)$$
$$X_t = X_{t-1} + K_t(z_t - X_{t-1})$$
$$P_t = P_t(1 - K_t) + Q.$$

Note the similarity between this Kalman filter and an EWMA estimator, taking $\alpha = K_t$. This Kalman filter can be considered as an adaptive EWMA estimator where $\alpha = f(Q, R)$ is calculated optimally when Q and R are known.

The performance of the Kalman filter depends on the accuracy of the a-priori assumptions:

- linearity of the difference stochastic equation

- estimation of covariances Q and R, assumed to be fixed, known, and follow normal distributions with zero mean.

When applying the Kalman filter to data streams that vary arbitrarily over time, both assumptions are problematic. The linearity assumption for sure, but also the assumption that parameters Q and R are fixed and known – in fact, estimating them from the data is itself a complex estimation problem [Rey06].

2.3 Frequent Pattern Mining

Patterns are graphs, composed by a labeled set of nodes (vertices) and a labeled set of edges. The number of nodes in a pattern is called its *size*. Examples of patterns are itemsets, sequences, and trees [ZPD+05]. Given two patterns t and t′, we say that t is a *subpattern* of t′, or t′ is a *super-pattern* of t, denoted by $t \preceq t'$ if there exists a 1-1 mapping from the nodes in t to a subset of the nodes in t′ that preserves node and edge labeling. As there may be many mappings with this property, we will define for each type of pattern a more specific definition of subpattern. Two patterns t, t′ are said to be *comparable* if $t \preceq t'$ or $t' \preceq t$. Otherwise, they are incomparable. Also $t \prec t'$ if t is a proper subpattern of t′ (that is, $t \preceq t'$ and $t \neq t'$).

The (infinite) set of all patterns will be denoted with $\mathcal{T}$, but actually all our developments will proceed in some finite subset of $\mathcal{T}$ which will act as our universe of discourse.

The input to our data mining process, now is a given finite dataset $\mathcal{D}$ of transactions, where each transaction $s \in \mathcal{D}$ consists of a transaction identifier, tid, and a pattern. Tids are supposed to run sequentially from 1 to the size of $\mathcal{D}$. From that dataset, our universe of discourse $\mathcal{U}$ is the set of all patterns that appear as subpattern of some pattern in $\mathcal{D}$.

Following standard usage, we say that a transaction s *supports* a pattern t if t is a subpattern of the pattern in transaction s. The number of transactions in the dataset $\mathcal{D}$ that support t is called the *support* of the pattern t. A subpattern t is called *frequent* if its support is greater than or equal to a given threshold min_sup. The frequent subpattern mining problem is to find all frequent subpatterns in a given dataset. Any subpattern of a frequent pattern is also frequent and, therefore, any superpattern of a non-frequent pattern is also nonfrequent (the *antimonotonicity* property).

We define a frequent pattern t to be *closed* if none of its proper superpatterns has the same support as it has. Generally, there are much fewer closed patterns than frequent ones. In fact, we can obtain all frequent subpatterns with their support from the set of frequent closed subpatterns with their supports. So, the set of frequent closed subpatterns maintains the same information as the set of all frequent subpatterns.

Itemsets are subsets of a set of items. Let $I = \{i_1, \cdots, i_n\}$ be a fixed set of items. All possible subsets $I' \subseteq I$ are itemsets. We can consider itemsets as patterns without edges, and without two nodes having the same label. In itemsets the notions of subpattern and super-pattern correspond to the notions of subset and superset.

Sequences are ordered list of itemsets. Let $I = \{i_1, \cdots, i_n\}$ be a fixed set of items. Sequences can be represented as $\langle (I_1)(I_2)...(I_n) \rangle$, where each I_i is a subset of I, and I_i comes before I_j if $i \leq j$. Without loss of generality we can assume that the items in each itemset are sorted in a certain order (such as alphabetic order). In sequences we are interested in a notion of subsequence defined as following: a sequence $s = \langle(I_1)(I_2)...(I_n)\rangle$ is a subsequence of $s' = \langle(I'_1)(I'_2)...(I'_n)\rangle$ i.e. $s \preceq s'$, if there exist integers $1 \leq j_1 < j_2 ... < j_n \leq m$ such that $I_1 \subseteq I'_{j_1}, ..., I_n \subseteq I'_{j_n}$.

Trees are connected acyclic graphs, *rooted trees* are trees with a vertex singled out as the root, *n-ary trees* are trees for which each node which is not a leaf has at most n children, and *unranked* trees are trees with unbounded arity. We say that $t_1, ..., t_k$ are the *components* of tree t if t is made of a node (the root) joined to the roots of all the t_i's. We can distinguish betweeen the cases where the components at each node form a sequence (ordered trees) or just a set (*unordered trees*).

2.4 Mining data streams: state of the art

The *Data Stream* model represents input data that arrives at high speed [Agg06, BW01, GGR02, Mut03]. This data is so massive that we may not be able to store all of what we see, and we don't have too much time to process it.

It requires that at a time t in a data stream with domain N, this three performance measures: the per-item processing time, storage and the computing time to be simultaneously $o(N,t)$, preferably, polylog(N,t).

The use of randomization often leads to simpler and more efficient algorithms in comparison to known deterministic algorithms [MR95]. If a randomized algorithm always return the right answer but the running times vary, it is known as a Las Vegas algorithm. A Monte Carlo algorithm has bounds on the running time but may not return the correct answer. One way to think of a randomized algorithm is simply as a probability distribution over a set of deterministic algorithms.

Given that a randomized algorithm returns a random variable as a result, we would like to have bounds on the tail probability of that random variable. These tell us that the probability that a random variable deviates from its expected value is small. Basic tools are Chernoff, Hoeffding, and Bernstein bounds [BLB03, CBL06]. Bernstein's bound is the most accurate if variance is known.

Theorem 1. *Let* $X = \sum_i X_i$ *where* $X_1, ..., X_n$ *are independent and indentically distributed in* $[0, 1]$. *Then*

1. **Chernoff** *For each* $\epsilon < 1$

$$\Pr[X > (1+\epsilon)E[X]] \leq \exp\left(-\frac{\epsilon^2}{3}E[X]\right)$$

2. **Hoeffding** *For each* $t > 0$

$$\Pr[X > E[X] + t] \leq \exp\left(-2t^2/n\right)$$

3. **Bernstein** Let $\sigma^2 = \sum_i \sigma_i^2$ *the variance of* X. *If* $X_i - E[X_i] \leq b$ *for each* $i \in [n]$ *then for each* $t > 0$

$$\Pr[X > E[X] + t] \leq \exp\left(-\frac{t^2}{2\sigma^2 + \frac{2}{3}bt}\right)$$

Surveys for mining data streams, with appropriate references, are given in [GG07, GZK05, Agg06].

2.4.1 Sliding Windows in data streams

An interesting approach to mining data streams is to use a sliding window to analyze them [BDMO03, DGIM02]. This technique is able to deal with concept drift. The main idea is instead of using all data seen so far, use only recent data. We can use a window of size W to store recent data, and deleting the oldest item when inserting the newer one. An element arriving at time t expires at time $t + W$.

Datar et al. [DGIM02] have considered the problem of maintaining statistics over sliding windows. They identified a simple counting problem whose solution is a prerequisite for efficient maintenance of a variety of more complex statistical aggregates: Given a stream of bits, maintain a count of the number of 1's in the last W elements seen from the stream. They showed that, using $O(\frac{1}{\epsilon} \log^2 W)$ bits of memory, it is possible to estimate the number of 1's to within a factor of $1 + \epsilon$. They also give a matching lower bound of $\Omega(\frac{1}{\epsilon} \log^2 W)$ memory bits for any deterministic or randomized algorithm. They extended their scheme to maintain the sum of the last W elements of a stream of integers in a known range $[0, B]$, and provide matching upper and lower bounds for this more general problem as well.

An important parameter to consider is the size W of the window. Usually it can be determined *a priori* by the user. This can work well if information on the time-scale of change is available, but this is rarely the case. Normally, the user is caught in a tradeoff without solution: choosing a small size (so that the window reflects accurately the current distribution) and choosing a large size (so that many examples are available to work on, increasing accuracy in periods of stability). A different strategy uses a *decay function* to weight the importance of examples according to their age (see e.g. [CS03]). If there is concept drift, the tradeoff shows up in the choice of a decay function that should match the unknown rate of change.

2.4.2 Classification in data streams

Classic decision tree learners like ID3, C4.5 [Qui93] and CART [BFOS94] assume that all training examples can be stored simultaneously in main memory, and are thus severely limited in the number of examples they can learn from. And in particular not applicable to data streams, where potentially there is no bound on number of examples.

Domingos and Hulten [DH00] developed Hoeffding trees, an incremental, anytime decision tree induction algorithm that is capable of learning from massive data streams, assuming that the distribution generating examples does not change over time. We describe it in some detail, since it will be the basis for our adaptive decision tree classifiers.

Hoeffding trees exploit the fact that a small sample can often be enough to choose an optimal splitting attribute. This idea is supported mathematically by the Hoeffding bound, which quantifies the number of observations (in our case, examples) needed to estimate some statistics within a prescribed precision (in our case, the goodness of an attribute). More precisely, the Hoeffding bound states that with probability $1-\delta$, the true mean of a random variable of range R will not differ from the estimated mean after n independent observations by more than:

$$\epsilon = \sqrt{\frac{R^2 \ln(1/\delta)}{2n}}.$$

A theoretically appealing feature of Hoeffding Trees not shared by other incremental decision tree learners is that it has sound guarantees of performance. Using the Hoeffding bound and the concept of intensional disagreement one can show that its output is asymptotically nearly identical to that of a non-incremental learner using infinitely many examples. The *intensional disagreement* Δ_i between two decision trees DT_1 and DT_2 is the probability that the path of an example through DT_1 will differ from its path through DT_2. Hoeffding Trees have the following theoretical guarantee:

Theorem 2. *If HT_δ is the tree produced by the Hoeffding tree algorithm with desired probability δ given infinite examples, DT is the asymptotic batch tree, and p is the leaf probability, then $E[\Delta_i(HT_\delta, DT)] \leq \delta/p$.*

VFDT (Very Fast Decision Trees) is the implementation of Hoeffding trees, with a few heuristics added, described in [DH00]; we basically identify both in this book. The pseudo-code of VFDT is shown in Figure 2.1. Counts n_{ijk} are the sufficient statistics needed to choose splitting attributes, in particular the information gain function G implemented in VFDT. Function $\epsilon(\delta, \dots)$ in line 4 is given by the Hoeffding bound and guarantees that whenever best and 2nd best attributes satisfy this condition, we can confidently conclude that best indeed has maximal gain. The sequence of examples S may be infinite, in which case the procedure never terminates, and at any point in time a parallel procedure can use the current tree to make class predictions.

Many other classification methods exist, but only a few can be applied to the data stream setting, without losing accuracy and in an efficient way.

2.4. MINING DATA STREAMS: STATE OF THE ART

VFDT(Stream, δ)
1   Let HT be a tree with a single leaf (root)
2   Init counts n_{ijk} at root to 0
3   **for** each example (x, y) in Stream
4   **do** VFDTGROW$((x, y), HT, \delta)$

VFDTGROW$((x, y), HT, \delta)$
1   Sort (x, y) to leaf l using HT
2   Update counts n_{ijk} at leaf l
3   **if** examples seen so far at l are not all of the same class
4   **then** Compute G for each attribute
5   **if** G(Best Attr.) − G(2nd best) $> \sqrt{\frac{R^2 \ln 1/\delta}{2n}}$
6   **then** Split leaf on best attribute
7   **for** each branch
8   **do** Start new leaf and initialize counts

Figure 2.1: The VFDT algorithm

We mention two more that, although not so popular, have the potential for adaptation to the data stream setting.

Last [Las02] has proposed a classification system IFN, which uses a info-fuzzy network, as a base classifier. IFN, or Info-Fuzzy Network, is an oblivious tree-like classification model, which is designed to minimize the total number of predicting attributes. The underlying principle of the IFN method is to construct a multi-layered network in order to test the Mutual Information (MI) between the input and output attributes. Each hidden layer is related to a specific input attribute and represents the interaction between this input attribute and the other ones. The IFN algorithm is using the pre-pruning strategy: a node is split if this procedure brings about a statistically significant decrease in the entropy value (or increase in the mutual information) of the target attribute. If none of the remaining input attributes provides a statistically significant increase in mutual information, the network construction stops. The output of this algorithm is a network, which can be used to predict the values of a target attribute similarly to the prediction technique used in decision trees.

AWSOM (Arbitrary Window Stream mOdeling Method) is a method for interesting pattern discovery from sensors proposed by Papadimitriou et al. [PFB03]. It is a one-pass algorithm that incrementally updates the patterns. This method requires only $O(\log n)$ memory where n is the length of the sequence. It uses wavelet coefficients as compact information representation and correlation structure detection, applying a linear regression model in the wavelet domain.

2.4.3 Clustering in data streams

An incremental k-means algorithm for clustering binary data streams was proposed by Ordonez [Ord03]. As this algorithm has several improvements to k-means algorithm, the proposed algorithm can outperform the scalable k-means in the majority of cases. The use of binary data simplifies the manipulation of categorical data and eliminates the need for data normalization. The complexity of the algorithm for n points in $\mathbf{R}^d$, is $O(dkn)$, where k is the number of centers. It updates the cluster centers and weights after examining each batch of $\sqrt{n}$ points rather than updating them one by one.

LOCALSEARCH is an algorithm for high quality data stream clustering proposed by O'Callaghan et al. [OMM+02]. An algorithm called STREAM starts by determining the size of the sample and then applies the LOCAL-SEARCH algorithm if the sample size is larger than a pre-specified equation result. This process is repeated for each data chunk. Finally, the LOCALSEARCH algorithm is applied to the cluster centers generated in the previous iterations.

2.5 Frequent pattern mining: state of the art

There exist abundant work in closure-based mining on structured data, particularly sequences [YHA03, BG07b], trees [CXYM01, TRS04, AU05], and graphs [YH03, YZH05]. One of the differences with closed itemset mining stems from the fact that the set theoretic intersection no longer applies, and whereas the intersection of sets is a set, the intersection of two sequences or two trees is not one sequence or one tree. This makes it nontrivial to justify the word "closed" in terms of a standard closure operator. Many papers resort to a support-based notion of closedness of a tree or sequence ([CXYM01], see below); others (like [AU05]) choose a variant of trees where a closure operator between trees can be actually defined (via least general generalization). In some cases, the trees are labeled, and strong conditions are imposed on the label patterns (such as nonrepeated labels in tree siblings [TRS04] or nonrepeated labels at all in sequences [GB04]).

Yan and Han [YH02, YH03] proposed two algorithms for mining frequent and closed graphs. The first one is called gSpan (graph-based Substructure pattern mining) and discovers frequent graph substructures without candidate generation; gSpan builds a new lexicographic order among graphs, and maps each graph to a unique minimum DFS code as its canonical label. Based on this lexicographic order, gSpan adopts the depth-first search strategy to mine frequent connected subgraphs. The second one is called CloseGraph and discovers closed graph patterns. CloseGraph is based on gSpan, and is based on the development of two pruning methods: equivalent occurrence and early termination. The early termination method is similar to the early termination by equivalence of projected databases method in CloSpan [YHA03], an algorithm for mining closed sequential patterns in large datasets published by the Illimine team. However, in graphs there are some cases where early termination may fail and miss some patterns. By detecting and eliminating these cases, CloseGraph guarantees the completeness and soundness of the closed graph patterns discovered.

In the case of trees, only labeled tree mining methods are considered in the literature. There are four broad kinds of subtrees: bottom-up subtrees, top-down subtrees, induced subtrees, and embedded subtrees. Bottom-up subtree mining is the simplest from the subtree mining point of view.

Algorithms for embedded labeled frequent trees include:

- Rooted Ordered Trees
  - **TreeMiner** [Zak02]: This algorithm, developed by Zaki, uses vertical representations for support counting, and follows the combined depth-first/breadth traversal idea to discover all embedded ordered subtrees.

- Rooted Unordered Trees
  - **SLEUTH** [Zak05]: This method, also by Zaki, extends TreeMiner to the unordered case using two different methods for generating canonical candidates: the class-based extension and the canonical extension.

Algorithms for induced labeled frequent trees include:

- Rooted Ordered Trees
  - **FREQT** [AAK+02]. Asai et al. developed FREQT. It uses an extension approach based on the rightmost path. FREQT uses an occurrence list base approach to determine the support of trees.

- Rooted Unordered Trees
  - **uFreqt** [NK03]: Nijssen et al. extended FREQT to the unordered case. Their method solves in the worst case, a maximum bipartite matching problem when counting tree supports.
  - **uNot** [AAUN03]: Asai et al. presented uNot in order to extend FREQT. It uses an occurrence list based approach wich is similar to Zaki's TreeMiner.

- **HybridTreeMiner** [CYM04]: Chi et al. proposed HybridTreeMiner, a method that generates candidates using both joins and extensions. It uses the combined depth-first/breadth-first traversal approach.

- **PathJoin** [XYLD03]: Xiao et al. developed PathJoin, assuming that no two siblings are indentically labeled. It presents the *maximal* frequent subtrees. A *maximal* frequent subtree is a frequent subtree none of whose proper supertrees are frequent.

A survey of works on frequent subtree mining can be found in [CMNK01].

Arimura and Uno proposed CLOATT [AU05] considering closed mining in attribute trees, which is a subclass of labeled ordered trees and can also be regarded as a fragment of description logic with functional roles only. These attribute trees are defined using a relaxed tree inclusion. Termier et al. [TRS04] considered the frequent closed tree discovery problem for a class of trees with the same constraint as attribute trees.

Labeled trees are trees in which each vertex is given a unique label. Unlabeled trees are trees in which each vertex has no label, or there is a unique label for all vertices. A comprehensive introduction to the algorithms on unlabeled trees can be found in [Val02].

2.5.1 CMTreeMiner

Chi et al. proposed CMTreeMiner [CXYM01], the first algorithm to discover all closed and maximal frequent labeled induced subtrees without first discovering all frequent subtrees. CMTreeMiner is to our knowledge, the state of art method for closed frequent tree mining. It shares many features with CloseGraph, and uses two pruning techniques: the *left-blanket* and *right-blanket* pruning. The *blanket* of a tree is defined as the set of immediate supertrees that are frequent, where an *immediate supertree* of a tree t is a tree that has one more vertex than t. The *left-blanket* of a tree t is the blanket where the vertex added is not in the right-most path of t (the path from the root to the rightmost vertex of t). The *right-blanket* of a tree t is the blanket where the vertex added is in the right-most path of t. The method is as follows: it computes, for each candidate tree, the set of trees that are occurrence-matched with its blanket's trees. If this set is not empty, they apply two pruning techniques using the left-blanket and right-blanket. If it is empty, then they check if the set of trees that are transaction-matched but not occurrence matched with its blanket's trees is also empty. If this is the case, there is no supertree with the same support and then the tree is closed.

CMTreeMiner is a labeled tree method and it was not designed for unlabeled trees. As explained in [CXYM01]:

Therefore, if the number of distinct labels decrease dramatically (so different occurrences for the same pattern increase dramatically), the memory usage of CMTreeMiner is expected to increase and its performance is expected to deteriorate. To study the performance under this special case and to modify CMTreeMiner to handle it is a topic for future work.

In this book we will propose closed frequent mining methods for unlabeled trees, that will outperform CMTreeMiner precisely in this case.

2.5.2 DRYADEPARENT

Termier et al. proposed DRYADEPARENT [TRS$^+$08] as a closed frequent attribute tree mining method comparable to CMTreeMiner. Attribute trees are trees such that two sibling nodes cannot have the same label. They extend to induced subtrees their previous algorithm DRYADE [TRS04].

The DRYADE and DRYADEPARENT algorithm are based on the computation of tiles (closed frequent attribute trees of depth 1) in the data and on an efficient hooking strategy that reconstructs the closed frequent trees from these tiles. Whereas CMTreeMiner uses a classical generate-and-test strategy to build candidate trees edge by edge, the hooking strategy of DRYADEPARENT finds a complete depth level at each iteration and does not need tree mapping tests. The authors claim that their experiments have shown that DRYADEPARENT is faster than CMTreeMiner in most settings and that the performances of DRYADEPARENT are robust with respect to the structure of the closed frequent trees to find, whereas the performances of CMTreeMiner are biased toward trees having most of their edges on their rightmost branch.

As attribute trees are trees such that two sibling nodes cannot have the same label, DRYADEPARENT is not a method appropriate for dealing with unlabeled trees.

2.5.3 Streaming Pattern Mining

There is a large body of work done on itemset mining. An important part of the most recent work is related to data streams; see the survey [JCN07b] and the references there. We can divide these data stream methods in two families depending if they use a landmark window or a sliding window. Only a small part of these methods deal with closed frequent mining. Moment [CWYM04], CFI-Stream [JG06], and IncMine [JCN07a] are the state-of-art algorithms for mining frequent closed itemsets over a sliding window. CFI-Stream stores only closed itemsets in memory, but must maintain all closed itemsets as does not implement a min-support threshold. Moment stores much more information besides the current closed frequent itemsets, but it has a min-support threshold to reduce the quantity of patterns found. IncMine proposes a notion of semi-FCIs that consists in increasing the minimum support threshold for an itemset as it is retained longer in the window.

A lot of research work exist on XML pattern mining. Asai et al. [AAA$^+$02] present StreamT, a tree online mining algorithm that uses a forgetting model and is able to maintain a sliding window, but it extracts only frequent trees, not closed ones. Hsieh et al. [HWC06] propose STMer, an alternative to StreamT to deal with frequent trees over data streams, but without using a sliding window. In [FQWZ07], Feng et al. present SOLARIA*, a frequent closed XML query pattern mining algorithm, but it is not an incremental method. Li. et al [LSL06] present Incre-FXQPMiner, an incremental mining algorithm of frequent XML query patterns, but it does not obtain the closed XML queries, neither uses a sliding window.

Part II
Evolving Data Stream Learning

3
Mining Evolving Data Streams

In order to deal with evolving data streams, the model learned from the streaming data must be able to capture up-to-date trends and transient patterns in the stream [Tsy04, WFYH03]. To do this, as we revise the model by incorporating new examples, we must also eliminate the effects of outdated examples representing outdated concepts. This is a nontrivial task. Also, we propose a new experimental data stream framework for studying concept drift.

3.1 Introduction

Dealing with time-changing data requires strategies for detecting and quantifying change, forgetting stale examples, and for model revision. Fairly generic strategies exist for detecting change and deciding when examples are no longer relevant. Model revision strategies, on the other hand, are in most cases method-specific.

Most strategies for dealing with time change contain hardwired constants, or else require input parameters, concerning the expected speed or frequency of the change; some examples are *a priori* definitions of sliding window lengths, values of decay or forgetting parameters, explicit bounds on maximum drift, etc. These choices represent preconceptions on how fast or how often the data are going to evolve and, of course, they may be completely wrong. Even more, no fixed choice may be right, since the stream may experience any combination of abrupt changes, gradual ones, and long stationary periods. More in general, an approach based on fixed parameters will be caught in the following tradeoff: the user would like to use values of parameters that give more accurate statistics (hence, more precision) during periods of stability, but at the same time use the opposite values of parameters to quickly react to changes, when they occur.

Many ad-hoc methods have been used to deal with drift, often tied to particular algorithms. In this chapter we propose a more general approach based on using two primitive design elements: change detectors and estimators. The idea is to encapsulate all the statistical calculations having to do with detecting change and keeping updated statistics from a stream an abstract data type that can then be used to replace, in a black-box way, the counters and accumulators that typically all machine learning and data mining algorithms use to make their decisions, including when change has occurred.

We believe that, compared to any previous approaches, our approach better isolates different concerns when designing new data mining algorithms, therefore reducing design time, increasing modularity, and facilitating analysis. Furthermore, since we crisply identify the nuclear problem in dealing with drift, and use a well-optimized algorithmic solution to tackle it, the resulting algorithms are more accurate, adaptive, and time- and memory-efficient than other ad-hoc approaches.

3.1.1 Theoretical approaches

The task of learning drifting or time-varying concepts has also been studied in computational learning theory. Learning a changing concept is infeasible, if no restrictions are imposed on the type of admissible concept changes, but drifting concepts are provably efficiently learnable (at least for certain concept classes), if the rate or the extent of drift is limited in particular ways.

Helmbold and Long [HL94] assume a possibly permanent but slow concept drift and define the extent of drift as the probability that two subsequent concepts disagree on a randomly drawn example. Their results include an upper bound for the extend of drift maximally tolerable by any learner and algorithms that can learn concepts that do not drift more than a certain constant extent of drift. Furthermore they show that it is sufficient for a learner to see a fixed number of the most recent examples. Hence a window of a certain minimal fixed size allows to learn concepts for which the extent of drift is appropriately limited. While Helmbold and Long restrict the extend of drift, Kuh, Petsche, and Rivest [KPR90] determine a maximal rate of drift that is acceptable by any learner, i. e. a maximally acceptable frequency of concept changes, which implies a lower bound for the size of a fixed window for a time-varying concept to be learnable, which is similar to the lower bound of Helmbold and Long.

3.2 Algorithms for mining with change

In this section we review some of the data mining methods that deal with data streams and concept drift. There are many algorithms in the literature that address this problem. We focus on the ones that they are more referred to in other works.

3.2.1 FLORA: Widmer and Kubat

FLORA [WK96] is a supervised incremental learning system that takes as input a stream of positive and negative example of a target concept that changes over time. The original FLORA algorithm uses a fixed moving window approach to process the data. The concept definitions are stored into three description sets:

- ADES description based on positive examples
- NDES descriptions based on negative examples
- PDES concept descriptions based on both positive and negative examples

The system uses the examples present in the moving window to incrementally update the knowledge about the concepts. The update of the concept descriptions involves two processes: a learning process (adjust concept description based on the new data) and a forgetting process (discard data that may be out of date). FLORA2 was introduced to address some of the problems associated with FLORA such as the fixed window size. FLORA2 has a heuristic routine to dynamically adjust its window size and uses a better generalization technique to integrate the knowledge extracted from the examples observed. The algorithm was further improved to allow previously extracted knowledge to help deal with recurring concepts (FLORA3) and to allow it to handle noisy data (FLORA4).

3.2.2 Suport Vector Machines: Klinkenberg

Klinkenberg and Joachims [KJ00] presented a method to handle concept drift with support vector machines. A proper introduction to SVM can be found in [Bur98].

Their method maintains a window on the training data with an appropriate size without using a complicated parameterization. The key idea is to automatically adjust the window size so that the estimated generalization error on new examples is minimized. To get an estimate of the generalization error, a special form of $\xi\alpha$-estimates is used. $\xi\alpha$-estimates are a particularly efficient method for estimating the performance of an SVM, estimating the leave-one-out-error of a SVM based solely on the one SVM solution learned with all examples.

Each example $z = (x, y)$ consists of a feature vector $x \in R^N$ and a label $y \in \{-1, +1\}$ indicating its classification. Data arrives over time in batches of equal size, each containing m examples. For each batch i the data is independently identically distributed with respect to a distribution $Pr_i(x, y)$. The goal of the learner $\mathcal{L}$ is to sequentially predict the labels of the next batch.

The window adaptive approach that employs this method, works that way: at batch t, it essentially tries various windows sizes, training a SVM for each resulting training set.

For each window size it computes a $\xi\alpha$-estimate based on the result of training, considering only the last batch for the estimation, that is the m most recent training examples $z_{(t,1)}, \ldots, z_{(t,m)}$.

This reflects the assumption that the most recent examples are most similar to the new examples in batch $t + 1$. The window size minimizing the $\xi\alpha$-estimate of the error rate is selected by the algorithm and used to train a classifier for the current batch.

The window adaptation algorithm is showed in figure 3.1.

SVMWINDOWSIZE(Stream S_{Train} consisting of t batches of m examples)
1   **for** $h \in \{0, \ldots, t-1\}$
2   **do** train SVM on examples $z_{(t-h,1)}, \ldots, z_{(t,m)}$
3   Compute $\xi\alpha$-estimate on examples $z_{(t-h,1)}, \ldots, z_{(t,m)}$
4   **return** Window size which minimizes $\xi\alpha$-estimate.

Figure 3.1: Window size adaption algorithm

3.2.3 OLIN: Last

Last in [Las02] describes an online classification system that uses the info-fuzzy network (IFN) explained in Section 2.4.2. The system called OLIN (On Line Information Network) gets a continuous stream of non-stationary data and builds a network based on a sliding window of the latest examples. The system dynamically adapts the size of the training window and the frequency of model re-construction to the current rate of concept drift

OLIN uses the statistical significance of the difference between the training and the validation accuracy of the current model as an indicator of concept stability.

OLIN adjusts dynamically the number of examples between model re-constructions by using the following heuristic: keep the current model for more examples if the concept appears to be stable and reduce drastically the size of the validation window, if a concept drift is detected.

OLIN generates a new model for every new sliding window. This approach ensures accurate and relevant models over time and therefore an increase in the classification accuracy. However, the OLIN algorithm has a major drawback, which is the high cost of generating new models. OLIN does not take into account the costs involved in replacing the existing model with a new one.

3.2.4 CVFDT: Domingos

Hulten, Spencer and Domingos presented Concept-adapting Very Fast Decision Trees CVFDT [HSD01] algorithm as an extension of VFDT to deal with concept change.

Figure 3.2 shows CVFDT algorithm. CVFDT keeps the model it is learning in sync with such changing concepts by continuously monitoring the quality of old search decisions with respect to a sliding window of data from the data stream, and updating them in a fine-grained way when it detects that the distribution of data is changing. In particular, it maintains sufficient statistics throughout time for every candidate M considered at every search step. After the first w examples, where w is the window width, it subtracts the oldest example from these statistics whenever a new one is added. After every Δn new examples, it determines again the best candidates at every previous search decision point. If one of them is better than an old winner by δ^* then one of two things has happened. Either the original decision was incorrect (which will happen a fraction δ of the time) or concept drift has occurred. In either case, it begins an alternate search starting from the new winners, while continuing to pursue the original search. Periodically it uses a number of new examples as a validation set to compare the performance of the models produced by the new and old searches. It prunes an old search (and replace it with the new one) when the new model is on average better than the old one, and it prunes the new search if after a maximum number of validations its models have failed to become more accurate on average than the old ones. If more than a maximum number of new searches is in progress, it prunes the lowest-performing ones.

3.2.5 UFFT: Gama

Gama, Medas and Rocha [GMR04] presented the Ultra Fast Forest of Trees (UFFT) algorithm.

UFFT is an algorithm for supervised classification learning, that generates a forest of binary trees. The algorithm is incremental, processing each example in constant time, works on-line, UFFT is designed for continuous data. It uses analytical techniques to choose the splitting criteria, and the information gain to estimate the merit of each possible splitting-test. For multi-class problems, the algorithm builds a binary tree for each possible pair of classes leading to a forest-of-trees. During the training phase the algorithm maintains a short term memory. Given a data stream, a limited number of the most recent examples are maintained in a data structure that supports constant time insertion and deletion. When a test is installed, a leaf is transformed into a decision node with two descendant leaves. The sufficient statistics of the leaf are initialized with the examples in the short term memory that will fall at that leaf.

CVFDT(Stream, δ)

1 Let HT be a tree with a single leaf(root)
2 Init counts n_{ijk} at root
3 **for** each example (x, y) in Stream
4   **do** Add, Remove and Forget Examples
5   CVFDTGROW((x, y), HT, δ)
6   CHECKSPLITVALIDITY(HT, n, δ)

CVFDTGROW((x, y), HT, δ)

1 Sort (x, y) to leaf l using HT
2 Update counts n_{ijk} at leaf l and nodes traversed in the sort
3 **if** examples seen so far at l are not all of the same class
4   **then** Compute G for each attribute
5   **if** G(Best Attr.)$-$G(2nd best) $> \sqrt{\frac{R^2 \ln 1/\delta}{2n}}$
6   **then** Split leaf on best attribute
7   **for** each branch
8   **do** Start new leaf and initialize counts
9   Create alternate subtree

CHECKSPLITVALIDITY(HT, n, δ)

1 **for** each node l in HT that it is not a leaf
2   **do for** each tree T_{alt} in ALT(l)
3   **do** CHECKSPLITVALIDITY(T_{alt}, n, δ)
4   **if** exists a new promising attributes at node l
5   **do** Start an alternate subtree

Figure 3.2: The CVFDT algorithm

The UFFT algorithm maintains, at each node of all decision trees, a Naïve Bayes classifier. Those classifiers were constructed using the sufficient statistics needed to evaluate the splitting criteria when that node was a leaf. After the leaf becomes a node, all examples that traverse the node will be classified by the Naïve Bayes. The basic idea of the drift detection method is to control this error-rate. If the distribution of the examples is stationary, the error rate of Naïve-Bayes decreases. If there is a change on the distribution of the examples the Naïve Bayes error increases. The system uses DDM, the drift detection method explained in Section 2.2.1. When it detects an statistically significant increase of the Naïve-Bayes error in a given node, an indication of a change in the distribution of the examples, this suggest that the splitting-test that has been installed at this node is no longer appropriate. The subtree rooted at that node is pruned, and the node becomes a leaf. All the sufficient statistics of the leaf are initialized. When a new training example becomes available, it will cross the corresponding binary decision trees from the root node till a leaf. At each node, the Naïve Bayes installed at that node classifies the example. The example will be correctly or incorrectly classified. For a set of examples the error is a random variable from Bernoulli trials. The Binomial distribution gives the general form of the probability for the random variable that represents the number of errors in a sample of n examples.

The sufficient statistics of the leaf are initialized with the examples in the short term memory that maintains a limited number of the most recent examples. It is possible to observe an increase of the error reaching the warning level, followed by a decrease. This method uses the information already available to the learning algorithm and does not require additional computational resources. An advantage of this method is it continuously monitors the online error of Naïve Bayes. It can detect changes in the class-distribution of the examples at any time. All decision nodes contain Naïve Bayes to detect changes in the class distribution of the examples that traverse the node, that correspond to detect shifts in different regions of the instance space. Nodes near the root should be able to detect abrupt changes in the distribution of the examples, while deeper nodes should detect smoothed changes.

3.3 A Methodology for Adaptive Stream Mining

The starting point of our work is the following observation: In the data stream mining literature, most algorithms incorporate one or more of the following ingredients: windows to remember recent examples; methods for detecting distribution change in the input; and methods for keeping updated estimations for some statistics of the input. We see them as the basis for solving the three central problems of

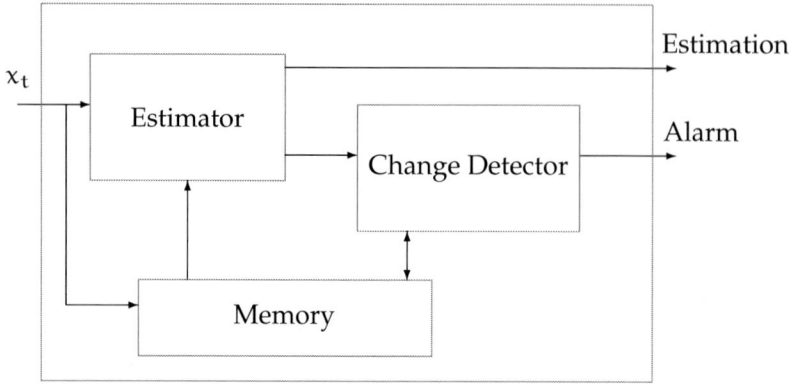

Figure 3.3: General Framework

- what to remember or forget,
- when to do the model upgrade, and
- how to do the model upgrade.

Our claim is that by basing mining algorithms on well-designed, well-encapsulated modules for these tasks, one can often get more generic and more efficient solutions than by using ad-hoc techniques as required.

3.3.1 Time Change Detectors and Predictors: A General Framework

Most approaches for predicting and detecting change in streams of data can be discussed in the general framework: The system consists of three modules: a Memory module, an Estimator Module, and a Change Detector or Alarm Generator module. These three modules interact as shown in Figure 3.3, which is analogous to Figure 8 in [SEG05].

In general, the input to this algorithm is a sequence $x_1, x_2, \ldots, x_t, \ldots$ of data items whose distribution varies over time in an unknown way. The outputs of the algorithm are, at each time step

- an estimation of some important parameters of the input distribution, and
- a signal alarm indicating that distribution change has recently occurred.

We consider a specific, but very frequent case, of this setting: that in which all the x_t are real values. The desired estimation is usually the expected value of the current x_t, and less often another distribution statistics

3.3. A METHODOLOGY FOR ADAPTIVE STREAM MINING

such as the variance. The only assumption on the distribution is that each x_t is drawn independently from each other.

Memory is the component where the algorithm stores all the sample data or summary that considers relevant at current time, that is, that presumably shows the current data distribution.

The Estimator component is an algorithm that estimates the desired statistics on the input data, which may change over time. The algorithm may or may not use the data contained in the Memory. The simplest Estimator algorithm for the expected is the *linear estimator,* which simply returns the average of the data items contained in the Memory. Other examples of run-time efficient estimators are Auto-Regressive, Auto Regressive Moving Average, and Kalman filters.

The change detector component outputs an alarm signal when it detects change in the input data distribution. It uses the output of the Estimator, and may or may not in addition use the contents of Memory.

In Table 3.1 we classify these predictors in four classes, depending on whether Change Detector and Memory modules exist:

	No memory	**Memory**
No Change Detector	*Type I* Kalman Filter	*Type III* Adaptive Kalman Filter
Change Detector	*Type II* Kalman Filter + CUSUM	*Type IV* ADWIN Kalman Filter + ADWIN

Table 3.1: Types of Time Change Predictor and some examples

- *Type I: Estimator only.* The simplest one is modelled by

$$\hat{x}_k = (1 - \alpha)\hat{x}_{k-1} + \alpha \cdot x_k.$$

The linear estimator corresponds to using $\alpha = 1/N$ where N is the width of a virtual window containing the last N elements we want to consider. Otherwise, we can give more weight to the last elements with an appropriate constant value of α. The Kalman filter tries to optimize the estimation using a non-constant α (the K value) which varies at each discrete time interval.

- *Type II: Estimator with Change Detector.* An example is the Kalman Filter together with a CUSUM test change detector algorithm, see for example [JMJH04].

- *Type III: Estimator with Memory.* We add Memory to improve the results of the Estimator. For example, one can build an Adaptive Kalman Filter that uses the data in Memory to compute adequate values for the process variance Q and the measure variance R. In particular, one can use the sum of the last elements stored into a memory window to model the Q parameter and the difference of the last two elements to estimate parameter R.

- *Type IV: Estimator with Memory and Change Detector.* This is the most complete type. Two examples of this type, from the literature, are:

    - A Kalman filter with a CUSUM test and fixed-length window memory, as proposed in [SEG05]. Only the Kalman filter has access to the memory.

    - A linear Estimator over fixed-length windows that flushes when change is detected [KBDG04], and a change detector that compares the running windows with a reference window.

In Chapter 4, we will present ADWIN, an adaptive sliding window method that works as a type IV change detector and predictor.

3.3.2 Window Management Models

Window strategies have been used in conjunction with mining algorithms in two ways: one, externally to the learning algorithm; the window system is used to monitor the error rate of the current model, which under stable distributions should keep decreasing or at most stabilize; when instead this rate grows significantly, change is declared and the base learning algorithm is invoked to revise or rebuild the model with fresh data. Note that in this case the window memory contains bits or real numbers (not full examples). Figure 3.4 shows this model.

The other way is to embed the window system *inside* the learning algorithm, to maintain the statistics required by the learning algorithm continuously updated; it is then the algorithm's responsibility to keep the model in synchrony with these statistics, as shown in Figure 3.5.

Learning algorithms that detect change, usually compare statistics of two windows. Note that the methods may be memoryless: they may keep window statistics without storing all their elements. There have been in the literature, some different window management strategies:

3.3. A METHODOLOGY FOR ADAPTIVE STREAM MINING

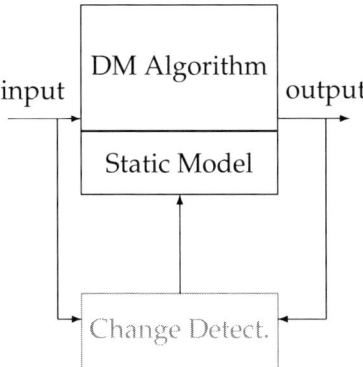

Figure 3.4: Data mining algorithm framework with concept drift.

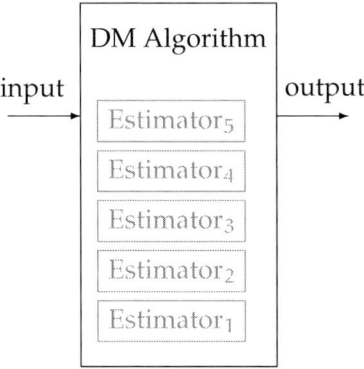

Figure 3.5: Data mining algorithm framework with concept drift using estimators replacing counters.

- Equal & fixed size subwindows: Kifer et al. [KBDG04] compares one reference, non-sliding, window of older data with a sliding window of the same size keeping the most recent data.

- Equal size adjacent subwindows: Dasu et al. [DKVY06] compares two adjacent sliding windows of the same size of recent data.

- Total window against subwindow: Gama et al. [GMCR04] compares the window that contains all the data with a subwindow of data from the beginning until it detects that the accuracy of the algorithm decreases.

The strategy of ADWIN, the method presented in next chapter, will be to compare all the adjacent subwindows in which is possible to partition the window containing all the data. Figure 3.6 shows these window management strategies.

Let $W = \boxed{101010110111111}$

- Equal & fixed size subwindows: $\boxed{1010}\boxed{1011011}\boxed{1111}$
- Equal size adjacent subwindows: $1010101\boxed{1011}\boxed{1111}$
- Total window against subwindow: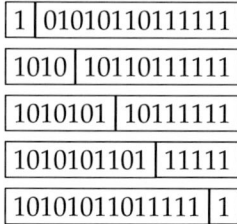
- `ADWIN`: All adjacent subwindows:

$$\boxed{1\,|\,01010110111111}$$
$$\boxed{1010\,|\,10110111111}$$
$$\boxed{1010101\,|\,10111111}$$
$$\boxed{1010101101\,|\,11111}$$
$$\boxed{10101011011111\,|\,1}$$

Figure 3.6: Different window management strategies

3.4 Optimal Change Detector and Predictor

We have presented in section 3.3 a general framework for time change detectors and predictors. Using this framework we can establish the main properties of an optimal change detector and predictor system as the following:

- High accuracy
- Fast detection of change
- Low false positives and negatives ratios
- Low computational cost: minimum space and time needed
- Theoretical guarantees
- No parameters needed
- Detector of type IV: Estimator with Memory and Change Detector

In the next chapter we design and propose `ADWIN`, a change detector and predictor with these characteristics, using an adaptive sliding window model. `ADWIN`'s window management strategy will be to compare all the adjacent subwindows in which is possible to partition the window containing all the data. It seems that this procedure may be the most accurate, since it looks at all possible subwindows partitions. On the other hand, time cost is the main disadvantage of this method. Considering this, we will provide another version working in the strict conditions of the Data Stream model, namely low memory and low processing per item.

3.5 Experimental Setting

This section proposes a new experimental data stream framework for studying concept drift. A majority of concept drift research in data streams mining is done using traditional data mining frameworks such as WEKA [WF05]. As the data stream setting has constraints that a traditional data mining environment does not, we believe that a new framework is needed to help to improve the empirical evaluation of these methods.

In data stream mining, we are interested in three main dimensions:

- accuracy

- amount of space necessary or computer memory

- the time required to learn from training examples and to predict

These properties may be interdependent: adjusting the time and space used by an algorithm can influence accuracy. By storing more pre-computed information, such as look up tables, an algorithm can run faster at the expense of space. An algorithm can also run faster by processing less information, either by stopping early or storing less, thus having less data to process. The more time an algorithm has, the more likely it is that accuracy can be increased.

In evolving data streams we are concerned about

- evolution of accuracy

- probability of false alarms

- probability of true detections

- average delay time in detection

Sometimes, learning methods do not have change detectors implemented inside, and then it may be hard to define ratios of false positives and negatives, and average delay time in detection. In these cases, learning curves may be a useful alternative for observing the evolution of accuracy in changing environments.

To summarize, the main properties of an ideal learning method for mining evolving data streams are the following: high accuracy and fast adaption to change, low computational cost in both space and time, theoretical performance guarantees, and minimal number of parameters.

In traditional batch learning the problem of limited data is overcome by analyzing and averaging multiple models produced with different random arrangements of training and test data. In the stream setting the problem of (effectively) unlimited data poses different challenges. One solution involves taking snapshots at different times during the induction of a model to see how much the model improves.

The evaluation procedure of a learning algorithm determines which examples are used for training the algorithm, and which are used to test the model output by the algorithm. The procedure used historically in batch learning has partly depended on data size. As data sizes increase, practical time limitations prevent procedures that repeat training too many times. It is commonly accepted with considerably larger data sources that it is necessary to reduce the numbers of repetitions or folds to allow experiments to complete in reasonable time. When considering what procedure to use in the data stream setting, one of the unique concerns is how to build a picture of accuracy over time. Two main approaches arise [Kir07]:

- **Holdout**: When traditional batch learning reaches a scale where cross-validation is too time consuming, it is often accepted to instead measure performance on a single holdout set. This is most useful when the division between train and test sets have been pre-defined, so that results from different studies can be directly compared.

- **Interleaved Test-Then-Train**: Each individual example can be used to test the model before it is used for training, and from this the accuracy can be incrementally updated. When intentionally performed in this order, the model is always being tested on examples it has not seen. This scheme has the advantage that no holdout set is needed for testing, making maximum use of the available data. It also ensures a smooth plot of accuracy over time, as each individual example will become increasingly less significant to the overall average.

As data stream classification is a relatively new field, such evaluation practices are not nearly as well researched and established as they are in the traditional batch setting. The majority of experimental evaluations use less than one million training examples. Some papers use more than this, up to ten million examples, and only very rarely is there any study like Domingos and Hulten [DH00, HSD01] that is in the order of tens of millions of examples. In the context of data streams this is disappointing, because to be truly useful at data stream classification the algorithms need to be capable of handling very large (potentially infinite) streams of examples. Demonstrating systems only on small amounts of data does not build a convincing case for capacity to solve more demanding data stream applications.

A claim of [Kir07] is that in order to adequately evaluate data stream classification algorithms they need to be tested on large streams, in the order of tens of millions of examples where possible, and under explicit memory limits. Any less than this does not actually test algorithms in a realistically challenging setting.

3.5.1 Concept Drift Framework

We present a new experimental framework for concept drift. Our goal is to introduce artificial drift to data stream generators in a straightforward way.

The framework approach most similar to the one presented in this Chapter is the one proposed by Narasimhamurthy et al. [NK07]. They proposed a general framework to generate data simulating changing environments. Their framework accommodates the STAGGER and Moving Hyperplane generation strategies. They consider a set of k data sources with known distributions. As these distributions at the sources are fixed, the data distribution at time t, $D^{(t)}$ is specified through $v_i(t)$, where $v_i(t) \in [0,1]$ specify the extent of the influence of data source i at time t:

$$D^{(t)} = \{v_1(t), v_2(t), \ldots, v_k(t)\}, \sum_i v_i(t) = 1$$

Their framework covers gradual and abrupt changes. Our approach is more concrete, we begin by dealing with a simple scenario: a data stream and two different concepts. Later, we will consider the general case with more than one concept drift events.

Considering data streams as data generated from pure distributions, we can model a concept drift event as a weighted combination of two pure distributions that characterizes the target concepts before and after the drift. In our framework, we need to define the probability that every new instance of the stream belongs to the new concept after the drift. We will use the sigmoid function, as an elegant and practical solution.

We see from Figure 3.7 that the sigmoid function

$$f(t) = 1/(1 + e^{-s(t-t_0)})$$

has a derivative at the point t_0 equal to $f'(t_0) = s/4$. The tangent of angle α is equal to this derivative, $\tan \alpha = s/4$. We observe that $\tan \alpha = 1/W$, and as $s = 4 \tan \alpha$ then $s = 4/W$. So the parameter s in the sigmoid gives the length of W and the angle α. In this sigmoid model we only need to specify

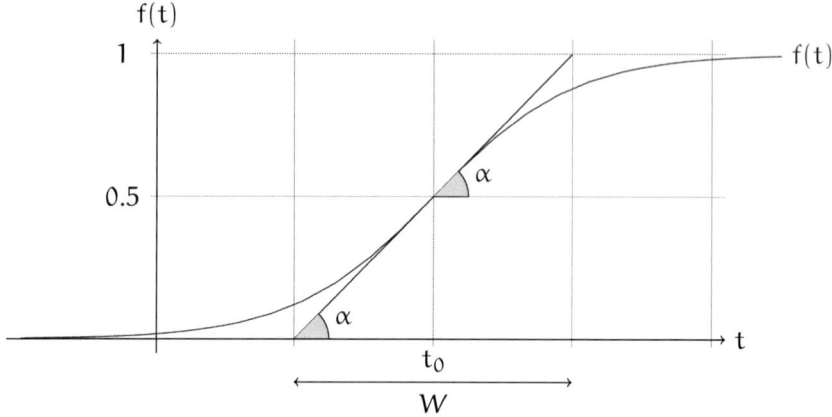

Figure 3.7: A sigmoid function $f(t) = 1/(1+e^{-s(t-t_0)})$.

two parameters : t_0 the point of change, and W the length of change. Note that
$$f(t_0 + \beta \cdot W) = 1 - f(t_0 - \beta \cdot W),$$
and that $f(t_0+\beta \cdot W)$ and $f(t_0-\beta \cdot W)$ are constant values that don't depend on t_0 and W:

$$f(t_0 + W/2) = 1 - f(t_0 - W/2) = 1/(1+e^{-2}) \approx 88.08\%$$
$$f(t_0 + W) = 1 - f(t_0 - W) = 1/(1+e^{-4}) \approx 98.20\%$$
$$f(t_0 + 2W) = 1 - f(t_0 - 2W) = 1/(1+e^{-8}) \approx 99.97\%$$

Definition 1. *Given two data streams a, b, we define $c = a \oplus_{t_0}^{W} b$ as the data stream built joining the two data streams a and b, where t_0 is the point of change, W is the length of change and*

- $\Pr[c(t) = a(t)] = e^{-4(t-t_0)/W}/(1+e^{-4(t-t_0)/W})$
- $\Pr[c(t) = b(t)] = 1/(1+e^{-4(t-t_0)/W})$.

We observe the following properties, if $a \neq b$:

- $a \oplus_{t_0}^{W} b \neq b \oplus_{t_0}^{W} a$
- $a \oplus_{t_0}^{W} a = a$
- $a \oplus_{0}^{0} b = b$
- $a \oplus_{t_0}^{W} (b \oplus_{t_0}^{W} c) \neq (a \oplus_{t_0}^{W} b) \oplus_{t_0}^{W} c$
- $a \oplus_{t_0}^{W} (b \oplus_{t_1}^{W} c) \approx (a \oplus_{t_0}^{W} b) \oplus_{t_1}^{W} c$ if $t_0 < t_1$ and $W \ll |t_1 - t_0|$

3.5. EXPERIMENTAL SETTING

In order to create a data stream with multiple concept changes, we can build new data streams joining different concept drifts:

$$(((a \oplus_{t_0}^{W_0} b) \oplus_{t_1}^{W_1} c) \oplus_{t_2}^{W_2} d)\ldots$$

3.5.2 Datasets for concept drift

Synthetic data has several advantages – it is easier to reproduce and there is little cost in terms of storage and transmission. For this framework, the data generators most commonly found in the literature have been collected.

SEA Concepts Generator This dataset contains abrupt concept drift, first introduced in [SK01]. It is generated using three attributes, where only the two first attributes are relevant. All three attributes have values between 0 and 10. The points of the dataset are divided into 4 blocks with different concepts. In each block, the classification is done using $f_1 + f_2 \leq \theta$, where f_1 and f_2 represent the first two attributes and θ is a threshold value. The most frequent values are 9, 8, 7 and 9.5 for the data blocks. In our framework, SEA concepts are defined as follows:

$$(((SEA_9 \oplus_{t_0}^{W} SEA_8) \oplus_{2t_0}^{W} SEA_7) \oplus_{3t_0}^{W} SEA_{9.5})$$

STAGGER Concepts Generator They were introduced by Schlimmer and Granger in [SG86]. The concept description in STAGGER is a collection of elements, where each individual element is a Boolean function of attribute-valued pairs that is represented by a disjunct of conjuncts. A typical example of a concept description covering either green rectangles or red triangles can be represented by (shape rectangle and colour green) or (shape triangles and colour red).

Rotating Hyperplane This dataset was used as testbed for CVFDT versus VFDT in [HSD01]. A hyperplane in d-dimensional space is the set of points x that satisfy

$$\sum_{i=1}^{d} w_i x_i = w_0 = \sum_{i=1}^{d} w_i$$

where x_i, is the ith coordinate of x. Examples for which $\sum_{i=1}^{d} w_i x_i \geq w_0$ are labeled positive, and examples for which $\sum_{i=1}^{d} w_i x_i < w_0$ are labeled negative. Hyperplanes are useful for simulating time-changing concepts, because we can change the orientation and position of the hyperplane in a smooth manner by changing the relative size of the weights. We introduce change to this dataset adding drift to each weight attribute $w_i = w_i + d\sigma$, where σ is the probability that the direction of change is reversed and d is the change applied to every example.

Random RBF Generator This generator was devised to offer an alternate complex concept type that is not straightforward to approximate with a decision tree model. The RBF (Radial Basis Function) generator works as follows: A fixed number of random centroids are generated. Each center has a random position, a single standard deviation, class label and weight. New examples are generated by selecting a center at random, taking weights into consideration so that centers with higher weight are more likely to be chosen. A random direction is chosen to offset the attribute values from the central point. The length of the displacement is randomly drawn from a Gaussian distribution with standard deviation determined by the chosen centroid. The chosen centroid also determines the class label of the example. This effectively creates a normally distributed hypersphere of examples surrounding each central point with varying densities. Only numeric attributes are generated. Drift is introduced by moving the centroids with constant speed. This speed is initialized by a drift parameter.

LED Generator This data source originates from the CART book [B+84]. An implementation in C was donated to the UCI [AN07] machine learning repository by David Aha. The goal is to predict the digit displayed on a seven-segment LED display, where each attribute has a 10% chance of being inverted. It has an optimal Bayes classification rate of 74%. The particular configuration of the generator used for experiments (led) produces 24 binary attributes, 17 of which are irrelevant.

Waveform Generator It shares its origins with LED, and was also donated by David Aha to the UCI repository. The goal of the task is to differentiate between three different classes of waveform, each of which is generated from a combination of two or three base waves. The optimal Bayes classification rate is known to be 86%. There are two versions of the problem, wave21 which has 21 numeric attributes, all of which include noise, and wave40 which introduces an additional 19 irrelevant attributes.

Function Generator It was introduced by Agrawal et al. in [AGI+92], and was a common source of data for early work on scaling up decision tree learners [AIS93, MAR96, SAM96, GRG98]. The generator produces a stream containing nine attributes, six numeric and three categorical. Although not explicitly stated by the authors, a sensible

3.5. EXPERIMENTAL SETTING

conclusion is that these attributes describe hypothetical loan applications. There are ten functions defined for generating binary class labels from the attributes. Presumably these determine whether the loan should be approved.

Data streams may be considered infinite sequences of (x, y) where x is the feature vector and y the class label. Zhang et al. [ZZS08] observe that $p(x, y) = p(x|t) \cdot p(y|x)$ and categorize concept drift in two types:

- *Loose Concept Drifting (LCD)* when concept drift is caused only by the change of the class prior probability $p(y|x)$,

- *Rigorous Concept Drifting (RCD)* when concept drift is caused by the change of the class prior probability $p(y|x)$ and the conditional probability $p(x|t)$

Note that the Random RBF Generator has RCD drift, and the rest of the dataset generators have LCD drift.

Real-World Data

It is not easy to find large real-world datasets for public benchmarking, especially with substantial concept change. The UCI machine learning repository [AN07] contains some real-world benchmark data for evaluating machine learning techniques. We will consider three : Forest Covertype, Poker-Hand, and Electricity.

Forest Covertype dataset It contains the forest cover type for 30 x 30 meter cells obtained from US Forest Service (USFS) Region 2 Resource Information System (RIS) data. It contains $581,012$ instances and 54 attributes, and it has been used in several papers on data stream classification [GRM03, OR01b].

Poker-Hand dataset It consists of $1,000,000$ instances and 11 attributes. Each record of the Poker-Hand dataset is an example of a hand consisting of five playing cards drawn from a standard deck of 52. Each card is described using two attributes (suit and rank), for a total of 10 predictive attributes. There is one Class attribute that describes the "Poker Hand". The order of cards is important, which is why there are 480 possible Royal Flush hands instead of 4.

Electricity dataset Another widely used dataset is the Electricity Market Dataset described by M. Harries [Har99] and used by Gama [GMCR04]. This data was collected from the Australian New South Wales Electricity Market. In this market, the prices are not fixed and are affected by demand and supply of the market. The prices in this market are set every five minutes. The ELEC2 dataset contains $45,312$ instances.

Each example of the dataset refers to a period of 30 minutes, i.e. there are 48 instances for each time period of one day. The class label identifies the change of the price related to a moving average of the last 24 hours. The class level only reflect deviations of the price on a one day average and removes the impact of longer term price trends.

The size of these datasets is small, compared to tens of millions of training examples of synthetic datasets: 45,312 for ELEC2 dataset, 581,012 for CoverType, and 1,000,000 for Poker-Hand. Another important fact is that we do not know when drift occurs or if there is any drift. We may simulate RCD concept drift, joining the three datasets, merging attributes, and supposing that each dataset corresponds to a different concept.

$$\text{CovPokElec} = (\text{CoverType} \oplus_{581,012}^{5,000} \text{Poker}) \oplus_{1,000,000}^{5,000} \text{ELEC2}$$

3.5.3 MOA Experimental Framework

Massive Online Analysis (MOA) [HKP07] is a framework for online learning from continuous data streams. The data stream evaluation framework and most of the classification algorithms evaluated in this book were implemented in the Java programming language extending the MOA framework. MOA includes a collection of offline and online methods as well as tools for evaluation. In particular, it implements boosting, bagging, and Hoeffding Trees, all with and without Naïve Bayes classifiers at the leaves.

MOA is related to WEKA, the Waikato Environment for Knowledge Analysis [WF05], which is an award-winning open-source workbench containing implementations of a wide range of batch machine learning methods. WEKA is also written in Java. The main benefits of Java are portability, where applications can be run on any platform with an appropriate Java virtual machine, and the strong and well-developed support libraries. Use of the language is widespread, and features such as the automatic garbage collection help to reduce programmer burden and error.

One of the key data structures used in MOA is the description of an example from a data stream. This structure borrows from WEKA, where an example is represented by an array of double precision floating point values. This provides freedom to store all necessary types of value – numeric attribute values can be stored directly, and discrete attribute values and class labels are represented by integer index values that are stored as floating point values in the array. Double precision floating point values require storage space of 64 bits, or 8 bytes. This detail can have implications for memory usage.

4

Adaptive Sliding Windows

Dealing with data whose nature changes over time is one of the core problems in data mining and machine learning. In this chapter we propose ADWIN, an adaptive sliding window algorithm, as an estimator with memory and change detector with the main properties of optimality explained in section 3.4. We study and develop also the combination of ADWIN with Kalman filters.

4.1 Introduction

Most strategies in the literature use variations of the sliding window idea: a window is maintained that keeps the most recently read examples, and from which older examples are dropped according to some set of rules. The contents of the window can be used for the three tasks: 1) to detect change (e.g., by using some statistical test on different subwindows), 2) obviously, to obtain updated statistics from the recent examples, and 3) to have data to rebuild or revise the model(s) after data has changed.

The simplest rule is to keep a window of some fixed size, usually determined *a priori* by the user. This can work well if information on the timescale of change is available, but this is rarely the case. Normally, the user is caught in a tradeoff without solution: choosing a small size (so that the window reflects accurately the current distribution) and choosing a large size (so that many examples are available to work on, increasing accuracy in periods of stability). A different strategy uses a *decay function* to weight the importance of examples according to their age (see e.g. [CS03]): the relative contribution of each data item is scaled down by a factor that depends on elapsed time. In this case, the tradeoff shows up in the choice of a decay constant that should match the unknown rate of change.

Less often, it has been proposed to use windows of variable size. In general, one tries to keep examples as long as possible, i.e., while not proven stale. This delivers the users from having to guess *a priori* an unknown parameter such as the time scale of change. However, most works along these lines that we know of (e.g., [GMCR04, KJ00, Las02, WK96]) are heuristics and have no rigorous guarantees of performance. Some works in computational learning theory (e.g. [BBDK00, HL94, HW95]) describe strategies with rigorous performance bounds, but to our knowledge they have never been tried in real learning/mining contexts and often assume a known bound on the rate of change.

We will present ADWIN, a parameter-free adaptive size sliding window, with theoretical garantees. We will use Kalman filters at the last part of this Chapter, in order to provide an adaptive weight for each item.

4.2 Maintaining Updated Windows of Varying Length

In this section we describe our algorithms for dynamically adjusting the length of a data window, make a formal claim about its performance, and derive an efficient variation.

We will use Hoeffding's bound in order to obtain formal guarantees, and a streaming algorithm. However, other tests computing differences between window distributions may be used.

4.2.1 Setting

The inputs to the algorithms are a confidence value $\delta \in (0,1)$ and a (possibly infinite) sequence of real values $x_1, x_2, x_3, \ldots, x_t, \ldots$ The value of x_t is available only at time t. Each x_t is generated according to some distribution D_t, independently for every t. We denote with μ_t and σ_t^2 the expected value and the variance of x_t when it is drawn according to D_t. We assume that x_t is always in $[0,1]$; by an easy rescaling, we can handle any case in which we know an interval $[a,b]$ such that $a \leq x_t \leq b$ with probability 1. Nothing else is known about the sequence of distributions D_t; in particular, μ_t and σ_t^2 are unknown for all t.

4.2.2 First algorithm: ADWIN0

Our algorithm keeps a sliding window W with the most recently read x_i. Let n denote the length of W, $\hat{\mu}_W$ the (observed) average of the elements in W, and μ_W the (unknown) average of μ_t for $t \in W$. Strictly speaking, these quantities should be indexed by t, but in general t will be clear from the context.

Since the values of μ_t can oscillate wildly, there is no guarantee that μ_W or $\hat{\mu}_W$ will be anywhere close to the instantaneous value μ_t, even for long W. However, μ_W is the expected value of $\hat{\mu}_W$, so μ_W and $\hat{\mu}_W$ *do* get close as W grows.

Algorithm ADWIN0 is presented in Figure 4.1. The idea is simple: whenever two "large enough" subwindows of W exhibit "distinct enough" averages, one can conclude that the corresponding expected values are different, and the older portion of the window is dropped. In other words,

4.2. MAINTAINING UPDATED WINDOWS OF VARYING LENGTH

ADWIN0: ADAPTIVE WINDOWING ALGORITHM
1   Initialize Window W
2   **for** each $t > 0$
3   **do** $W \leftarrow W \cup \{x_t\}$ (i.e., add x_t to the head of W)
4   **repeat** Drop elements from the tail of W
5   **until** $|\hat{\mu}_{W_0} - \hat{\mu}_{W_1}| < \epsilon_{cut}$ holds
6   for every split of W into $W = W_0 \cdot W_1$
7   output $\hat{\mu}_W$

Figure 4.1: Algorithm ADWIN0.

W is kept as long as possible while the null hypothesis "μ_t has remained constant in W" is sustainable up to confidence δ.[1] "Large enough" and "distinct enough" above are made precise by choosing an appropriate statistical test for distribution change, which in general involves the value of δ, the lengths of the subwindows, and their contents. We choose one particular statistical test for our implementation, but this is not the essence of our proposal – many other tests could be used. At every step, ADWIN0 simply outputs the value of $\hat{\mu}_W$ as an approximation to μ_W.

The value of ϵ_{cut} for a partition $W_0 \cdot W_1$ of W is computed as follows: Let n_0 and n_1 be the lengths of W_0 and W_1 and n be the length of W, so $n = n_0 + n_1$. Let $\hat{\mu}_{W_0}$ and $\hat{\mu}_{W_1}$ be the averages of the values in W_0 and W_1, and μ_{W_0} and μ_{W_1} their expected values. To obtain totally rigorous performance guarantees we define:

$$m = \frac{1}{1/n_0 + 1/n_1} \text{ (harmonic mean of } n_0 \text{ and } n_1\text{),}$$

$$\delta' = \frac{\delta}{n}, \text{ and } \epsilon_{cut} = \sqrt{\frac{1}{2m} \cdot \ln \frac{4}{\delta'}}.$$

Our statistical test for different distributions in W_0 and W_1 simply checks whether the observed average in both subwindows differs by more than the threshold ϵ_{cut}. The role of δ' is to avoid problems with multiple hypothesis testing (since we will be testing n different possibilities for W_0 and W_1 and we want global error below δ). Later we will provide a more sensitive test based on the normal approximation that, although not 100% rigorous, is perfectly valid in practice.

Now we state our main technical result about the performance of ADWIN0:

Theorem 3. *At every time step we have*

---

[1]It would easy to use instead the null hypothesis "there has been no change greater than ϵ", for a user-specified ϵ expressing the smallest change that deserves reaction.

1. **(False positive rate bound).** *If μ_t remains constant within W, the probability that* `ADWIN0` *shrinks the window at this step is at most δ.*

2. **(False negative rate bound).** *Suppose that for some partition of W in two parts $W_0 W_1$ (where W_1 contains the most recent items) we have $|\mu_{W_0} - \mu_{W_1}| > 2\epsilon_{cut}$. Then with probability $1 - \delta$* `ADWIN0` *shrinks W to W_1, or shorter.*

Proof. **Part 1)** Assume $\mu_{W_0} = \mu_{W_1} = \mu_W$ as null hypothesis. We show that for any partition W as $W_0 W_1$ we have probability at most δ/n that `ADWIN0` decides to shrink W to W_1, or equivalently,

$$\Pr[|\hat{\mu}_{W_1} - \hat{\mu}_{W_0}| \geq \epsilon_{cut}] \leq \delta/n.$$

Since there are at most n partitions $W_0 W_1$, the claim follows by the union bound. Note that, for every real number $k \in (0, 1)$, $|\hat{\mu}_{W_1} - \hat{\mu}_{W_0}| \geq \epsilon_{cut}$ can be decomposed as

$$\Pr[|\hat{\mu}_{W_1} - \hat{\mu}_{W_0}| \geq \epsilon_{cut}]$$
$$\leq \Pr[|\hat{\mu}_{W_1} - \mu_W| \geq k\epsilon_{cut}] + \Pr[|\mu_W - \hat{\mu}_{W_0}| \geq (1-k)\epsilon_{cut}].$$

Applying the Hoeffding bound, we have then

$$\Pr[|\hat{\mu}_{W_1} - \hat{\mu}_{W_0}| \geq \epsilon_{cut}] \leq 2\exp(-2(k\,\epsilon_{cut})^2 n_0) + 2\exp(-2((1-k)\epsilon_{cut})^2 n_1)$$

To approximately minimize the sum, we choose the value of k that makes both probabilities equal, i.e. such that

$$(k\,\epsilon_{cut})^2 n_0 = ((1-k)\,\epsilon_{cut})^2 n_1.$$

which is $k = \sqrt{n_1/n_0}/(1 + \sqrt{n_1/n_0})$. For this k, we have precisely

$$(k\,\epsilon_{cut})^2 n_0 = \frac{n_1 n_0}{(\sqrt{n_0} + \sqrt{n_1})^2}\,\epsilon_{cut}^2 \leq \frac{n_1 n_0}{(n_0 + n_1)}\,\epsilon_{cut}^2 = m\,\epsilon_{cut}^2.$$

Therefore, in order to have

$$\Pr[|\hat{\mu}_{W_1} - \hat{\mu}_{W_0}| \geq \epsilon_{cut}] \leq \frac{\delta}{n}$$

it suffices to have

$$4\exp(-2m\,\epsilon_{cut}^2) \leq \frac{\delta}{n}$$

which is satisfied by

$$\epsilon_{cut} = \sqrt{\frac{1}{2m} \ln \frac{4n}{\delta}}.$$

Part 2) Now assume $|\mu_{W_0} - \mu_{W_1}| > 2\epsilon_{cut}$. We want to show that $\Pr[|\hat{\mu}_{W_1} - \hat{\mu}_{W_0}| \leq \epsilon_{cut}] \leq \delta$, which means that with probability at least $1 - \delta$ change

4.2. MAINTAINING UPDATED WINDOWS OF VARYING LENGTH

is detected and the algorithm cuts W to W_1. As before, for any $k \in (0,1)$, we can decompose $|\hat{\mu}_{W_0} - \hat{\mu}_{W_1}| \leq \epsilon_{cut}$ as

$$\Pr[|\hat{\mu}_{W_0} - \hat{\mu}_{W_1}| \leq \epsilon_{cut}]$$
$$\leq \Pr[(|\hat{\mu}_{W_0} - \mu_{W_0}| \geq k\epsilon_{cut}) \cup (|\hat{\mu}_{W_1} - \mu_{W_1}| \geq (1-k)\epsilon_{cut})]$$
$$\leq \Pr[|\hat{\mu}_{W_0} - \mu_{W_0}| \geq k\epsilon_{cut}] + \Pr[|\hat{\mu}_{W_1} - \mu_{W_1}| \geq (1-k)\epsilon_{cut}].$$

To see the first inequality, observe that if $|\hat{\mu}_{W_0} - \hat{\mu}_{W_1}| \leq \epsilon_{cut}$, $|\hat{\mu}_{W_0} - \mu_{W_0}| \leq k\epsilon_{cut}$, and $|\hat{\mu}_{W_1} - \mu_{W_1}| \leq (1-k)\epsilon_{cut}$ hold, by the triangle inequality we have

$$|\mu_{W_0} - \mu_{W_1}| \leq |\hat{\mu}_{W_0} + k\epsilon_{cut} - \hat{\mu}_{W_1} + (1-k)\epsilon_{cut}| \leq |\hat{\mu}_{W_0} - \hat{\mu}_{W_1}| + \epsilon_{cut} \leq 2\epsilon_{cut},$$

contradicting the hypothesis. Using the Hoeffding bound, we have then

$$\Pr[|\hat{\mu}_{W_0} - \hat{\mu}_{W_1}| \geq \epsilon_{cut}]$$
$$\leq 2\exp(-2(k\,\epsilon_{cut})^2 n_0) + 2\exp(-2((1-k)\,\epsilon_{cut})^2 n_1).$$

Now, choose k as before to make both terms equal. By the calculations in Part 1 we have

$$\Pr[|\hat{\mu}_{W_0} - \hat{\mu}_{W_1}| \geq \epsilon_{cut}] \leq 4\exp(-2m\,\epsilon_{cut}^2) \leq \frac{\delta}{n} \leq \delta,$$

as desired. □

In practice, the definition of ϵ_{cut} as above is too conservative. Indeed, it is based on the Hoeffding bound, which is valid for all distributions but greatly overestimates the probability of large deviations for distributions of small variance; in fact, it is equivalent to assuming always the worst-case variance $\sigma^2 = 1/4$. In practice, one can observe that $\mu_{W_0} - \mu_{W_1}$ tends to a normal distribution for large window sizes, and use

$$\epsilon_{cut} = \sqrt{\frac{2}{m} \cdot \sigma_W^2 \cdot \ln\frac{2}{\delta'}} + \frac{2}{3m}\ln\frac{2}{\delta'}, \qquad (4.1)$$

where σ_W^2 is the observed variance of the elements in window W. Thus, the term with the square root is essentially equivalent to setting ϵ_{cut} to k times the standard deviation, for k depending on the desired confidence δ, as is done in [GMCR04]. The extra additive term protects the cases where the window sizes are too small to apply the normal approximation, as an alternative to the traditional use of requiring, say, sample size at least 30; it can be formally derived from the so-called Bernstein bound. Additionally, one (somewhat involved) argument shows that setting $\delta' = \delta/(\ln n)$ is enough in this context to protect from the multiple hypothesis testing problem; anyway, in the actual algorithm that we will run (ADWIN), only

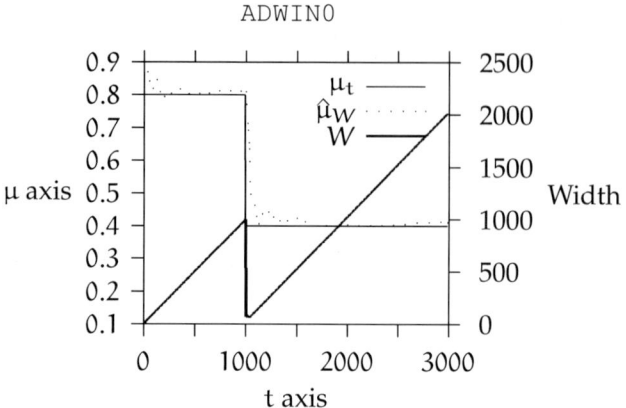

Figure 4.2: Output of algorithm ADWIN0 with abrupt change.

$O(\log n)$ subwindows are checked, which justifies using $\delta' = \delta/(\ln n)$. Theorem 3 holds for this new value of ϵ_{cut}, up to the error introduced by the normal approximation. We have used these better bounds in all our implementations.

Let us consider how ADWIN0 behaves in two special cases: sudden (but infrequent) changes, and slow gradual changes. Suppose that for a long time μ_t has remained fixed at a value μ, and that it suddenly jumps to a value $\mu' = \mu + \epsilon$. By part (2) of Theorem 3 and Equation 4.1, one can derive that the window will start shrinking after $O(\mu \ln(1/\delta)/\epsilon^2)$ steps, and in fact will be shrunk to the point where only $O(\mu \ln(1/\delta)/\epsilon^2)$ examples prior to the change are left. From then on, if no further changes occur, no more examples will be dropped so the window will expand unboundedly.

In case of a gradual change with slope α following a long stationary period at μ, observe that the average of W_1 after n_1 steps is $\mu + \alpha n_1/2$; we have $\epsilon (= \alpha n_1/2) \geq O(\sqrt{\mu \ln(1/\delta)/n_1})$ iff $n_1 = O(\mu \ln(1/\delta)/\alpha^2)^{1/3}$. So n_1 steps after the change the window will start shrinking, and will remain at approximately size n_1 from then on. A dependence on α of the form $O(\alpha^{-2/3})$ may seem odd at first, but one can show that this window length is actually optimal in this setting, even if α is known: it minimizes the sum of variance error (due to short window) and error due to out-of-date data (due to long windows in the presence of change). Thus, in this setting, ADWIN0 provably adjusts automatically the window setting to its optimal value, up to multiplicative constants.

Figures 4.2 and 4.3 illustrate these behaviors. In Figure 4.2, a sudden change from $\mu_{t-1} = 0.8$ to $\mu_t = 0.4$ occurs, at $t = 1000$. One can see that the window size grows linearly up to $t = 1000$, that ADWIN0 cuts the window severely 10 steps later (at $t = 1010$), and that the window expands again linearly after time $t = 1010$. In Figure 4.3, μ_t gradually descends from 0.8

4.2. MAINTAINING UPDATED WINDOWS OF VARYING LENGTH

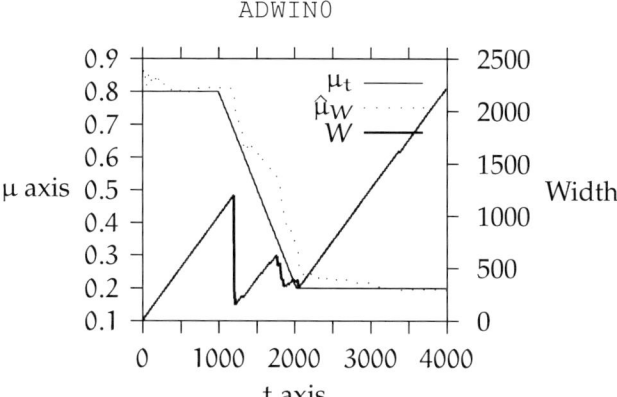

Figure 4.3: Output of algorithm ADWIN0 with slow gradual changes.

to 0.2 in the range t ∈ [1000..2000]. In this case, ADWIN0 cuts the window sharply at t around 1200 (i.e., 200 steps after the slope starts), keeps the window length bounded (with some random fluctuations) while the slope lasts, and starts growing it linearly again after that. As predicted by theory, detecting the change is harder in slopes than in abrupt changes.

4.2.3 ADWIN0 for Poisson processes

A Poisson process is the stochastic process in which events occur continuously and independently of one another. A well-known example is radioactive decay of atoms. Many processes are not exactly Poisson processes, but similar enough that for certain types of analysis they can be regarded as such; e.g., telephone calls arriving at a switchboard, webpage requests to a search engine, or rainfall.

Using the Chernoff bound for Poisson processes [MN02]

$$\Pr\{X \geq cE[X]\} \leq \exp(-(c\ln(c) + 1 - c)E[X])$$

we find a similar ϵ_{cut} for Poisson processes.

First, we look for a simpler form of this bound. Let $c = 1 + \epsilon$ then

$$c\ln(c) - c + 1 = (1 + \epsilon) \cdot \ln(1 + \epsilon) - \epsilon$$

Using the Taylor expansion of $\ln(x)$

$$\ln(1 + x) = \sum (-1)^{n+1} \cdot \frac{x^n}{n} = x - \frac{x^2}{2} + \frac{x^3}{3} - \cdots$$

we get the following simpler expression:

$$\Pr\{X \geq (1+\epsilon)E[X]\} \leq \exp(-\epsilon^2 E[X]/2)$$

Now, let S_n be the sum of n Poisson processes. As S_n is also a Poisson process

$$E[S_n] = \lambda_{S_n} = nE[X] = n \cdot \lambda_X$$

and then we obtain

$$\Pr\{S_n \geq (1+\epsilon)E[S_n]\} \leq \exp(-\epsilon^2 E[S_n]/2)$$

In order to obtain a formula for ϵ_{cut}, let $Y = S_n/n$

$$\Pr\{Y \geq (1+\epsilon)E[Y]\} \leq \exp(-\epsilon^2 \cdot n \cdot E[Y]/2)$$

And finally, with this bound we get the following ϵ_{cut} for ADWIN0

$$\epsilon_{cut} = \sqrt{\frac{2\lambda}{m} \ln \frac{2}{\delta}}$$

where $1/m = 1/n_0 + 1/n_1$, and λ is the mean of the window data.

4.2.4 Improving time and memory requirements

Our first version of ADWIN0 is computationally expensive, because it checks exhaustively all "large enough" subwindows of the current window for possible cuts. Furthermore, the contents of the window is kept explicitly, with the corresponding memory cost as the window grows. To reduce these costs we present a new version ADWIN using ideas developed in data stream algorithmics [BBD+02, Mut03, BDM02, DGIM02] to find a good cut-point quickly. Figure 4.4 shows the ADWIN algorithm. We next provide a sketch of how this algorithm and these data structures work.

Our data structure is a variation of exponential histograms [DGIM02], a data structure that maintains an approximation of the number of 1's in a sliding window of length W with logarithmic memory and update time. We adapt this data structure in a way that can provide this approximation simultaneously for about $O(\log W)$ subwindows whose lengths follow a geometric law, *with no memory overhead* with respect to keeping the count for a single window. That is, our data structure will be able to give the number of 1s among the most recently $t-1$, $t - \lfloor c \rfloor$, $t - \lfloor c^2 \rfloor$,..., $t - \lfloor c^i \rfloor$, ... read bits, with the same amount of memory required to keep an approximation for the whole W. Note that keeping exact counts for a fixed-window size is provably impossible in sublinear memory. We go around this problem by shrinking or enlarging the window strategically so that what would otherwise be an approximate count happens to be exact.

ADWIN: ADAPTIVE WINDOWING ALGORITHM
1   Initialize W as an empty list of buckets
2   Initialize WIDTH, VARIANCE and TOTAL
3   **for** each $t > 0$
4   **do** SETINPUT(x_t, W)
5   output $\hat{\mu}_W$ as TOTAL/WIDTH and ChangeAlarm

SETINPUT(item e, List W)
1   INSERTELEMENT(e, W)
2   **repeat** DELETEELEMENT(W)
3   **until** $|\hat{\mu}_{W_0} - \hat{\mu}_{W_1}| < \epsilon_{cut}$ holds
4   for every split of W into $W = W_0 \cdot W_1$

INSERTELEMENT(item e, List W)
1   create a new bucket b with content e and capacity 1
2   $W \leftarrow W \cup \{b\}$ (i.e., add e to the head of W)
3   update WIDTH, VARIANCE and TOTAL
4   COMPRESSBUCKETS(W)

DELETEELEMENT(List W)
1   remove a bucket from tail of List W
2   update WIDTH, VARIANCE and TOTAL
3   ChangeAlarm $\leftarrow$ **true**

COMPRESSBUCKETS(List W)
1   Traverse the list of buckets in increasing order
2   **do** If there are more than M buckets of the same capacity
3   **do** merge buckets
4   COMPRESSBUCKETS(sublist of W not traversed)

Figure 4.4: Algorithm ADWIN.

More precisely, to design the algorithm one chooses a parameter M. This parameter controls both 1) the amount of memory used (it will be $O(M \log W/M)$ words, and 2) the closeness of the cutpoints checked (the basis c of the geometric series above, which will be about $c = 1 + 1/M$). Note that the choice of M does *not* reflect any assumption about the time-scale of change: Since points are checked at a geometric rate anyway, this policy is essentially scale-independent.

More precisely, in the boolean case, the information on the number of 1's is kept as a series of buckets whose size is always a power of 2. We keep at most M buckets of each size 2^i, where M is a design parameter. For each bucket we record two (integer) elements: *capacity* and *content* (size, or number of 1s it contains).

Thus, we use about $M \cdot \log(W/M)$ buckets to maintain our data stream sliding window. ADWIN checks as a possible cut every border of a bucket, i.e., window lengths of the form $M(1 + 2 + \cdots + 2^{i-1}) + j \cdot 2^i$, for $0 \leq j \leq M$. It can be seen that these $M \cdot \log(W/M)$ points follow approximately a geometric law of basis $\cong 1 + 1/M$.

Let's look at an example: a sliding window with 14 elements. We register it as:

| 1010101 | 101 | 11 | 1 | 1 |

Content: 4   2   2   1   1
Capacity: 7   3   2   1   1

Each time a new element arrives, if the element is "1", we create a new bucket of *content* 1 and *capacity* the number of elements arrived since the last "1". After that we compress the rest of buckets: When there are $M + 1$ buckets of size 2^i, we merge the two oldest ones (adding its capacity) into a bucket of size 2^{i+1}. So, we use $O(M \cdot \log W/M)$ memory words if we assume that a word can contain a number up to W. In [DGIM02], the window is kept at a fixed size W. The information missing about the last bucket is responsible for the approximation error. Here, each time we detect change, we reduce the window's length deleting the last bucket, instead of (conceptually) dropping a single element as in a typical sliding window framework. This lets us keep an exact counting, since when throwing away a whole bucket we know that we are dropping exactly 2^i "1"s.

We summarize these results with the following theorem.

Theorem 4. *The* ADWIN *algorithm maintains a data structure with the following properties:*

- *It uses $O(M \cdot \log(W/M))$ memory words (assuming a memory word can contain numbers up to W).*

- *It can process the arrival of a new element in $O(1)$ amortized time and $O(\log W)$ worst-case time.*

4.2. MAINTAINING UPDATED WINDOWS OF VARYING LENGTH

- It can provide the exact counts of 1's for all the subwindows whose lengths are of the form $\lfloor (1+1/M)^i \rfloor$, in $O(1)$ time per query.

Since ADWIN tries $O(\log W)$ cutpoints, the total processing time per example is $O(\log W)$ (amortized) and $O(\log W)$ (worst-case).

In our example, suppose $M=2$, if a new element "1" arrives then

| 1010101 | 101 | 11 | 1 | 1 | 1 |

Content: 4   2   2   1 1 1
Capacity: 7 3   2   1 1 1

There are 3 buckets of 1, so we compress it:

| 1010101 | 101 | 11 | 11 | 1 |

Content: 4   2   2   2   1
Capacity: 7 3   2   2   1

and now as we have 3 buckets of size 2, we compress it again

| 1010101 | 10111 | 11 | 1 |

Content: 4   4   2   1
Capacity: 7 5   2   1

And finally, if we detect change, we reduce the size of our sliding window deleting the last bucket:

| 10111 | 11 | 1 |

Content: 4   2   1
Capacity: 5 2   1

In the case of real values, we also maintain buckets of two elements: *capacity* and *content*. We store at *content* the sum of the real numbers we want to summarize. We restrict *capacity* to be a power of two. As in the boolean case, we use $O(\log W)$ buckets, and check $O(\log W)$ possible cuts. The memory requirement for each bucket is $\log W + R + \log \log W$ bits per bucket, where R is number of bits used to store a real number.

Figure 4.5 shows the output of ADWIN to a sudden change, and Figure 4.6 to a slow gradual change. The main difference with ADWIN output is that as ADWIN0 reduces one element by one each time it detects changes, ADWIN deletes an entire bucket, which yields a slightly more jagged graph in the case of a gradual change. The difference in approximation power between ADWIN0 and ADWIN is almost negligible, so we use ADWIN exclusively for our experiments.

Finally, we state our main technical result about the performance of ADWIN, in a similar way to the Theorem 3:

Theorem 5. *At every time step we have*

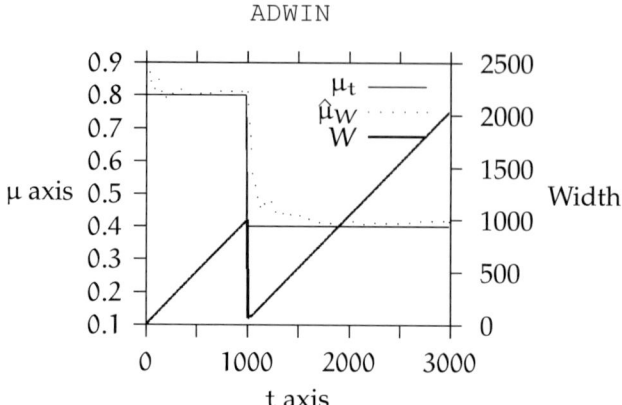

Figure 4.5: Output of algorithm ADWIN with abrupt change

1. (False positive rate bound). *If μ_t remains constant within W, the probability that* ADWIN *shrinks the window at this step is at most* $M/n \cdot \log(n/M) \cdot \delta$.

2. (False negative rate bound). *Suppose that for some partition of W in two parts $W_0 W_1$ (where W_1 contains the most recent items) we have $|\mu_{W_0} - \mu_{W_1}| > 2\epsilon_{cut}$. Then with probability $1 - \delta$* ADWIN *shrinks W to W_1, or shorter.*

Proof. **Part 1)** Assume $\mu_{W_0} = \mu_{W_1} = \mu_W$ as null hypothesis. We have shown in the proof of Theorem 3 that for any partition W as $W_0 W_1$ we have probability at most δ/n that ADWIN0 decides to shrink W to W_1, or equivalently,

$$\Pr[|\hat{\mu}_{W_1} - \hat{\mu}_{W_0}| \geq \epsilon_{cut}] \leq \delta/n.$$

Since ADWIN checks at most $M \log(n/M)$ partitions $W_0 W_1$, the claim follows.

Part 2) The proof is similar to the proof of Part 2 of Theorem 3. □

4.3 Experimental Validation of ADWIN

In this section, we are going to consider the performance of ADWIN in a data stream environment. We are interested in:

- evolution of accuracy
- probability of false alarms

4.3. EXPERIMENTAL VALIDATION OF ADWIN

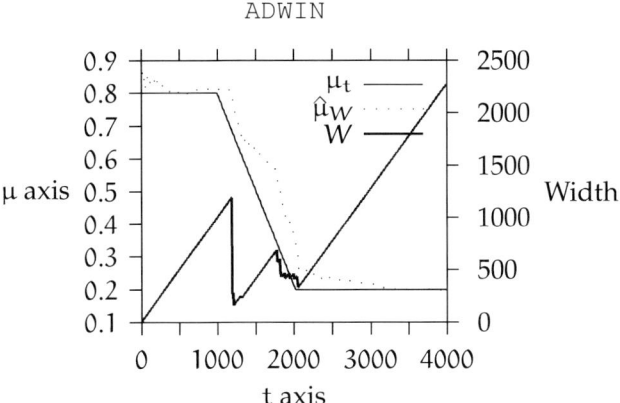

Figure 4.6: Output of algorithm ADWIN with slow gradual changes

- probability of true detections for different rates of drift
- average delay time in detection

We construct the following experiments to test the performance of our algorithms:

1. Rate of false positives: we show that the ratio of false positives is as predicted by theory.

2. Accuracy: we compare the estimation accuracy of ADWIN to estimations obtained from fixed-size windows with or without flushing when change is detected. ADWIN often does better than the best fixed-size window.

3. Small probabilities: we show that when the input samples to estimators are generated from small probabilities, then ADWIN beats almost all fixed-size window estimators, with or without flushing.

4. Probability of true detections and average delay time for different rates of drift: we compare the number of true detections and average delay time with DDM, and we observe that ADWIN detects more changes than DDM, but its average delay time of detection sometimes is higher.

5. Accuracy on mining methods as Naïve Bayes and k–means Clustering.

We use, somewhat arbitrarily, $M = 5$ for all experiments.

In the first experiment, we investigate the rate of false positives of ADWIN. This is a very important measure, specially when there is a cost associated with a reported change. To do this, we feed ADWIN a data stream of 100,000 bits, generated from a stationary Bernoulli distribution with parameter μ, and different confidence parameters δ.

Table 4.1 shows the ratio of false positives obtained. In all cases, it is below δ as predicted by the theory, and in fact much smaller for small values of μ.

μ	$\delta = 0.05$	$\delta = 0.1$	$\delta = 0.3$
0.01	0.00000	0.00000	0.00000
0.1	0.00002	0.00004	0.00019
0.3	0.00003	0.00008	0.00036
0.5	0.00004	0.00009	0.00040

Table 4.1: Rate of false positives. All standard deviations in this table are below 0.0002

In the second set of experiments, we want to compare ADWIN as an estimator with estimations obtained from fixed-size window, and with fixed-size window which are flushed when change is detected. In the last case, we use a pair of windows (X, Y) of a fixed size W. Window X is used as a reference window that contains the first W elements of the stream that occurred after the last detected change. Window Y is a sliding window that contains the latest W items in the data stream. To detect change we check whether the difference of the averages of the two windows exceeds threshold ϵ_{cut}. If it does, we copy the content of window Y into reference window X, and empty the sliding window Y. This scheme is as in [KBDG04], and we refer to it as "fixed-size windows with flushing".

We build a framework with a stream of synthetic data, and estimators of each class: an estimator that uses ADWIN, an array of estimators of fixed-size windows for different sizes, and also an array of fixed-size windows with flushing. Our synthetic data streams consist of some triangular wavelets, of different periods, some square wavelets, also of different periods, and a staircase wavelet of different values. We test the estimator's performance over a sample of 10^6 points, feeding the same synthetic data stream to each one of the estimators tested. We compute the error estimation as the average distance (both L_1 and L_2) from the true probability generating the data stream to the estimation. Finally, we compare these measures for the different estimators. Tables 4.2, 4.3, 4.4 and 4.5 shows these results using L_1 and L_2 distances and $\delta = 0.1, 0.3$. For the ADWIN estimator, besides the distance to the true distribution, we list as information the window length averaged over the whole run.

4.3. EXPERIMENTAL VALIDATION OF ADWIN

Stream	Period	ADWIN		Fixed-sized Window					Fixed-sized flushing Window				
			Width	32	128	512	2048	8192	32	128	512	2048	8192
Scale	5000	0,05	503	0,07	0,04	0,06	0,17	0,16	0,07	0,04	0,05	0,11	0,15
Triangular	128	0,15	74	0,13	0,17	0,16	0,16	0,16	0,13	0,17	0,16	0,16	0,16
Triangular	512	0,09	140	0,08	0,12	0,16	0,16	0,16	0,09	0,12	0,16	0,16	0,16
Triangular	2048	0,05	314	0,07	0,06	0,11	0,16	0,16	0,07	0,06	0,09	0,16	0,16
Triangular	8192	0,03	657	0,07	0,04	0,04	0,11	0,16	0,07	0,04	0,04	0,06	0,16
Triangular	32768	0,02	935	0,07	0,03	0,02	0,04	0,11	0,07	0,03	0,02	0,02	0,03
Triangular	131072	0,02	1.099	0,07	0,03	0,02	0,02	0,03	0,07	0,03	0,02	0,01	0,01
Triangular	524288	0,02	1.107	0,07	0,03	0,02	0,01	0,01	0,07	0,03	0,02	0,01	0,01
Triangular	43	0,17	148	0,20	0,17	0,16	0,16	0,16	0,20	0,17	0,16	0,16	0,16
Triangular	424	0,10	127	0,09	0,13	0,15	0,16	0,16	0,10	0,13	0,15	0,16	0,16
Triangular	784	0,07	180	0,08	0,09	0,19	0,16	0,16	0,08	0,10	0,15	0,16	0,16
Triangular	5000	0,03	525	0,07	0,04	0,06	0,16	0,17	0,07	0,04	0,05	0,09	0,15
Square	128	0,14	45	0,18	0,30	0,30	0,30	0,30	0,20	0,30	0,30	0,30	0,30
Square	512	0,06	129	0,09	0,16	0,30	0,30	0,30	0,09	0,14	0,30	0,30	0,30
Square	2048	0,03	374	0,06	0,06	0,16	0,30	0,30	0,07	0,06	0,08	0,30	0,30
Square	8192	0,02	739	0,06	0,04	0,05	0,15	0,30	0,06	0,04	0,03	0,04	0,30
Square	32768	0,02	1.144	0,06	0,03	0,02	0,04	0,15	0,06	0,03	0,02	0,01	0,02
Square	131072	0,02	1.248	0,06	0,03	0,02	0,02	0,04	0,06	0,03	0,02	0,01	0,01

Table 4.2: Comparative of ADWIN with other estimators using L_1 and $\delta = 0.1$. All standard deviations in this table are below 0.011

Stream	Period	ADWIN		Fixed-sized Window					Fixed-sized flushing Window				
			Width	32	128	512	2048	8192	32	128	512	2048	8192
Scale	5000	0,05	213	0,07	0,04	0,06	0,17	0,16	0,07	0,04	0,05	0,10	0,15
Triangular	128	0,13	48	0,13	0,17	0,16	0,16	0,16	0,13	0,17	0,16	0,16	0,16
Triangular	512	0,08	93	0,08	0,12	0,16	0,16	0,16	0,09	0,12	0,16	0,16	0,16
Triangular	2048	0,06	156	0,07	0,06	0,11	0,16	0,16	0,07	0,06	0,09	0,16	0,16
Triangular	8192	0,05	189	0,07	0,04	0,04	0,11	0,16	0,07	0,04	0,04	0,06	0,16
Triangular	32768	0,05	218	0,07	0,03	0,02	0,04	0,11	0,07	0,03	0,02	0,02	0,03
Triangular	131072	0,05	215	0,07	0,03	0,02	0,02	0,03	0,07	0,03	0,02	0,01	0,01
Triangular	524288	0,05	217	0,07	0,03	0,02	0,01	0,01	0,07	0,03	0,02	0,01	0,01
Triangular	43	0,17	49	0,20	0,17	0,16	0,16	0,16	0,20	0,17	0,16	0,16	0,16
Triangular	424	0,09	85	0,09	0,13	0,15	0,16	0,16	0,10	0,14	0,15	0,16	0,16
Triangular	784	0,07	109	0,08	0,09	0,19	0,16	0,16	0,08	0,10	0,15	0,16	0,16
Triangular	5000	0,05	184	0,07	0,04	0,06	0,16	0,17	0,07	0,04	0,05	0,09	0,15
Square	128	0,12	37	0,18	0,30	0,30	0,30	0,30	0,20	0,30	0,30	0,30	0,30
Square	512	0,07	93	0,09	0,16	0,30	0,30	0,30	0,09	0,14	0,30	0,30	0,30
Square	2048	0,05	175	0,06	0,06	0,16	0,30	0,30	0,07	0,06	0,08	0,30	0,30
Square	8192	0,05	220	0,06	0,04	0,05	0,15	0,30	0,06	0,04	0,03	0,04	0,30
Square	32768	0,05	273	0,06	0,03	0,02	0,04	0,15	0,06	0,03	0,02	0,02	0,02
Square	131072	0,04	250	0,06	0,03	0,02	0,02	0,04	0,06	0,03	0,01	0,01	0,01

Table 4.3: Comparative of ADWIN with other estimators using L_1 and $\delta = 0.3$. All standard deviations in this table are below 0.014

4.3. EXPERIMENTAL VALIDATION OF ADWIN

Stream	Period	ADWIN		Fixed-sized Window					Fixed-sized flushing Window				
			Width	32	128	512	2048	8192	32	128	512	2048	8192
Scale	5000	0.06	501	0.08	0.04	0.06	0.19	0.19	0.08	0.05	0.07	0.13	0.17
Triangular	128	0.19	75	0.18	0.19	0.19	0.19	0.19	0.18	0.19	0.19	0.19	0.19
Triangular	512	0.12	140	0.12	0.17	0.19	0.19	0.19	0.12	0.17	0.19	0.19	0.19
Triangular	2048	0.08	320	0.09	0.09	0.16	0.19	0.19	0.09	0.10	0.14	0.19	0.19
Triangular	8192	0.05	666	0.08	0.06	0.09	0.16	0.19	0.09	0.06	0.08	0.11	0.19
Triangular	32768	0.04	905	0.08	0.05	0.05	0.08	0.16	0.08	0.05	0.04	0.06	0.08
Triangular	131072	0.04	1,085	0.08	0.04	0.03	0.04	0.08	0.08	0.04	0.03	0.03	0.04
Triangular	524288	0.04	1,064	0.08	0.04	0.02	0.02	0.03	0.08	0.04	0.02	0.02	0.02
Triangular	43	0.20	146	0.23	0.20	0.19	0.19	0.19	0.23	0.20	0.19	0.19	0.19
Triangular	424	0.13	126	0.12	0.18	0.17	0.19	0.19	0.13	0.18	0.17	0.19	0.19
Triangular	784	0.11	181	0.11	0.14	0.22	0.19	0.19	0.11	0.14	0.19	0.19	0.19
Triangular	5000	0.06	511	0.09	0.07	0.11	0.20	0.20	0.09	0.07	0.10	0.14	0.19
Square	128	0.21	45	0.25	0.30	0.30	0.30	0.30	0.26	0.30	0.30	0.30	0.30
Square	512	0.12	129	0.14	0.25	0.30	0.30	0.30	0.15	0.23	0.30	0.30	0.30
Square	2048	0.07	374	0.09	0.13	0.25	0.30	0.30	0.10	0.12	0.18	0.30	0.30
Square	8192	0.05	765	0.08	0.07	0.12	0.24	0.30	0.08	0.07	0.09	0.13	0.30
Square	32768	0.04	1,189	0.07	0.05	0.06	0.12	0.24	0.07	0.04	0.05	0.07	0.09
Square	131072	0.04	1,281	0.07	0.04	0.03	0.06	0.12	0.07	0.04	0.03	0.03	0.05

Table 4.4: Comparative of ADWIN with other estimators using L_2 and $\delta = 0.1$ All standard deviations in this table are below 0.007

Stream	Period	ADWIN		Fixed-sized Window					Fixed-sized flushing Window				
			Width	32	128	512	2048	8192	32	128	512	2048	8192
Scale	5000	0.08	210	0.08	0.04	0.06	0.18	0.19	0.08	0.05	0.07	0.13	0.17
Triangular	128	0.17	48	0.18	0.19	0.19	0.19	0.19	0.18	0.19	0.19	0.19	0.19
Triangular	512	0.12	93	0.12	0.17	0.19	0.19	0.19	0.12	0.17	0.19	0.19	0.19
Triangular	2048	0.09	153	0.09	0.09	0.16	0.19	0.19	0.09	0.10	0.14	0.19	0.19
Triangular	8192	0.08	193	0.08	0.06	0.09	0.16	0.19	0.09	0.06	0.08	0.11	0.19
Triangular	32768	0.08	213	0.08	0.05	0.05	0.08	0.16	0.08	0.05	0.04	0.06	0.08
Triangular	131072	0.08	223	0.08	0.04	0.03	0.04	0.08	0.08	0.04	0.03	0.03	0.04
Triangular	524288	0.08	222	0.08	0.04	0.02	0.02	0.03	0.08	0.04	0.02	0.02	0.02
Triangular	43	0.21	49	0.23	0.19	0.19	0.19	0.19	0.23	0.19	0.19	0.19	0.19
Triangular	424	0.12	85	0.12	0.18	0.17	0.19	0.19	0.13	0.18	0.17	0.19	0.19
Triangular	784	0.11	109	0.11	0.14	0.22	0.19	0.19	0.11	0.14	0.19	0.19	0.19
Triangular	5000	0.08	181	0.09	0.07	0.11	0.20	0.20	0.09	0.07	0.10	0.14	0.19
Square	128	0.18	37	0.25	0.30	0.30	0.30	0.30	0.26	0.30	0.30	0.30	0.30
Square	512	0.12	93	0.14	0.25	0.30	0.30	0.30	0.15	0.23	0.30	0.30	0.30
Square	2048	0.09	174	0.09	0.13	0.25	0.30	0.30	0.10	0.12	0.18	0.30	0.30
Square	8192	0.08	243	0.08	0.07	0.12	0.25	0.30	0.08	0.07	0.09	0.13	0.30
Square	32768	0.08	262	0.07	0.05	0.06	0.12	0.24	0.07	0.05	0.05	0.07	0.09
Square	131072	0.08	253	0.07	0.04	0.03	0.06	0.12	0.07	0.04	0.03	0.03	0.04

Table 4.5: Comparative of ADWIN with other estimators using L_2 and $\delta = 0.3$. All standard deviations in this table are below 0.007

4.3. EXPERIMENTAL VALIDATION OF ADWIN

The general pattern for the triangular or square wavelets is as follows. For any fixed period P, the best fixed-size estimator is that whose window size is a certain fraction of P. ADWIN usually sometimes does worse than this best fixed-size window, but only slightly, and often does better than even the best fixed size that we try. Additionally, it does better than any window of fixed size W when P is much larger or much smaller than W, that is, when W is a "wrong" time scale. The explanation is simple: if W is too large the estimator does not react quickly enough to change, and if W is too small the variance within the window implies a bad estimation. One can check that ADWIN adjusts its window length to about P/4 when P is small, but keeps it much smaller than P for large P, in order again to minimize the variance / time-sensitivity tradeoff.

In the third type of experiments, we use small probabilities to generate input to estimators. We feed our estimators with samples from distributions with small probabilities of getting 1, so we can compare ADWIN to fixed-size strategies in the situation when getting a 1 is a rare event. To deal with this case nonadaptively, one should decide *a priori* on a very large fixed window size, which is a waste if it turns out that there happen to be many 1s. We measure the relative error of the estimator, that is |True Probability - Estimated Probability|/ True Probability. Table 4.6 shows the results. ADWIN beats almost all fixed-size window estimators, with or without flushing. This confirms that ADWIN's capacity of shrinking or enlarging its window size can be a very useful tool for to accurately track the probability of infrequent events.

Prob.	ADWIN	Fixed-sized Window					Fixed-sized flushing Window				
		32	128	512	2048	8192	32	128	512	2048	8192
1/32	0.06	0.72	0.38	0.20	0.10	0.05	0.72	0.38	0.20	0.10	0.05
1/64	0.04	1.21	0.53	0.27	0.14	0.07	1.21	0.53	0.27	0.14	0.07
1/128	0.02	1.56	0.73	0.39	0.20	0.10	1.56	0.73	0.39	0.20	0.10
1/256	0.02	1.76	1.21	0.53	0.28	0.14	1.76	1.21	0.53	0.28	0.14
1/512	0.03	1.89	1.56	0.74	0.40	0.22	1.89	1.56	0.74	0.40	0.22
1/1024	0.04	1.89	1.72	1.18	0.52	0.28	1.89	1.72	1.18	0.52	0.28
1/2048	0.04	1.97	1.88	1.55	0.70	0.36	1.97	1.88	1.55	0.70	0.36
1/4096	0.10	1.97	1.93	1.76	1.22	0.55	1.97	1.93	1.76	1.22	0.55
1/8192	0.10	1.93	1.91	1.83	1.50	0.66	1.93	1.91	1.83	1.50	0.66
1/16384	0.22	2.08	2.06	2.02	1.83	1.31	2.08	2.06	2.02	1.83	1.31
1/32768	0.37	1.85	1.85	1.83	1.75	1.49	1.85	1.85	1.83	1.75	1.49

Table 4.6: Relative error using small probabilities. All standard deviations in this table are below 0.17.

In the fourth type of experiments, we test ADWIN as a change detector rather than as an estimator, and compare it to DDM method [GMCR04] described in section 2.2.1. The measures of interest here are the rate of changes detected and the mean time until detection.

To do this, we feed ADWIN and DDM change detector with four data streams of lengths L = 2,000, 10,000, 100,000 and 1,000,000 bits, generated from a Bernoulli distribution of parameter μ. We keep μ = 0.2 stationary during the first L − 1,000 time steps, and then make it increase linearly during the last 1,000 steps. We try different slopes: 0 (no change), 10^{-4}, $2 \cdot 10^{-4}$, $3 \cdot 10^{-4}$, and $4 \cdot 10^{-4}$.

To compare the rate of false negatives on an equal foot, we adjust ADWIN confidence parameter δ to have the same rate of false positives as DDM method.

Table 4.7 shows the results. Rows are grouped in four parts, corresponding to the four values of L that we tested. For each value of L, we give the number of changes detected in the last 1,000 samples (summed over all runs) and the mean and standard distribution of the time until the change is detected, in those runs where there is detection.

The first column gives the ratio of false positives. One observation we made is that DDM method tends to detect many more changes early on (when the window is small) and less changes as the window grows. This explains that, on the first column, even if the ratio of false positives is the same, the average time until the first false positive is produced is much smaller for DDM method.

The last four columns describe the results when change does occur, with different slopes. ADWIN detects change more often, with the exception of the L = 2,000 experiment. As the number of samples increases, the percentage of changes detected decreases in DDM methodology; as discussed early, this is to be expected since it takes a long time for DDM method to overcome the weight of past examples. In contrast, ADWIN maintains a good rate of detected changes, largely independent of the number of the number of past samples L − 1,000. One can observe the same phenomenon as before: even though DDM method detects less changes, the average time until detection (when detection occurs) is smaller.

4.4 Example 1: Incremental Naïve Bayes Predictor

We test the accuracy performance of ADWIN inside an incremental Naïve Bayes learning method, in two ways: as a change detector and comparing it with DDM, and as estimator of the probabilities needed by the Naïve Bayes learning method. We test our method using synthetic and real datasets.

Let $x_1, \ldots, x_k$ be k discrete attributes, and assume that x_i can take n_i different values. Let C be the class attribute, which can take n_C differ-

4.4. EXAMPLE 1: INCREMENTAL NAÏVE BAYES PREDICTOR

		Slope			
	0	10^{-4}	$2 \cdot 10^{-4}$	$3 \cdot 10^{-4}$	$4 \cdot 10^{-4}$
$2 \cdot 10^3$ samples, 10^3 trials					
Detection time (DDM)	854 ± 462	532 ± 271	368 ± 248	275 ± 206	232 ± 178
%runs detected (DDM)	10.6	58.6	97.2	100	100
Detection time (ADWIN)	975 ± 607	629 ± 247	444 ± 210	306 ± 171	251 ± 141
%runs detected (ADWIN)	10.6	39.1	94.6	93	95
10^4 samples, 100 trials					
Detection time (DDM)	$2,019 \pm 2,047$	498 ± 416	751 ± 267	594 ± 287	607 ± 213
%runs detected (DDM)	14	13	38	71	84
Detection time (ADWIN)	$4,673 \pm 3,142$	782 ± 195	595 ± 100	450 ± 96	367 ± 80
%runs detected (ADWIN)	14	40	79	90	87
10^5 samples, 100 trials					
Detection time (DDM)	$12,164 \pm 17,553$	127 ± 254	206 ± 353	440 ± 406	658 ± 422
%runs detected (DDM)	12	4	7	11	8
Detection time (ADWIN)	$47,439 \pm 32,609$	878 ± 102	640 ± 101	501 ± 72	398 ± 69
%runs detected (ADWIN)	12	28	89	84	89
10^6 samples, 100 trials					
Detection time (DDM)	$56,794 \pm 142,876$	1 ± 1	1 ± 0	1 ± 0	180 ± 401
%runs detected (DDM)	22	5	5	3	5
Detection time (ADWIN)	$380,738 \pm 289,242$	898 ± 80	697 ± 110	531 ± 89	441 ± 71
%runs detected (ADWIN)	22	15	77	80	83

Table 4.7: Change detection experiments. Each entry contains "x±y" where x is average and y is standard deviation.

ent values. Recall that upon receiving an unlabelled instance $I = (x_1 = v_1, \ldots, x_k = v_k)$, the Naïve Bayes predictor computes a "probability" of I being in class c as:

$$\Pr[C = c|I] \cong \prod_{i=1}^{k} \Pr[x_i = v_i | C = c]$$

$$= \Pr[C = c] \cdot \prod_{i=1}^{k} \frac{\Pr[x_i = v_i \wedge C = c]}{\Pr[C = c]}$$

The values $\Pr[x_i = v_j \wedge C = c]$ and $\Pr[C = c]$ are estimated from the training data. Thus, the summary of the training data is simply a 3-dimensional table that stores for each triple (x_i, v_j, c) a count $N_{i,j,c}$ of training instances with $x_i = v_j$, together with a 1-dimensional table for the counts of $C = c$. This algorithm is naturally incremental: upon receiving a new example (or a batch of new examples), simply increment the relevant counts. Predictions can be made at any time from the current counts.

We compare two time-change management strategies. The first one uses a static model to make predictions. This model is rebuilt every time that an external change detector module detects a change. We use DDM detection method and ADWIN as change detectors. DDM method generates a warning example some time before actually declaring change; see section 2.2.1 for the details; the examples received between the warning and the change signal are used to rebuild the model. In ADWIN, we use the examples currently stored in the window to rebuild the static model.

The second one is incremental: we simply create an instance $A_{i,j,c}$ of ADWIN for each count $N_{i,j,c}$, and one for each value c of C. When a labelled example is processed, add a 1 to $A_{i,j,c}$ if $x_i = v \wedge C = c$, and a 0 otherwise, and similarly for N_c. When the value of $\Pr[x_i = v_j \wedge C = c]$ is required to make a prediction, compute it using the estimate of $N_{i,j,c}$ provided by $A_{i,j,c}$. This estimate varies automatically as $\Pr[x_i = v_j \wedge C = c]$ changes in the data.

Note that different $A_{i,j,c}$ may have windows of different lengths at the same time. This will happen when the distribution is changing at different rates for different attributes and values, and there is no reason to sacrifice accuracy in all of the counts $N_{i,j,c}$, only because a few of them are changing fast. This is the intuition why this approach may give better results than one monitoring the global error of the predictor: it has more accurate information on at least some of the statistics that are used for the prediction.

4.4.1 Experiments on Synthetic Data

For the experiments with synthetic data we use a changing concept based on a rotating hyperplane explained in [HSD01]. A hyperplane in d-dimen-

4.4. EXAMPLE 1: INCREMENTAL NAÏVE BAYES PREDICTOR

sional space is the set of points x that satisfy

$$\sum_{i=1}^{d} w_i x_i \geq w_0$$

where x_i, is the ith coordinate of x. Examples for which $\sum_{i=1}^{d} w_i x_i \geq w_0$ are labeled positive, and examples for which $\sum_{i=1}^{d} w_i x_i < w_0$ are labeled negative. Hyperplanes are useful for simulating time-changing concepts because we can change the orientation and position of the hyperplane in a smooth manner by changing the relative size of the weights.

We use 2 classes, d = 8 attributes, and 2 values (0 and 1) per attribute. The different weights w_i of the hyperplane vary over time, at different moments and different speeds for different attributes i. All w_i start at 0.5 and we restrict to two w_i's varying at the same time, to a maximum value of 0.75 and a minimum of 0.25.

To test the performance of our two Naïve Bayes methodologies we do the following: At every time t, we build a static Naïve Bayes model M_t using a data set of 10,000 points generated from the distribution at time t. Model M_t is taken as a "baseline" of how well a Naïve Bayes model can do on this distribution. Then we generate 1000 fresh points from the current distribution and use them to compute the error rate of both the static model M_t and the different models built dynamically from the points seen so far. The ratio of these error rates is averaged over all the run.

Table 4.8 shows accuracy results. The "%Static" column shows the accuracy of the static model M_t – it is the same for all rows, except for small random fluctuations. The "%Dynamic" column is the accuracy of the model built dynamically using the estimator in the row. The last column in the table shows the quotient of columns 1 and 2, i.e., the relative accuracy of the dynamically vs. statically built models. In all NB experiments we show in boldface the result for `ADWIN` and the best result. It can be seen that the incremental time-change management model (using one instance of `ADWIN` per count) outperforms fixed-size windows and the models based on detecting change and rebuilding the model. Among these, the one using `ADWIN` as a change detector is better than that using DDM's method.

We test our methods on the SEA Concepts dataset described in Section 3.5.2. Figure 4.7 shows the learning curve of this experiment. We observe that `ADWIN` outperforms others estimators using fixed-size windows or flushing fixed-size windows.

4.4.2 Real-world data experiments

We test the performance of our Naïve Bayes predictors using the Electricity Market Dataset described in Section 3.5.2.

	Width	%Static	%Dyn.	Dyn./Stat.
DDM Change Detection		94.74%	58.02%	61.24%
ADWIN Change Detection		94.73%	70.72%	74.66%
ADWIN for counts		94.77%	**94.16%**	**99.36%**
Fixed-sized Window	32	94.74%	70.34%	74.24%
Fixed-sized Window	128	94.76%	80.12%	84.55%
Fixed-sized Window	512	94.73%	88.20%	93.10%
Fixed-sized Window	2048	94.75%	92.82%	97.96%
Fixed-sized flushing Window	32	94.74%	70.34%	74.25%
Fixed-sized flushing Window	128	94.75%	80.13%	84.58%
Fixed-sized flushing Window	512	94.73%	88.17%	93.08%
Fixed-sized flushing Window	2048	94.72%	92.86%	98.03%

Table 4.8: Naïve Bayes, synthetic data benchmark

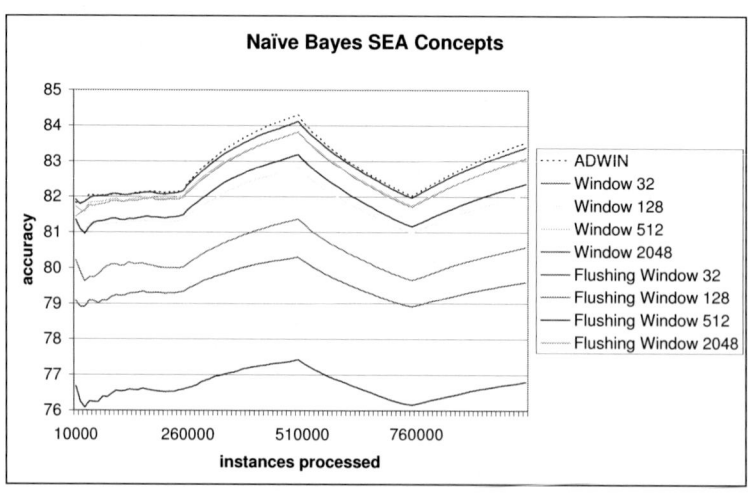

Figure 4.7: Accuracy on SEA Concepts dataset with three concept drifts.

4.4. EXAMPLE 1: INCREMENTAL NAÏVE BAYES PREDICTOR

	Width	%Static	%Dyn.	Dyn./Stat.
DDM Change Detection		91.62%	45.94%	50.14%
ADWIN Change Detection		91.62%	60.29%	65.81%
ADWIN for counts		91.62%	**76.61%**	**83.62%**
Fixed-sized Window	32	91.55%	**79.13%**	**86.44%**
Fixed-sized Window	128	91.55%	72.29%	78.97%
Fixed-sized Window	512	91.55%	68.34%	74.65%
Fixed-sized Window	2048	91.55%	65.02%	71.02%
Fixed-sized flushing Window	32	91.55%	78.57%	85.83%
Fixed-sized flushing Window	128	91.55%	73.46%	80.24%
Fixed-sized flushing Window	512	91.55%	69.65%	76.08%
Fixed-sized flushing Window	2048	91.55%	66.54%	72.69%

Table 4.9: Naïve Bayes, Electricity data benchmark, testing on last 48 items

At each time step, we train a static model using the last 48 samples received. We compare this static model with other models, also on the last 48 samples. Table 4.9 shows accuracy results of the different methods on this dataset. Again, in each column (a test), we show in boldface the result for ADWIN and for the best result.

The results are similar to those obtained with the hyperplane dataset: ADWIN applied in the incremental time-change model (to estimate probabilities) does much better than all the others, with the exception of the shortest fixed-length window, which achieves 86.44% of the static performance compared to ADWIN's 83.62%. The reason for this anomaly is due to the nature of this particular dataset: by visual inspection, one can see that it contains a lot of short runs (length 10 to 20) of identical values, and therefore a myopic strategy (i.e., a short window) gives best results. ADWIN behaves accordingly and shortens its window as much as it can, but the formulas involved do not allow windows as short as 10 elements. In fact, we have tried replicating each instance in the dataset 10 times (so there are runs of length 100 to 200 of equal values), and then case ADWIN becomes the winner again.

We also test the prediction accuracy of these methods. We compare, as before, a static model generated at each time t to the other models, and evaluate them asking to predict the instance that will arrive at time $t + 1$. The static model is computed training on the last 24 samples. The results are in Table 4.10. In this experiment, ADWIN outperforms clearly other time-change models. Generally, the incremental time-change management model does much better than the static model that refreshes its NB model when change is detected.

	Width	%Static	%Dyn.	Dyn./Stat.
DDM Change Detection		94.40%	45.87%	48.59%
`ADWIN` Change Detection		94.40%	46.86%	49.64%
`ADWIN` for counts		94.39%	**72.71%**	**77.02%**
Fixed-sized Window	32	94.39%	71.54%	75.79%
Fixed-sized Window	128	94.39%	68.78%	72.87%
Fixed-sized Window	512	94.39%	67.14%	71.13%
Fixed-sized Window	2048	94.39%	64.25%	68.07%
Fixed-sized flushing Window	32	94.39%	71.62%	75.88%
Fixed-sized flushing Window	128	94.39%	70.12%	74.29%
Fixed-sized flushing Window	512	94.39%	68.02%	72.07%
Fixed-sized flushing Window	2048	94.39%	65.60%	69.50%

Table 4.10: Naïve Bayes, Electricity data benchmark, testing on next instance

4.5 Example 2: Incremental k-means Clustering

In contrast to Naïve Bayes, it is not completely obvious how to give an incremental version of the k-means clustering algorithm.

We adapt in essence the incremental version from [Ord03]. In that version, every new example is added to the cluster with nearest centroid, and every r steps a recomputation phase occurs, which recomputes both the assignment of points to clusters and the centroids. To balance accuracy and computation time, r is chosen in [Ord03] to be the square root of the number of points seen so far. In our case, this latter rule is extended to react to changes in the data distribution.

We incorporate adaptive windowing to this algorithm in the following way. Let k and d be the number of centroids and attributes. We add an instance W_{ij} of our algorithm for every attribute centroid i and every attribute j, hence kd instances. The algorithm still interleaves phases in which centroids are just incrementally modified with incoming points and phases where global recomputation of centroids takes place. The second type of phase can occur each time we detect change. We use two criteria. First, when any of the $W_{i\ell}$ windows shrinks, we take this as a signal that the position of centroid i may have changed. In the case of estimators that use windows of a fixed size s, when any of the windows is full of new s elements we take this as as indicator of change in the position of centroids. And in the estimators that use windows of a fixed size with change detection, every time it detects change, we use this as a signal that the position of a centroid may have changed.

The second criterion is to recompute when the average point distance to theirs centroids has changed more than an ϵ factor where ϵ is user-specified. This is taken as an indication that a certain number of points may change from cluster i to cluster j or vice-versa if recomputation takes place now.

4.5.1 Experiments

We build a model of k-means clustering, using a window estimator for each centroid coordinate. We compare the performance of our model with a static one, measuring the sum of the distances of each data point to each centroid assigned.

The synthetic data used in our experiments consist of a sample of 10^6 points generated from a k-gaussian distribution with some fixed variance σ^2, and centered in our k moving centroids. Each centroid moves according to a constant velocity. We try different velocities v and values of σ in different experiments. Table 4.11 and 4.12 shows the results of computing the distance from 100 random points to their centroids. We observe that ADWIN outperforms other estimators in essentially all settings.

	Width	$\sigma = 0.15$ Static	Dyn.	$\sigma = 0.3$ Static	Dyn.	$\sigma = 0.6$ Static	Dyn.
ADWIN		9.72	16.63	19.42	26.71	38.83	47.32
Fixed-sized Window	32	9.72	18.46	19.42	27.92	38.83	48.79
Fixed-sized Window	128	9.72	26.08	19.42	35.87	38.83	58.65
Fixed-sized Window	512	9.72	28.20	19.42	38.13	38.83	61.22
Fixed-sized Window	2048	9.72	29.84	19.42	39.24	38.83	61.96
Fixed-sized Window	8192	9.72	32.79	19.42	40.58	38.83	63.09
Fixed-sized Window	32768	9.72	35.12	19.42	40.93	38.83	64.40
Fixed-sized flushing Window	32	9.72	29.29	19.42	34.19	38.83	57.54
Fixed-sized flushing Window	128	9.72	31.49	19.42	39.06	38.83	61.18
Fixed-sized flushing Window	512	9.72	30.10	19.42	39.47	38.83	62.44
Fixed-sized flushing Window	2048	9.72	29.68	19.42	39.38	38.83	62.01
Fixed-sized flushing Window	8192	9.72	31.54	19.42	39.86	38.83	62.82
Fixed-sized flushing Window	32768	9.72	36.21	19.42	41.11	38.83	65.54

Table 4.11: k-means sum of distances to centroids, with $k = 5$, 10^6 samples and change's velocity of 10^{-5}.

4.6 K-ADWIN = ADWIN + Kalman Filtering

ADWIN is basically a linear Estimator with Change Detector that makes an efficient use of Memory. It seems a natural idea to improve its performance by replacing the linear estimator by an adaptive Kalman filter, where the

		$\sigma = 0.15$		$\sigma = 0.3$		$\sigma = 0.6$	
	Width	Static	Dyn.	Static	Dyn.	Static	Dyn.
ADWIN		19.41	28.13	19.41	28.60	19.41	27.63
Fixed-sized Window	32	19.41	30.60	19.41	29.89	19.41	28.62
Fixed-sized Window	128	19.41	39.28	19.41	37.62	19.41	36.41
Fixed-sized Window	512	19.41	41.74	19.41	39.47	19.41	38.32
Fixed-sized Window	2048	19.41	42.36	19.41	39.76	19.41	38.67
Fixed-sized Window	8192	19.41	42.73	19.41	40.24	19.41	38.21
Fixed-sized Window	32768	19.41	44.13	19.41	41.81	19.41	37.12
Fixed-sized flushing Window	32	19.41	38.82	19.41	34.92	19.41	29.44
Fixed-sized flushing Window	128	19.41	41.30	19.41	38.79	19.41	42.72
Fixed-sized flushing Window	512	19.41	42.14	19.41	39.80	19.41	44.04
Fixed-sized flushing Window	2048	19.41	42.43	19.41	40.37	19.41	44.37
Fixed-sized flushing Window	8192	19.41	43.18	19.41	40.92	19.41	44.45
Fixed-sized flushing Window	32768	19.41	44.94	19.41	70.07	19.41	44.47

Table 4.12: k-means sum of distances to centroids, with k = 5, 10^6 samples and $\sigma = 0.3$.

parameters Q and R of the Kalman filter are computed using the information in ADWIN's memory.

We have set $R = W^2/50$ and $Q = 200/W$, where W is the length of the window maintained by ADWIN. While we cannot rigorously prove that these are the optimal choices, we have informal arguments that these are about the "right" forms for R and Q, on the basis of the theoretical guarantees of ADWIN.

Let us sketch the argument for Q. Theorem 3, part (2) gives a value ϵ for the maximum change that may have occurred within the window maintained by ADWIN. This means that the process variance within that window is at most ϵ^2, so we want to set $Q = \epsilon^2$. In the formula for ϵ, consider the case in which $n_0 = n_1 = W/2$, then we have

$$\epsilon \geq 4 \cdot \sqrt{\frac{3(\mu_{W_0} + \epsilon)}{W/2}} \cdot \ln \frac{4W}{\delta}$$

Isolating from this equation and distinguishing the extreme cases in which $\mu_{W_0} \gg \epsilon$ or $\mu_{W_0} \ll \epsilon$, it can be shown that $Q = \epsilon^2$ has a form that varies between c/W and d/W^2. Here, c and d are constant for constant values of δ, and $c = 200$ is a reasonable estimation. This justifies our choice of $Q = 200/W$. A similar, slightly more involved argument, can be made to justify that reasonable values of R are in the range W^2/c to W^3/d, for somewhat large constants c and d.

When there is no change, ADWIN window's length increases, so R increases too and K decreases, reducing the significance of the most recent data arrived. Otherwise, if there is change, ADWIN window's length reduces, so does R, and K increases, which means giving more importance to the last data arrived.

4.6.1 Experimental Validation of K-ADWIN

We compare the behaviours of the following types of estimators:

- *Type I*: Kalman filter with different but fixed values of Q and R. The values Q = 1, R = 1000 seemed to obtain the best results with fixed parameters.

- *Type I*: Exponential filters with $\alpha = 0.1, 0.25, 0.5$. This filter is similar to Kalman's with $K = \alpha, R = (1-\alpha)P/\alpha$.

- *Type II*: Kalman filter with a CUSUM test Change Detector algorithm. We tried initially the parameters $\upsilon = 0.005$ and $h = 0.5$ as in [JMJH04], but we changed to $h = 5$ which systematically gave better results.

- *Type III*: Adaptive Kalman filter with R as the difference of $x_t - x_{t-1}$ and Q as the sum of the last 100 values obtained in the Kalman filter. We use a fixed window of 100 elements.

- *Types III and IV*: Linear Estimators over fixed-length windows, without and with flushing when changing w.r.t. a reference window is detected. Details are explained in Section 4.3.

- *Type IV*: ADWIN and K-ADWIN. K-ADWIN uses a Kalman filter with $R = W^2/50$ and $Q = 200/W$, where W is the length of the ADWIN window.

We build a framework with a stream of synthetic data consisting of some triangular wavelets, of different periods, some square wavelets, also of different periods, and a staircase wavelet of different values. We generate 10^6 points and feed all them to all of the estimators tested. We calculate the mean L_1 distances from the prediction of each estimator to the original distribution that generates the data stream. Finally, we compare these measures for the different estimators.

Table 4.13 shows the results for $\delta = 0.3$ and L_1. In each column (a test), we show in boldface the result for K-ADWIN and for the best result.

A summary of the results is as follows: The results for K-ADWIN, ADWIN, the Adaptive Kalman filter, and the best fixed-parameter Kalman filter are the best ones in most cases. They are all very close to each other and they outwin each other in various ways, always by a small margin. They all do about as well as the best fixed-size window, and in most cases they win by a large amount. The exception are wavelets of very long periods, in which a very large fixed-size window wins. This is to be expected: when change is extremely rare, it is best to use a large window. Adaptivity necessarily introduces a small penalty, which is a waste in this particular case.

CHAPTER 4. ADAPTIVE SLIDING WINDOWS

	Stair	Triangular					Square				
	5000	128	512	2048	8192	32768	128	512	2048	8192	32768	131072
ADWIN	0.04	0.16	0.09	**0.05**	**0.03**	0.03	0.16	**0.07**	**0.03**	**0.02**	0.02	0.02
Kalman Q = 1, R = 1000	0.05	0.14	**0.08**	0.06	0.05	0.05	0.22	0.10	0.05	0.04	0.04	0.04
Kalman Q = 1, R = 100	0.08	**0.11**	0.09	0.08	0.08	0.08	**0.13**	0.09	0.08	0.07	0.07	0.07
Kalman Q = .25, R = .25	0.28	0.27	0.27	0.27	0.27	0.27	0.22	0.22	0.22	0.22	0.22	0.22
Exp. Estim. α = .1	0.09	**0.11**	0.09	0.09	0.09	0.09	**0.13**	0.09	0.08	0.07	0.07	0.07
Exp. Estim. α = .5	0.23	0.23	0.23	0.23	0.23	0.23	0.19	0.19	0.19	0.19	0.19	0.19
Exp. Estim. α = .25	0.15	0.15	0.14	0.14	0.14	0.14	0.14	0.13	0.12	0.12	0.12	0.12
Adaptive Kalman	**0.03**	0.16	0.11	0.06	0.04	0.03	0.28	0.17	0.06	0.04	0.03	0.03
CUSUM Kalman	0.08	0.15	0.12	0.08	0.06	0.05	0.24	0.18	0.11	0.06	0.04	0.04
K-ADWIN	**0.05**	**0.14**	**0.10**	**0.06**	**0.04**	**0.04**	**0.17**	**0.09**	**0.05**	**0.04**	**0.03**	**0.03**
Fixed-sized W = 32	0.07	0.13	**0.08**	0.07	0.07	0.07	0.18	0.09	0.06	0.06	0.06	0.06
Fixed-sized W = 128	0.04	0.17	0.12	0.06	0.04	0.03	0.30	0.16	0.06	0.04	0.03	0.03
Fixed-sized W = 512	0.06	0.16	0.16	0.11	0.04	**0.02**	0.30	0.30	0.16	0.05	0.02	0.02
Fixed-sized W = 2048	0.17	0.16	0.16	0.16	0.11	0.04	0.30	0.30	0.30	0.15	0.04	0.02
Fixed-sized W = 8192	0.16	0.16	0.16	0.16	0.16	0.11	0.30	0.30	0.30	0.30	0.15	0.04
Fix. flushing W = 32	0.07	0.14	0.09	0.07	0.07	0.07	0.20	0.09	0.07	0.06	0.06	0.06
Fix. flushing W = 128	0.04	0.17	0.12	0.06	0.04	0.03	0.30	0.13	0.05	0.03	0.03	0.03
Fix. flushing W = 512	0.05	0.16	0.16	0.08	0.04	**0.02**	0.30	0.30	0.07	0.03	0.02	**0.01**
Fix. flushing W = 2048	0.10	0.16	0.16	0.16	0.05	**0.02**	0.30	0.30	0.30	0.04	**0.01**	**0.01**
Fix. flushing W = 8192	0.15	0.16	0.16	0.16	0.16	0.03	0.30	0.30	0.30	0.30	0.02	**0.01**

Table 4.13: Comparative of different estimators using L_1 and $\delta = 0.3$. All standard deviations in this table are below 0.014.

4.6.2 Example 1: Naïve Bayes Predictor

We test our algorithms on a classical Naïve Bayes predictor as explained in Section 4.4. We use 2 classes, 8 attributes, and 2 values per attribute. The different weights w_i of the hyperplane vary over time, at different moments and different speeds for different attributes i. All w_i start at 0.5 and we restrict to two w_i's varying at the same time, to a maximum value of 0.75 and a minimum of 0.25.

We prepare the following experiment in order to test our Naïve Bayes predictor: At every time t we build a static Naïve Bayes model M_t using a data set of 1000 points generated from the distribution at time t. Model M_t is taken as a "baseline" of how well a Naïve Bayes model can do on this distribution. Then we generate 2000 fresh points, and compute the error rate of both this static model M_t and the different sliding-window models built from the t points seen so far. The ratio of these error rates is averaged over all the run.

Table 4.14 shows accuracy results. The "%Static" column shows the accuracy of the statically built model – it is the same for all rows, except for small variance. The "%Dynamic" column is the accuracy of the dynamically built model, using the estimator in the row. The last column in the table shows the quotient of columns 1 and 2, i.e., the relative accuracy of the estimator-based model Naïve Bayes model with respect that of the statically computed one. Again, in each column (a test), we show in boldface the result for K-ADWIN and for the best result.

The results can be summarized as follows: K-ADWIN outperforms plain ADWIN by a small margin, and they both do much better than all the memoryless Kalman filters. Thus, having a memory clearly helps in this case. Strangely enough, the winner is the longest fixed-length window, which achieves 98.73% of the static performance compared to K-ADWIN's 97.77%. We have no clear explanation of this fact, but believe it is an artifact of our benchmark: the way in which we vary the attributes' distributions might imply that simply taking the average of an attribute's value over a large window has best predictive power. More experiments with other change schedules should confirm or refute this idea.

4.6.3 Example 2: k-means Clustering

The synthetic data used in our experiments consist of a sample of 10^5 points generated from a k-gaussian distribution with some fixed variance σ^2, and centered in our k moving centroids. Each centroid moves according to a constant velocity. We try different velocities v and values of σ in different experiments.

On this data stream, we run one instance of the incremental k-means clusterer with each of the estimator types we want to test. Each instance of

	Width	%Static	%Dyn.	Dyn./Stat.
ADWIN		83,36%	80,30%	96,33%
Kalman $Q = 1, R = 1000$		83,22%	71,13%	85,48%
Kalman $Q = 1, R = 1$		83,21%	56,91%	68,39%
Kalman $Q = .25, R = .25$		83,26%	56,91%	68,35%
Exponential Estimator $\alpha = .1$		83,33%	64,19%	77,03%
Exponential Estimator $\alpha = .5$		83,32%	57,30%	68,77%
Exponential Estimator $\alpha = .25$		83,26%	59,68%	71,68%
Adaptive Kalman		83,24%	76,21%	91,56%
CUSUM Kalman		83,30%	50,65%	60,81%
K-ADWIN		**83,24%**	**81,39%**	**97,77%**
Fixed-sized Window	32	83,28%	67,64%	81,22%
Fixed-sized Window	128	83,30%	75,40%	90,52%
Fixed-sized Window	512	83,28%	80,47%	96,62%
Fixed-sized Window	2048	83,24%	**82,19%**	**98,73%**
Fixed-sized flushing Window	32	83,28%	67,65%	81,23%
Fixed-sized flushing Window	128	83,29%	75,57%	90,73%
Fixed-sized flushing Window	512	83,26%	80,46%	96,64%
Fixed-sized flushing Window	2048	83,25%	82,04%	98,55%

Table 4.14: Naïve Bayes benchmark

the clusterer uses itself an estimator for each centroid coordinate. At every time step, we feed the current example to each of the clusterers, we generate a sample of points from the current distribution (which we know) and use a traditional k-means clusterer to cluster this sample. Then, we compute the sum of the distances of each data point to each centroid assigned, for this statically built clustering and for each of the clustering dynamically built using different estimators. The statically built clustering is thus a baseline on how good the clustering could be without distribution drift.

Table 4.15 shows the results of computing the distance from 100 random points to their centroids. Again, in each column (a test), we show in boldface the result for K-ADWIN and for the best result.

The results can be summarized as follows: The winners are the best fixed-parameter Kalman filter and, for small variance, K-ADWIN. ADWIN follows closely in all cases. These three do much better than any fixed-size window strategy, and somewhat better than Kalman filters with suboptimal fixed-size parameters.

4.6.4 K-ADWIN Experimental Validation Conclusions

The main conclusions of K-ADWIN experiments are the following:

4.6. K-ADWIN = ADWIN + KALMAN FILTERING

	Width	σ = 0.15 Static	σ = 0.15 Dyn.	σ = 0.3 Static	σ = 0.3 Dyn.	σ = 0.6 Static	σ = 0.6 Dyn.
ADWIN		9,72	21,54	19,41	28,58	38,83	46,48
Kalman Q = 1, R = 1000		9,72	19,72	19,41	27,92	38,83	**46,02**
Kalman Q = 1, R = 100		9,71	17,60	19,41	**27,18**	38,77	46,16
Kalman Q = .25, R = .25		9,71	22,63	19,39	30,21	38,79	49,88
Exponential Estimator α = .1		9,71	21,89	19,43	27,28	38,82	46,98
Exponential Estimator α = .5		9,72	20,58	19,41	29,32	38,81	46,47
Exponential Estimator α = .25		9,72	17,69	19,42	27,66	38,82	46,18
Adaptive Kalman		9,72	18,98	19,41	31,16	38,82	51,96
CUSUM Kalman		9,72	18,29	19,41	33,82	38,85	50,38
K-ADWIN		**9,72**	**17,30**	**19,40**	28,34	38,79	47,45
Fixed-sized Window	32	9,72	25,70	19,40	39,84	38,81	57,58
Fixed-sized Window	128	9,72	36,42	19,40	49,70	38,81	68,59
Fixed-sized Window	512	9,72	38,75	19,40	52,35	38,81	71,32
Fixed-sized Window	2048	9,72	39,64	19,40	53,28	38,81	73,10
Fixed-sized Window	8192	9,72	43,39	19,40	55,66	38,81	76,90
Fixed-sized Window	32768	9,72	53,82	19,40	64,34	38,81	88,17
Fixed-sized flushing Window	32	9,72	35,62	19,40	47,34	38,81	65,37
Fixed-sized flushing Window	128	9,72	40,42	19,40	52,03	38,81	70,47
Fixed-sized flushing Window	512	9,72	39,12	19,40	53,05	38,81	72,81
Fixed-sized flushing Window	2048	9,72	40,99	19,40	56,82	38,81	75,35
Fixed-sized flushing Window	8192	9,72	45,48	19,40	60,23	38,81	91,49
Fixed-sized flushing Window	32768	9,72	73,17	19,40	84,55	38,81	110,77

Table 4.15: k-means sum of distances to centroids, with k = 5, 10^5 samples and change's velocity of 10^{-3}.

- In all three types of experiments (tracking, Naïve Bayes, and k-means), K-ADWIN either gives best results or is very close in performance to the best of the estimators we try. And each of the other estimators is clearly outperformed by K-ADWIN in at least some of the experiments. In other words, no estimator ever does much better than K-ADWIN, and each of the others is outperformed by K-ADWIN in at least one context.

- More precisely, for the tracking problem, K-ADWIN and ADWIN automatically do about as well as the Kalman filter with the best set of fixed covariance parameters (parameters which, in general, can only be determined after a good number of experiments). And these three do far better than any fixed-size window.

- In the Naïve Bayes experiments, K-ADWIN does somewhat better than ADWIN and far better than any memoryless Kalman filter. This is, then, a situation where having a memory clearly helps.

- In the k-means case, again K-ADWIN performs about as well as the best (and difficult to find) Kalman filter, and they both do much better than fixed-size windows.

4.7 Time and Memory Requirements

In the experiments above we have only discussed the performance in terms of error rate, and not time or memory usage. Certainly, this was not our main goal and we have in no way tried to optimize our implementations in either time or memory (as is clearly indicated by the choice of Java as programming language). Let us, however, mention some rough figures about time and memory, since they suggest that our approach can be fairly competitive after some optimization work.

All programs were implemented in Java Standard Edition. The experiments were performed on a 3.0 GHz Pentium PC machine with 1 Gigabyte main memory, running Microsoft Windows XP. The Sun Java 2 Runtime Environment, Standard Edition (build 1.5.0 06-b05) was used to run all benchmarks.

Consider first the experiments on ADWIN alone. A bucket formed by an integer plus a real number uses 9 bytes. Therefore, about 540 bytes store a sliding window of 60 buckets. In the boolean case, we could use only 5 bytes per bucket, which reduces our memory requirements to 300 bytes per window of 60 buckets. Note that 60 buckets, with our choice of $M = 5$ suffice to represent a window of length about $2^{60/5} = 4096$.

In the experiment comparing different estimators (Tables 4.2,4.3,4.4 and 4.5), the average number of buckets used by ADWIN was 45,11, and the average time spent was 23 seconds to process the 10^6 samples, which is quite remarkable. In the Naïve Bayes experiment (Table 4.8), it took an average of 1060 seconds and 2000 buckets to process 10^6 samples by 34 estimators. This means less than 32 seconds and 60 buckets per estimator. The results for k-means were similar: We executed the k-means experiments with $k = 5$ and two attributes, with 10 estimators and 10^6 sample points using about an average of 60 buckets and 11.3 seconds for each instance of ADWIN.

Finally, we compare the time needed by an ADWIN, a simple counter, and an EWMA with Cusum change detector and predictor. We do the following experiment: we feed an ADWIN estimator, a simple counter and a EWMA with Cusum with 1,000,000 samples from a distribution that has an abrupt change every n samples. Table 4.16 shows the results when the samples are retrieved from memory, and Table 4.17 when the samples are stored and retrieved from disk. We test also the overhead due to the fact of using objects, instead of native numbers in Java. Note that the time difference between ADWIN and the other methods is not constant, and it depends on the scale of change. The time difference between a EWMA and Cusum estimator and a simple counter estimator is small. We observe that

4.7. TIME AND MEMORY REQUIREMENTS

Change scale n	ADWIN	Counter	EWMA +Cusum	Counter Object	EWMA+Cusum Object
30	72,396	23	40	82	108
50	72,266	21	32	58	71
75	12,079	17	23	54	66
100	12,294	16	23	50	67
1,000	22,070	15	20	52	89
10,000	38,096	16	20	63	64
100,000	54,886	16	27	54	64
1,000,000	71,882	15	20	59	64

Table 4.16: Time in miliseconds on ADWIN experiment reading examples from memory

Change scale n	ADWIN	Counter	EWMA+ Cusum
30	83,769	10,999	11,021
50	83,934	11,004	10,964
75	23,287	10,939	11,002
100	23,709	11,086	10,989
1,000	33,303	11,007	10,994
10,000	49,248	10,930	10,999
100,000	66,296	10,947	10,923
1,000,000	83,169	10,926	11,037

Table 4.17: Time in miliseconds on ADWIN experiment reading examples from disk

the simple counter is the fastest method, and that `ADWIN` needs more time to process the samples when there is constant change or when there is no change at all.

5
Decision Trees

In this chapter we propose and illustrate a method for developing decision trees algorithms that can adaptively learn from data streams that change over time. We take the Hoeffding Tree learner, an incremental decision tree inducer for data streams, and use as a basis it to build two new methods that can deal with distribution and concept drift: a sliding window-based algorithm, Hoeffding Window Tree, and an adaptive method, Hoeffding Adaptive Tree. Our methods are based on the methodology explained in Chapter 3. We choose ADWIN as an implementation with theoretical guarantees in order to extend such guarantees to the resulting adaptive learning algorithm. A main advantage of our methods is that they require no guess about how fast or how often the stream will change; other methods typically have several user-defined parameters to this effect.

In our experiments, the new methods never do worse, and in some cases do much better, than CVFDT, a well-known method for tree induction on data streams with drift.

5.1 Introduction

We apply the framework presented in Chapter 3 to give two decision tree learning algorithms that can cope with concept and distribution drift on data streams: Hoeffding Window Trees in Section 5.2 and Hoeffding Adaptive Trees in Section 5.3. Decision trees are among the most common and well-studied classifier models. Classical methods such as C4.5 are not apt for data streams, as they assume all training data are available simultaneously in main memory, allowing for an unbounded number of passes, and certainly do not deal with data that changes over time. In the data stream context, a reference work on learning decision trees is the Hoeffding Tree or Very Fast Decision Tree method (VFDT) for fast, incremental learning [DH00]. The Hoeffding Tree was described in Section 2.4.2. The methods we propose are based on VFDT, enriched with the change detection and estimation building blocks mentioned above.

We try several such building blocks, although the best suited for our purposes is the ADWIN algorithm, described in Chapter 4. This algorithm is parameter-free in that it automatically and continuously detects the rate of change in the data streams rather than using apriori guesses, thus allowing the client algorithm to react adaptively to the data stream it is processing. Additionally, ADWIN has rigorous guarantees of performance (Theorem 3 in Section 4.2.2). We show that these guarantees can be transferred to decision tree learners as follows: if a change is followed by a long enough stable period, the classification error of the learner will tend, and the same rate, to the error rate of VFDT.

5.2 Decision Trees on Sliding Windows

We propose a general method for building incrementally a decision tree based on a sliding window keeping the last instances on the stream. To specify one such method, we specify how to:

- place one or more change detectors at every node that will raise a hand whenever something worth attention happens at the node
- create, manage, switch and delete alternate trees
- maintain estimators of only relevant statistics at the nodes of the current sliding window

We call *Hoeffding Window Tree* any decision tree that uses Hoeffding bounds, maintains a sliding window of instances, and that can be included in this general framework. Figure 5.1 shows the pseudo-code of HOEFFDING WINDOW TREE. Note that δ' should be the *Bonferroni correction* of δ to account for the fact that many tests are performed and we want all of them to be simultaneously correct with probability $1 - \delta$. It is enough e.g. to divide δ by the number of tests performed so far. The need for this correction is also acknowledged in [DH00], although in experiments the more convenient option of using a lower δ was taken. We have followed the same option in our experiments for fair comparison.

5.2.1 HWT-ADWIN : Hoeffding Window Tree using ADWIN

We use ADWIN to design HWT-ADWIN, a new Hoeffding Window Tree that uses ADWIN as a change detector. The main advantage of using a change detector as ADWIN is that it has theoretical guarantees, and we can extend this guarantees to the learning algorithms.

Example of performance Guarantee

Let HWT*ADWIN be a variation of HWT-ADWIN with the following condition: every time a node decides to create an alternate tree, an alternate tree

5.2. DECISION TREES ON SLIDING WINDOWS

HOEFFDING WINDOW TREE(Stream, δ)
1   Let HT be a tree with a single leaf(root)
2   Init estimators A_{ijk} at root
3   **for** each example (x, y) in Stream
4   **do** HWTREEGROW((x, y), HT, δ)

HWTREEGROW((x, y), HT, δ)
1   Sort (x, y) to leaf l using HT
2   Update estimators A_{ijk}
3   at leaf l and nodes traversed in the sort
4   **if** current node l has an alternate tree T_{alt}
5   HWTREEGROW((x, y), T_{alt}, δ)
6   Compute G for each attribute
    ▷ Evaluate condition for splitting leaf l
7   **if** G(Best Attr.)−G(2nd best) $> \epsilon(\delta', \dots)$
8   **then** Split leaf on best attribute
9   **for** each branch of the split
10   **do** Start new leaf
11   and initialize estimators
12 **if** one change detector has detected change
13   **then** Create an alternate subtree T_{alt} at leaf l if there is none
14 **if** existing alternate tree T_{alt} is more accurate
15   **then** replace current node l with alternate tree T_{alt}

Figure 5.1: Hoeffding Window Tree algorithm

is also started at the root. In this section we show an example of performance guarantee about the error rate of HWT*ADWIN. Informally speaking, it states that after a change followed by a stable period, HWT*ADWIN's error rate will decrease at the same rate as that of VFDT, after a transient period that depends only on the magnitude of the change.

We consider the following scenario: Let C and D be arbitrary concepts, that can differ both in example distribution and label assignments. Suppose the input data sequence S is generated according to concept C up to time t_0, that it abruptly changes to concept D at time $t_0 + 1$, and remains stable after that. Let HWT*ADWIN be run on sequence S, and e_1 be error(HWT*ADWIN,S,t_0), and e_2 be error(HWT*ADWIN,S,$t_0 + 1$), so that $e_2 - e_1$ measures how much worse the error of HWT*ADWIN has become after the concept change.

Here error(HWT*ADWIN,S,t) denotes the classification error of the tree kept by HWT*ADWIN at time t on S. Similarly, error(VFDT,D,t) denotes the expected error rate of the tree kept by VFDT after being fed with t random examples coming from concept D.

Theorem 6. *Let S, t_0, e_1, and e_2 be as described above, and suppose t_0 is sufficiently large w.r.t. $e_2 - e_1$. Then for every time $t > t_0$, we have*

$$error(HWT^*ADWIN, S, t) \leq \min\{e_2, e_{VFDT}\}$$

with probability at least $1 - \delta$, where

- $e_{VFDT} = error(VFDT, D, t - t0 - g(e_2 - e_1)) + O(\frac{1}{\sqrt{t-t_0}})$
- $g(e_2 - e_1) = 8/(e_2 - e_1)^2 \ln(4t_0/\delta)$

The following corollary is a direct consequence, since $O(1/\sqrt{t-t_0})$ tends to 0 as t grows.

Corollary 1. *If error(VFDT,D,t) tends to some quantity $\epsilon \leq e_2$ as t tends to infinity, then error(HWT*ADWIN ,S,t) tends to ϵ too.*

Proof. We know by the ADWIN False negative rate bound that with probability $1-\delta$, the ADWIN instance monitoring the error rate at the root shrinks at time $t_0 + n$ if

$$|e_2 - e_1| > 2\epsilon_{cut} = \sqrt{2/m \ln(4(t-t_0)/\delta)}$$

where m is the harmonic mean of the lengths of the subwindows corresponding to data before and after the change. This condition is equivalent to

$$m > 4/(e_1 - e_2)^2 \ln(4(t-t_0)/\delta)$$

If t_0 is sufficiently large w.r.t. the quantity on the right hand side, one can show that m is, say, less than n/2 by definition of the harmonic mean. Then

5.2. DECISION TREES ON SLIDING WINDOWS

some calculations show that for $n \geq g(e_2 - e_1)$ the condition is fulfilled, and therefore by time $t_0 + n$ `ADWIN` will detect change.

After that, HWT*`ADWIN` will start an alternative tree at the root. This tree will from then on grow as in VFDT, because HWT*`ADWIN` behaves as VFDT when there is no concept change. While it does not switch to the alternate tree, the error will remain at e_2. If at any time $t_0 + g(e_1 - e_2) + n$ the error of the alternate tree is sufficiently below e_2, with probability $1 - \delta$ the two `ADWIN` instances at the root will signal this fact, and HWT*`ADWIN` will switch to the alternate tree, and hence the tree will behave as the one built by VFDT with t examples. It can be shown, again by using the False Negative Bound on `ADWIN`, that the switch will occur when the VFDT error goes below $e_2 - O(1/\sqrt{n})$, and the theorem follows after some calculation. □

5.2.2 CVFDT

As an extension of VFDT to deal with concept change Hulten, Spencer, and Domingos presented Concept-adapting Very Fast Decision Trees CVFDT [HSD01] algorithm. We have presented it on Section 3.2. We review it here briefly and compare it to our method.

CVFDT works by keeping its model consistent with respect to a sliding window of data from the data stream, and creating and replacing alternate decision subtrees when it detects that the distribution of data is changing at a node. When new data arrives, CVFDT updates the sufficient statistics at its nodes by incrementing the counts n_{ijk} corresponding to the new examples and decrementing the counts n_{ijk} corresponding to the oldest example in the window, which is effectively forgotten. CVFDT is a Hoeffding Window Tree as it is included in the general method previously presented.

Two external differences among CVFDT and our method is that CVFDT has no theoretical guarantees (as far as we know), and that it uses a number of parameters, with default values that can be changed by the user - but which are fixed for a given execution. Besides the example window length, it needs:

1. T_0: after each T_0 examples, CVFDT traverses all the decision tree, and checks at each node if the splitting attribute is still the best. If there is a better splitting attribute, it starts growing an alternate tree rooted at this node, and it splits on the currently best attribute according to the statistics in the node.

2. T_1: after an alternate tree is created, the following T_1 examples are used to build the alternate tree.

3. T_2: after the arrival of T_1 examples, the following T_2 examples are used to test the accuracy of the alternate tree. If the alternate tree

is more accurate than the current one, CVDFT replaces it with this alternate tree (we say that the alternate tree is promoted).

The default values are $T_0 = 10,000$, $T_1 = 9,000$, and $T_2 = 1,000$. One can interpret these figures as the preconception that often about the last $50,000$ examples are likely to be relevant, and that change is not likely to occur faster than every $10,000$ examples. These preconceptions may or may not be right for a given data source.

The main internal differences of HWT-ADWIN respect CVFDT are:

- The alternates trees are created as soon as change is detected, without having to wait that a fixed number of examples arrives after the change. Furthermore, the more abrupt the change is, the faster a new alternate tree will be created.

- HWT-ADWIN replaces the old trees by the new alternates trees as soon as there is evidence that they are more accurate, rather than having to wait for another fixed number of examples.

These two effects can be summarized saying that HWT-ADWIN adapts to the scale of time change in the data, rather than having to rely on the *a priori* guesses by the user.

5.3 Hoeffding Adaptive Trees

In this section we present Hoeffding Adaptive Tree as a new method that evolving from Hoeffding Window Tree, adaptively learn from data streams that change over time without needing a fixed size of sliding window. The optimal size of the sliding window is a very difficult parameter to guess for users, since it depends on the rate of change of the distribution of the dataset.

In order to avoid to choose a size parameter, we propose a new method for managing statistics at the nodes. The general idea is simple: we place instances of estimators of frequency statistics at every node, that is, replacing each n_{ijk} counters in the Hoeffding Window Tree with an instance A_{ijk} of an estimator.

More precisely, we present three variants of a *Hoeffding Adaptive Tree* or HAT, depending on the estimator used:

- HAT-INC: it uses a linear incremental estimator

- HAT-EWMA: it uses an Exponential Weight Moving Average (EWMA)

- HAT-ADWIN : it uses an ADWIN estimator. As the ADWIN instances are also change detectors, they will give an alarm when a change in the attribute-class statistics at that node is detected, which indicates also a possible concept change.

The main advantages of this new method over a Hoeffding Window Tree are:

- All relevant statistics from the examples are kept in the nodes. There is no need of an optimal size of sliding window for all nodes. Each node can decide which of the last instances are currently relevant for it. There is no need for an additional window to store current examples. For medium window sizes, this factor substantially reduces our memory consumption with respect to a Hoeffding Window Tree.

- A Hoeffding Window Tree, as CVFDT for example, stores in main memory only a bounded part of the window. The rest (most of it, for large window sizes) is stored in disk. For example, CVFDT has one parameter that indicates the amount of main memory used to store the window (default is 10,000). Hoeffding Adaptive Trees keeps all its data in main memory.

5.3.1 Example of performance Guarantee

In this subsection we show a performance guarantee on the error rate of HAT-ADWIN on a simple situation. Roughly speaking, it states that after a distribution and concept change in the data stream, followed by a stable period, HAT-ADWIN will start, in reasonable time, growing a tree identical to the one that VFDT would grow if starting afresh from the new stable distribution. Statements for more complex scenarios are possible, including some with slow, gradual, changes.

Theorem 7. *Let D_0 and D_1 be two distributions on labelled examples. Let S be a data stream that contains examples following D_0 for a time T, then suddenly changes to using D_1. Let t be the time that until VFDT running on a (stable) stream with distribution D_1 takes to perform a split at the node. Assume also that VFDT on D_0 and D_1 builds trees that differ on the attribute tested at the root. Then with probability at least $1 - \delta$:*

- *By time $t' = T + c \cdot V^2 \cdot t \log(tV)$, HAT-ADWIN will create at the root an alternate tree labelled with the same attribute as VFDT(D_1). Here $c \leq 20$ is an absolute constant, and V the number of values of the attributes.*[1]

- *this alternate tree will evolve from then on identically as does that of VFDT(D_1), and will eventually be promoted to be the current tree if and only if its error on D_1 is smaller than that of the tree built by time T.*

If the two trees do not differ at the roots, the corresponding statement can be made for a pair of deeper nodes.

---

[1] This value of t' is a very large overestimate, as indicated by our experiments. We are working on an improved analysis, and hope to be able to reduce t' to $T + c \cdot t$, for $c < 4$.

Lemma 1. *In the situation above, at every time $t + T > T$, with probability $1 - \delta$ we have at every node and for every counter (instance of* `ADWIN`*) $A_{i,j,k}$*

$$|A_{i,j,k} - P_{i,j,k}| \leq \sqrt{\frac{\ln(1/\delta')\,T}{t(t+T)}}$$

where $P_{i,j,k}$ is the probability that an example arriving at the node has value j in its ith attribute and class k.

Observe that for fixed δ' and T this bound tends to 0 as t grows.

To prove the theorem, use this lemma to prove high-confidence bounds on the estimation of $G(a)$ for all attributes at the root, and show that the attribute best chosen by VFDT on D_1 will also have maximal $G(\text{best})$ at some point, so it will be placed at the root of an alternate tree. Since this new alternate tree will be grown exclusively with fresh examples from D_1, it will evolve as a tree grown by VFDT on D_1.

5.3.2 Memory Complexity Analysis

Let us compare the memory complexity Hoeffding Adaptive Trees and Hoeffding Window Trees. We take CVFDT as an example of Hoeffding Window Tree. Denote with

- E : size of an example
- A : number of attributes
- V : maximum number of values for an attribute
- C : number of classes
- T : number of nodes

A Hoeffding Window Tree as CVFDT uses memory $O(WE + TAVC)$, because it uses a window W with E examples, and each node in the tree uses AVC counters. A Hoeffding Adaptive Tree does not need to store a window of examples, but uses instead memory $O(\log W)$ at each node as it uses an `ADWIN` as a change detector, so its memory requirement is $O(TAVC + T \log W)$. For medium-size W, the $O(WE)$ in CVFDT can often dominate. HAT-`ADWIN` has a complexity of $O(TAVC \log W)$.

5.4 Experimental evaluation

We tested Hoeffding Adaptive Trees using synthetic and real datasets. In the experiments with synthetic datasets, we use the SEA Concepts [SK01] and a changing concept dataset based on a rotating hyperplane explained

5.4. EXPERIMENTAL EVALUATION

in Section 4.4.1. In the experiments with real datasets we use two UCI datasets [AN07] Adult and Poker-Hand from the UCI repository of machine learning databases. In all experiments, we use the values $\delta = 10^{-4}$, $T_0 = 20,000$, $T_1 = 9,000$, and $T_2 = 1,000$, following the original CVFDT experiments [HSD01].

In all tables, the result for the best classifier for a given experiment is marked in **boldface,** and the best choice for CVFDT window length is shown in *italics*.

We included two versions of the CVFDT algorithm:

- CVFDT ORIGINAL: version of CVFDT available from the VFML [HD03] software web page

- CVFDT: we have slightly modified the CVFDT implementation to follow strictly the CVFDT algorithm explained in the original paper by Hulten, Spencer and Domingos [HSD01]. The version available of CVFDT from VFML doesn't create alternatives tree for the root node, since it keeps the alternative tree for a node at its parent node data.

We included an improvement over CVFDT (which could be made on the two versions of CVFDT as well). If the two best attributes at a node happen to have exactly the same gain, the tie may be never resolved and split does not occur. CVFDT use a parameter τ to solve ties: it splits on the current best attribute if the difference between the observed heuristic values of the two best attributes is lower than τ:

$$\Delta G = G(\text{best}) - G(\text{second best}) < \tau$$

Note that this rule considers the difference between the best and second-best values, not the difference of the best attribute with respect to $\epsilon(\delta, \ldots)$. In our experiments we added an additional split rule: when G(best) exceeds by three times the current value of $\epsilon(\delta, \ldots)$, a split is forced anyway. We have tested the three versions of Hoeffding Adaptive Tree, HAT-INC, HAT-EWMA($\alpha = .01$), HAT-ADWIN, each with and without the addition of Naïve Bayes (NB) classifiers at the leaves. As a general comment on the results, the use of NB classifiers does not always improve the results, although it does make a good difference in some cases; this was observed in [HKP05], where a more detailed analysis can be found.

First, we experiment using the SEA concepts, a dataset with abrupt concept drift, first introduced in [SK01]. This artificial dataset is generated using three attributes, where only the two first attributes are relevant. All three attributes have values between 0 and 10. We generate 400,000 random samples. We divide all the points in blocks with different concepts. In each block, we classify using $f_1 + f_2 \leq \theta$, where f_1 and f_2 represent the first two attributes and θ is a threshold value. We use threshold values 9, 8,

7 and 9.5 for the data blocks. We inserted about 10% class noise into each block of data.

Table 5.1: SEA on-line errors using discrete attributes with 10% noise

	CHANGE SPEED		
	1,000	10,000	100,000
HAT-INC	16.99%	16.08%	14.82%
HAT-EWMA	16.98%	15.83%	**14.64 %**
HAT-ADWIN	16.86%	**15.39%**	14.73 %
HAT-INC NB	16.88%	15.93%	14.86%
HAT-EWMA NB	**16.85%**	15.91%	14.73 %
HAT-ADWIN NB	16.90%	15.76%	14.75 %
CVFDT $|W| = 1,000$	19.47%	*15.71%*	15.81%
CVFDT $|W| = 10,000$	17.03%	17.12%	*14.80%*
CVFDT $|W| = 100,000$	16.97%	17.15%	17.09%
CVFDT ORIGINAL $|W| = 1,000$	25.93%	17.05%	17.01%
CVFDT ORIGINAL $|W| = 10,000$	24.42%	17.41%	16.98%
CVFDT ORIGINAL $|W| = 100,000$	27.73%	14.90%	17.20%

We test our methods using discrete and continuous attributes. The on-line errors results for discrete attributes are shown in Table 5.1. On-line errors are the errors measured each time an example arrives with the current decision tree, before updating the statistics. Each column reflects a different speed of concept change. We observe that CVFDT best performance is not always with the same example window size, and that there is no optimal window size. The different versions of Hoeffding Adaptive Trees have a very similar performance, essentially identical to that of CVFDT with optimal window size for that speed of change. More graphically, Figure 5.2 shows its learning curve using continuous attributes for a speed of change of 100, 000. CVFDT uses a window of size 100, 000. Note that at the points where the concept drift appears HWT-ADWIN, decreases its error faster than CVFDT, due to the fact that it detects change faster.

Another frequent dataset is the rotating hyperplane, used as testbed for CVFDT versus VFDT in [HSD01] – see Section 4.4.1 for an explanation. We experiment with abrupt and with gradual drift. In the first set of experiments, we apply abrupt change. We use 2 classes, d = 5 attributes, and 5 discrete values per attribute. We do not insert class noise into the data. After every N examples arrived, we abruptly exchange the labels of positive and negative examples, i.e., move to the complementary concept. So, we classify the first N examples using $\sum_{i=1}^{d} w_i x_i \geq w_0$, the next N examples using $\sum_{i=1}^{d} w_i x_i \leq w_0$, and so on. The on-line error rates are shown in Ta-

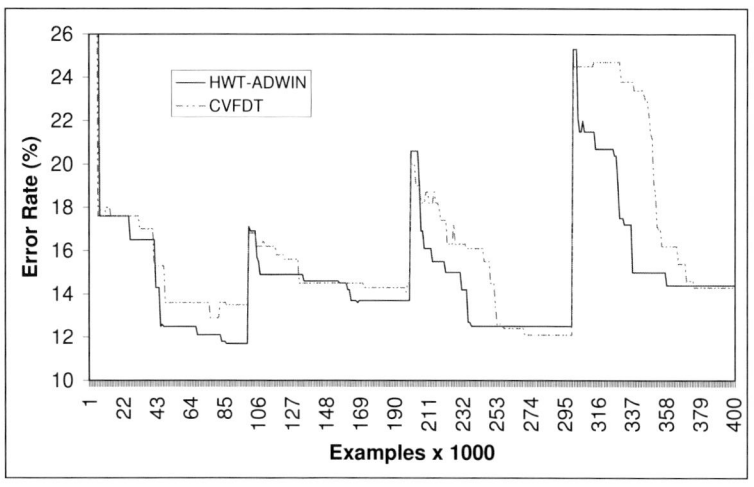

Figure 5.2: Learning curve of SEA Concepts using continuous attributes

ble 5.2, where each column reflects a different value of N, the period among classification changes. We detect that Hoeffding Adaptive Tree methods substantially outperform CVFDT in all speed changes.

In the second type of experiments, we introduce gradual drift. We vary the weight of the first attribute over time slowly, from 0 to 1, then back from 1 to 0, and so on, linearly as a triangular wave. We adjust the rest of weights in order to have the same number of examples for each class.

The on-line error rates are shown in Table 5.3. Observe that, in contrast to previous experiments, HAT-EWMA and HAT-ADWIN do much better than HAT-INC, when using NB at the leaves. We believe this will happen often in the case of gradual changes, because gradual changes will be detected earlier in individual attributes than in the overall error rate.

We test Hoeffding Adaptive Trees on two real datasets in two different ways: with and without concept drift. We tried some of the largest UCI datasets [AN07], and report results on Adult and Poker-Hand. For the Covertype and Census-Income datasets, the results we obtained with our method were essentially the same as for CVFDT (ours did better by fractions of 1% only) – we do not claim that our method is always better than CVFDT, but this confirms our belief that it is never much worse.

An important problem with most of the real-world benchmark data sets is that there is little concept drift in them [Tsy04] or the amount of drift is

Table 5.2: On-line errors of Hyperplane Experiments with abrupt concept drift

	CHANGE SPEED		
	1,000	10,000	100,000
HAT-INC	46.39%	31.38%	21.17%
HAT-EWMA	42.09%	31.40%	21.43 %
HAT-ADWIN	41.25%	30.42%	21.37 %
HAT-INC NB	46.34%	31.54%	22.08%
HAT-EWMA NB	**35.28%**	**24.02%**	15.69 %
HAT-ADWIN NB	35.35%	24.47%	**13.87 %**
CVFDT $\|W\| = 1,000$	50.01%	*39.53%*	33.36%
CVFDT $\|W\| = 10,000$	50.09%	49.76%	*28.63%*
CVFDT $\|W\| = 100,000$	49.89%	49.88%	46.78%
CVFDT ORIGINAL $\|W\| = 1,000$	*49.94%*	*36.55%*	*33.89%*
CVFDT ORIGINAL $\|W\| = 10,000$	*49.98%*	*49.80%*	*28.73%*
CVFDT ORIGINAL $\|W\| = 100,000$	*50.11%*	*49.96%*	*46.64%*

Table 5.3: On-line errors of Hyperplane Experiments with gradual concept drift

	CHANGE SPEED		
	1,000	10,000	100,000
HAT-INC	9.42%	9.40%	9.39%
HAT-EWMA	9.48%	9.43%	9.36 %
HAT-ADWIN	9.50%	9.46%	9.25 %
HAT-INC NB	9.37%	9.43%	9.42%
HAT-EWMA NB	**8.64%**	**8.56%**	8.23 %
HAT-ADWIN NB	8.65%	8.57%	**8.17 %**
CVFDT $\|W\| = 1,000$	24.95%	22.65%	22.24%
CVFDT $\|W\| = 10,000$	14.85%	15.46%	*13.53%*
CVFDT $\|W\| = 100,000$	*10.50%*	*10.61%*	*10.85%*
CVFDT ORIGINAL $\|W\| = 1,000$	*30.11%*	*28.19%*	*28.19%*
CVFDT ORIGINAL $\|W\| = 10,000$	*18.93%*	*19.96%*	*18.60%*
CVFDT ORIGINAL $\|W\| = 100,000$	*10.92%*	*11.00%*	*11.36%*

5.4. EXPERIMENTAL EVALUATION

unknown, so in many research works, concept drift is introduced artificially. We simulate concept drift by ordering the datasets by one of its attributes, the *education* attribute for Adult, and the first (unnamed) attribute for Poker-Hand. Note again that while using CVFDT one faces the question of which parameter values to use, our method just needs to be told "go" and will find the right values online.

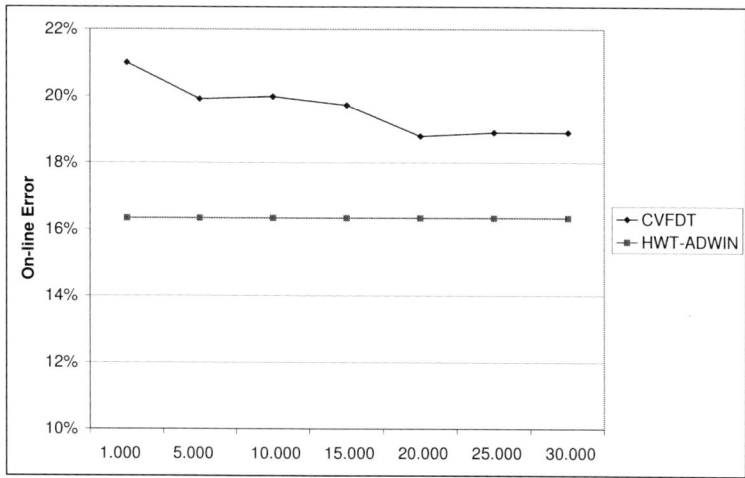

Figure 5.3: On-line error on UCI Adult dataset, ordered by the *education* attribute.

The Adult dataset aims to predict whether a person makes over 50k a year, and it was created based on census data. Adult consists of 48,842 instances, 14 attributes (6 continuous and 8 nominal) and missing attribute values. In Figure 5.3 we compare HWT-ADWIN error rate to CVFDT using different window sizes. We observe that CVFDT on-line error decreases when the example window size increases, and that HWT-ADWIN on-line error is lower for all window sizes.

The Poker-Hand dataset consists of 1,025,010 instances and 11 attributes. Each record of the Poker-Hand dataset is an example of a hand consisting of five playing cards drawn from a standard deck of 52. Each card is described using two attributes (suit and rank), for a total of 10 predictive attributes. There is one Class attribute that describes the "Poker Hand". The order of cards is important, which is why there are 480 possible Royal Flush hands instead of 4.

Table 5.4: On-line classification errors for CVFDT and Hoeffding Adaptive Trees on Poker-Hand data set.

	NO DRIFT	ARTIFICIAL DRIFT
HAT-INC	38.32%	39.21%
HAT-EWMA	39.48%	40.26%
HAT-ADWIN	38.71%	41.85%
HAT-INC NB	41.77%	42.83%
HAT-EWMA NB	24.49%	**27.28%**
HAT-ADWIN NB	**16.91%**	33.53%
CVFDT $|W| = 1,000$	49.90%	49.94%
CVFDT $|W| = 10,000$	*49.88%*	*49.88 %*
CVFDT $|W| = 100,000$	49.89%	52.13 %
CVFDT ORIGINAL $|W| = 1,000$	49.89%	49.92%
CVFDT ORIGINAL $|W| = 10,000$	*49.88%*	*49.88 %*
CVFDT ORIGINAL $|W| = 100,000$	*49.88%*	*52.09 %*

Table 5.4 shows the results on Poker-Hand dataset. It can be seen that CVFDT remains at 50% error, while the different variants of Hoeffding Adaptive Trees are mostly below 40% and one reaches 17% error only.

5.5 Time and memory

In this section, we discuss briefly the time and memory performance of Hoeffding Adaptive Trees. All programs were implemented in C modifying and expanding the version of CVFDT available from the VFML [HD03] software web page. The experiments were performed on a 2.0 GHz Intel Core Duo PC machine with 2 Gigabyte main memory, running Ubuntu 8.04.

Consider the experiments on SEA Concepts, with different speed of changes: $1,000, 10,000$ and $100,000$. Figure 5.4 shows the memory used on these experiments. As expected by memory complexity described in section 5.3.2, HAT-INC and HAT-EWMA, are the methods that use less memory. The reason for this fact is that it doesn't keep examples in memory as CVFDT, and that it doesn't store ADWIN data for all attributes, attribute values and classes, as HAT-ADWIN. We have used the default $10,000$ for the amount of window examples kept in memory, so the memory used by CVFDT is essentially the same for $W = 10,000$ and $W = 100,000$, and about 10 times larger than the memory used by HAT-INC memory.

Figure 5.5 shows the number of nodes used in the experiments of SEA

5.5. TIME AND MEMORY

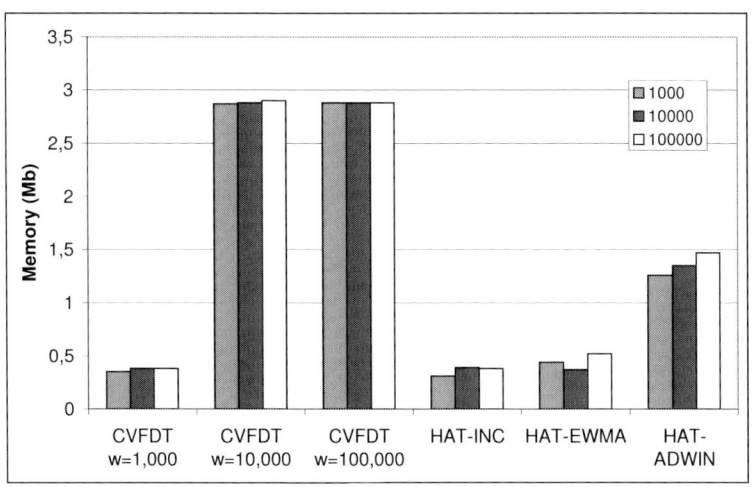

Figure 5.4: Memory used on SEA Concepts experiments

Concepts. We see that the number of nodes is similar for all methods, confirming that the good results on memory of HAT-INC is not due to smaller size of trees.

Finally, with respect to time we see that CVFDT is still the fastest method, but HAT-INC and HAT-EWMA have a very similar performance to CVFDT, a remarkable fact given that they are monitoring all the change that may occur in any node of the main tree and all the alternate trees. HAT-ADWIN increases time by a factor of 4, so it is still usable if time or data speed is not the main concern.

In summary, Hoeffding Adaptive Trees are always as accurate as CVFDT and, in some cases, they have substantially lower error. Their running time is similar in HAT-EWMA and HAT-INC and only slightly higher in HAT-ADWIN, and their memory consumption is remarkably smaller, often by an order of magnitude.

We can conclude that HAT-ADWIN is the most powerful method, but HAT-EWMA is a faster method that gives approximate results similar to HAT-ADWIN.

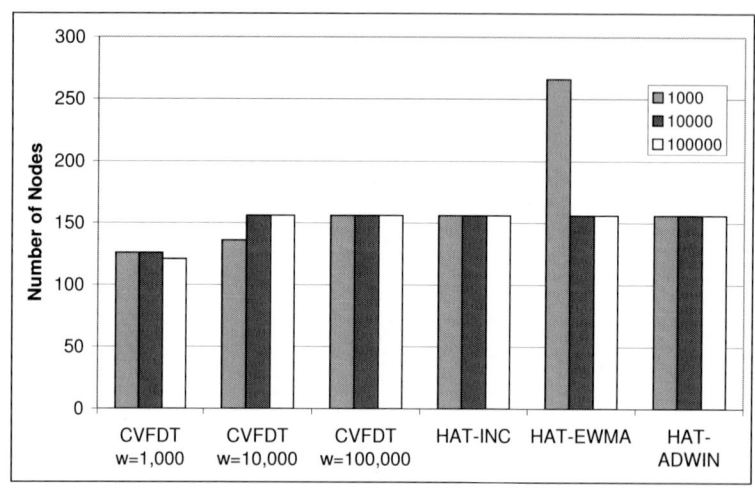

Figure 5.5: Number of Nodes used on SEA Concepts experiments

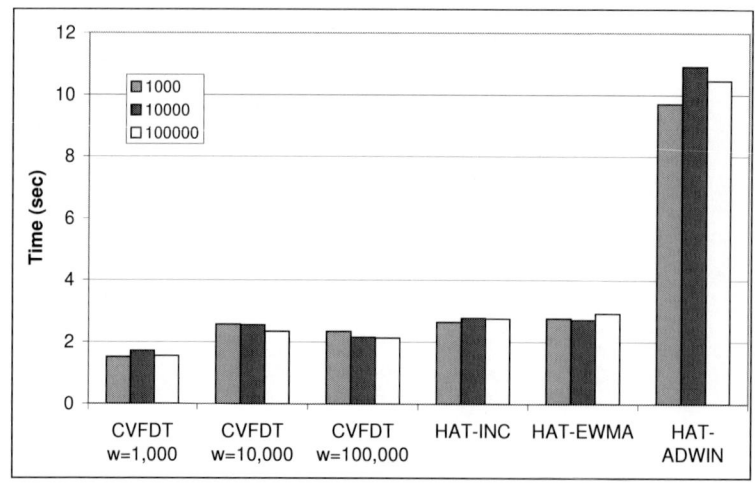

Figure 5.6: Time on SEA Concepts experiments

6
Ensemble Methods

Ensemble methods are combinations of several models whose individual predictions are combined in some manner (e.g., averaging or voting) to form a final prediction. Ensemble learning classifiers often have better accuracy and they are easier to scale and parallelize than single classifier methods.

This chapter proposes two new variants of Bagging. Using the new experimental framework presented in Section 3.5, an evaluation study on synthetic and real-world datasets comprising up to ten million examples shows that the new ensemble methods perform very well compared to several known methods.

6.1 Bagging and Boosting

Bagging and Boosting are two of the best known ensemble learning algorithms. In [OR01a] Oza and Russell developed online versions of bagging and boosting for Data Streams. They show how the process of sampling bootstrap replicates from training data can be simulated in a data stream context. They observe that the probability that any individual example will be chosen for a replicate tends to a Poisson(1) distribution.

For the boosting method, Oza and Russell note that the weighting procedure of AdaBoost actually divides the total example weight into two halves – half of the weight is assigned to the correctly classified examples, and the other half goes to the misclassified examples. They use the Poisson distribution for deciding the random probability that an example is used for training, only this time the parameter changes according to the boosting weight of the example as it is passed through each model in sequence.

Pelossof et al. presented in [PJVR08] Online Coordinate Boosting, a new online boosting algorithm for adapting the weights of a boosted classifier, which yields a closer approximation to Freund and Schapire's AdaBoost algorithm. The weight update procedure is derived by minimizing AdaBoost's loss when viewed in an incremental form. This boosting method may be reduced to a form similar to Oza and Russell's algorithm.

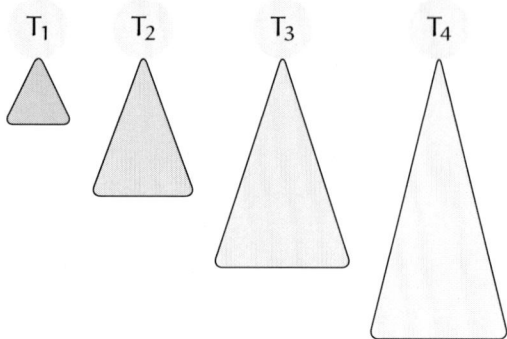

Figure 6.1: An ensemble of trees of different size

Chu and Zaniolo proposed in [CZ04] Fast and Light Boosting for adaptive mining of data streams. It is based on a dynamic sample-weight assignment scheme that is extended to handle concept drift via change detection. The change detection approach aims at significant data changes that could cause serious deterioration of the ensemble performance, and replaces the obsolete ensemble with one built from scratch.

6.2 New method of Bagging using trees of different size

In this section, we introduce the Adaptive-Size Hoeffding Tree (ASHT). It is derived from the Hoeffding Tree algorithm with the following differences:

- it has a maximum number of split nodes, or *size*
- after one node splits, if the number of split nodes of the ASHT tree is higher than the maximum value, then it deletes some nodes to reduce its size

The intuition behind this method is as follows: smaller trees adapt more quickly to changes, and larger trees do better during periods with no or little change, simply because they were built on more data. Trees limited to size s will be reset about twice as often as trees with a size limit of $2s$. This creates a set of different reset-speeds for an ensemble of such trees, and therefore a subset of trees that are a good approximation for the current rate of change. It is important to note that resets will happen all the time, even for stationary datasets, but this behaviour should not have a negative impact on the ensemble's predictive performance.

When the tree size exceeds the maximun size value, there are two different delete options:

6.2. NEW METHOD OF BAGGING USING TREES OF DIFFERENT SIZE

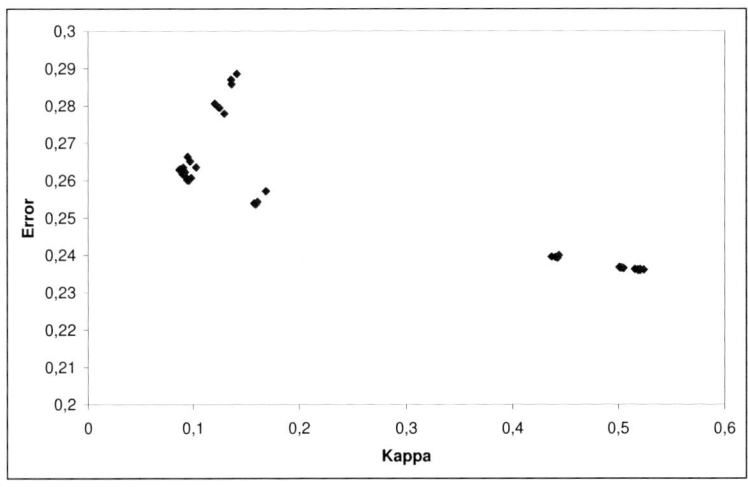

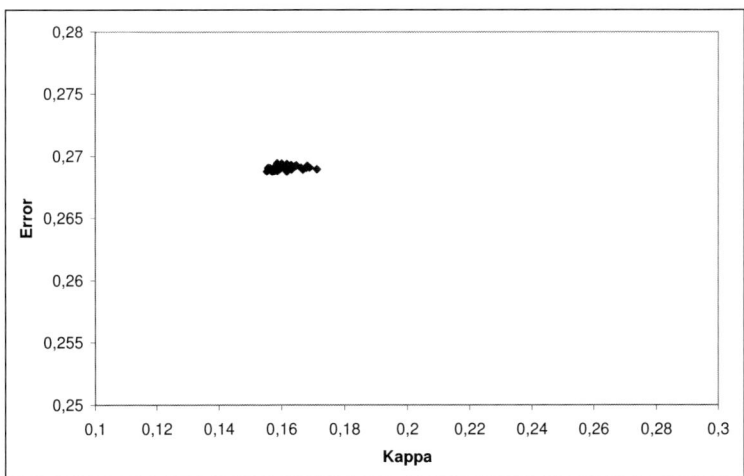

Figure 6.2: Kappa-Error diagrams for ASHT bagging (left) and bagging (right) on dataset RandomRBF with drift, plotting 90 pairs of classifiers.

- delete the oldest node, the root, and all of its children except the one where the split has been made. After that, the root of the child not deleted becomes the new root delete the oldest node, the root, and all of its children.

- delete all the nodes of the tree, i.e., restart from a new root.

We present a new bagging method that uses these Adaptive-Size Hoeffding Trees and that sets the size for each tree (Figure 6.1). The maximum allowed size for the n-th ASHT tree is twice the maximum allowed size for the $(n-1)$-th tree. Moreover, each tree has a weight proportional to the inverse of the square of its error, and it monitors its error with an exponential weighted moving average (EWMA) with $\alpha = .01$. The size of the first tree is 2.

With this new method, we attempt to improve bagging performance by increasing tree diversity. It has been observed that boosting tends to produce a more diverse set of classifiers than bagging, and this has been cited as a factor in increased performance [MD97].

We use the Kappa statistic κ to show how using trees of different size, we increase the diversity of the ensemble. Let's consider two classifiers h_a and h_b, a data set containing m examples, and a contingency table where cell C_{ij} contains the number of examples for which $h_a(x) = i$ and $h_b(x) = j$. If h_a and h_b are identical on the data set, then all non-zero counts will appear along the diagonal. If h_a and h_b are very different, then there should be a large number of counts off the diagonal. We define

$$\Theta_1 = \frac{\sum_{i=1}^{L} C_{ii}}{m}$$

$$\Theta_2 = \sum_{i=1}^{L} \left(\sum_{j=1}^{L} \frac{C_{ij}}{m} \cdot \sum_{j=1}^{L} \frac{C_{ji}}{m} \right)$$

We could use Θ_1 as a measure of agreement, but in problems where one class is much more common than others, all classifiers will agree by chance, so all pair of classifiers will obtain high values for Θ_1. To correct this, the κ statistic is defined as follows:

$$\kappa = \frac{\Theta_1 - \Theta_2}{1 - \Theta_2}$$

κ uses Θ_2, the probability that two classifiers agree by chance, given the observed counts in the table. If two classifiers agree on every example then $\kappa = 1$, and if their predictions coincide purely by chance, then $\kappa = 0$.

We use the Kappa-Error diagram to compare the diversity of normal bagging with bagging using trees of different size. The Kappa-Error diagram is a scatterplot where each point corresponds to a pair of classifiers.

The x coordinate of the pair is the κ value for the two classifiers. The y coordinate is the average of the error rates of the two classifiers.

Figure 6.2 shows the Kappa-Error diagram for the Random RBF dataset with drift parameter or change speed equal to 0.001.We observe that bagging classifiers are very similar to one another and that the decision tree classifiers of different size are very diferent from one another.

6.3 New method of Bagging using ADWIN

ADWIN Bagging is the online bagging method implemented in MOA with the addition of the ADWIN algorithm as a change detector and as an estimator for the weights of the boosting method. When a change is detected, the worst classifier of the ensemble of classifiers is removed and a new classifier is added to the ensemble.

6.4 Adaptive Hoeffding Option Trees

Hoeffding Option Trees [PHK07] are regular Hoeffding trees containing additional option nodes that allow several tests to be applied, leading to multiple Hoeffding trees as separate paths. They consist of a single structure that efficiently represents multiple trees. A particular example can travel down multiple paths of the tree, contributing, in different ways, to different options.

An *Adaptive Hoeffding Option Tree* is a Hoeffding Option Tree with the following improvement: each leaf stores an estimation of the current error. It uses an EWMA estimator with $\alpha = .2$. The weight of each node in the voting process is proportional to the square of the inverse of the error.

6.5 Comparative Experimental Evaluation

Massive **O**nline **A**nalysis (MOA) [HKP07] was introduced in Section 3.5.3. The data stream evaluation framework introduced there and all algorithms evaluated in this chapter were implemented in the Java programming language extending the MOA framework. We compare the following methods: Hoeffding Option Trees, bagging and boosting, and DDM and ADWIN bagging.

We use a variety of datasets for evaluation, as explained in Section 3.5.2. The experiments were performed on a 2.0 GHz Intel Core Duo PC machine with 2 Gigabyte main memory, running Ubuntu 8.10. The evaluation methodology used was Interleaved Test-Then-Train: every example was used for testing the model before using it to train. This interleaved test followed by train procedure was carried out on 10 million examples from the hyperplane and RandomRBF datasets, and one million examples from

CHAPTER 6. ENSEMBLE METHODS

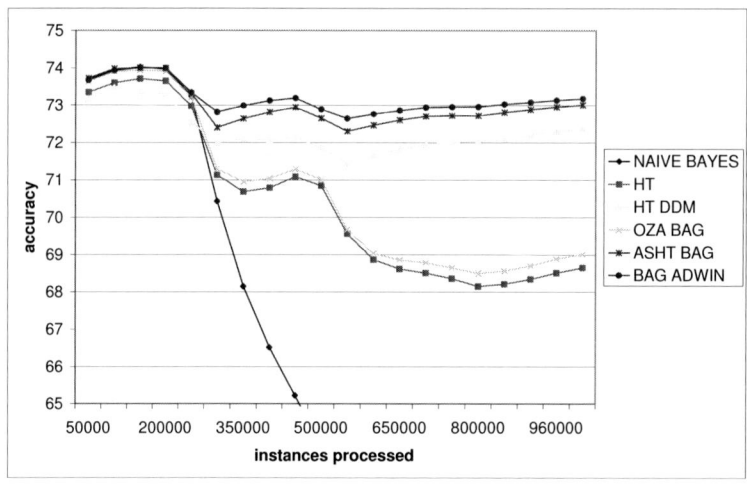

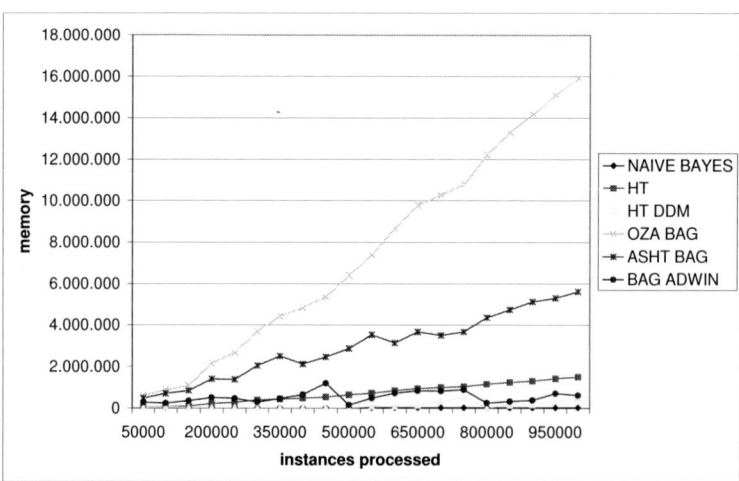

Figure 6.3: Accuracy and size on dataset LED with three concept drifts.

6.5. COMPARATIVE EXPERIMENTAL EVALUATION

the LED and SEA datasets. Tables 6.1 and 6.2 reports the final accuracy, and speed of the classification models induced on synthetic data. Table 6.3 shows the results for real datasets: Forest CoverType, Poker Hand, Electricity and CovPokElec. Additionally, the learning curves and model growth curves for LED dataset are plotted (Figure 6.3). For some datasets the differences in accuracy, as seen in Tables 6.1, 6.2 and 6.3, are marginal.

The first, and baseline, algorithm (HT) is a single Hoeffding tree, enhanced with adaptive Naive Bayes leaf predictions. Parameter settings are $n_{min} = 1000$, $\delta = 10^{-8}$ and $\tau = 0.05$. The HT DDM and HT EDDM are Hoeffding Trees with drift detection methods as explained in Section 2.2.1. HOT, is the Hoeffding option tree algorithm, restricted to a maximum of five option paths (HOT5) or fifty option paths (HOT50). AdaHOT is the Adaptive Hoeffding Tree explained in Section 6.4.

Bag10 is Oza and Russell online bagging using ten classifiers and Bag5 only five. BagADWIN is the online bagging version using ADWIN explained in Section 6.3. We implemented the following variants of bagging with Hoeffding trees of different size (ASHT): Bag ASHT is the base method, which deletes its root node and all its children except the one where the last split occurred, Bag ASHT W uses weighted classifiers, Bag ASHT R replaces oversized trees with new ones, and Bag ASHT W+R uses both weighted classifiers and replaces oversized trees with new ones. And finally, we tested three methods of boosting: Oza Boosting, Online Coordinate Boosting, and Fast and Light Boosting.

Bagging is clearly the best method in terms of accuracy. This superior position is, however, achieved at high cost in terms of memory and time. ADWIN Bagging and ASHT Bagging are the most accurate methods for most datasets, but they are slow. ADWIN Bagging is slower than ASHT Bagging and for some datasets it needs more memory. ASHT Bagging using weighted classifiers and replacing oversized trees with new ones seems to be the most accurate ASHT bagging method. We observe that bagging using 5 trees of different size may be sufficient, as its error is not much higher than for 10 trees, but it is nearly twice as fast. Also Hoeffding trees using drift detection methods are faster but less accurate methods.

In [PHK07], a range of option limits were tested and averaged across all datasets without concept drift to determine the optimal number of paths. This optimal number of options was five. Dealing with concept drift, we observe that increasing the number of options to 50, we obtain a significant improvement in accuracy for some datasets.

CHAPTER 6. ENSEMBLE METHODS

	Hyperplane Drift .0001			Hyperplane Drift .001			SEA W =50			SEA W 50000		
	Time	Acc.	Mem.	Time	Acc.	Mem.	Time	Acc.	Mem.	Time	Acc.	Mem.
DecisionStump	50.84	65.80	0.01	54.76	62.51	0.01	4.32	66.34	0.01	4.52	66.37	0.01
NaiveBayes	86.97	84.37	0.01	86.87	73.69	0.01	5.32	83.87	0.00	5.52	83.87	0.00
NB$_{\text{ADWIN}}$	308.85	91.40	0.06	295.19	90.68	0.06	12.24	88.33	0.02	12.40	87.58	0.02
HT	157.71	86.39	9.57	159.43	80.70	10.41	6.96	84.89	0.34	7.20	84.87	0.33
HT DDM	174.10	89.28	0.04	180.51	88.48	0.01	8.30	88.27	0.17	7.88	88.07	0.16
HT EDDM	207.47	88.95	13.23	193.07	87.64	2.52	8.56	87.97	0.18	8.52	87.64	0.06
HAT	500.81	89.88	1.72	431.6	88.72	0.15	21.2	88.91	0.17	20.96	88.32	0.18
HOT5	307.98	86.85	20.87	480.19	81.91	32.02	11.46	84.92	0.38	12.46	84.91	0.37
HOT50	890.86	87.37	32.04	3440.37	81.77	32.15	22.54	85.20	0.84	22.78	85.18	0.83
AdaHOT5	322.48	86.91	21.00	486.46	82.46	32.03	11.46	84.94	0.38	12.48	84.94	0.38
AdaHOT50	865.86	87.44	32.04	3369.89	83.47	32.15	22.70	85.35	0.86	22.80	85.30	0.84
Bag HT	1236.92	87.68	108.75	1253.07	81.80	114.14	31.06	85.45	3.38	30.88	85.34	3.36
Bag$_{\text{ADWIN}}$ 10 HT	1306.22	91.16	11.40	1308.08	90.48	5.52	54.51	88.58	1.90	53.15	**88.53**	0.88
Bag10 ASHT	1060.37	91.11	2.68	1070.44	90.08	2.69	34.99	87.83	1.04	35.30	87.57	0.91
Bag10 ASHT W	1055.87	91.40	2.68	1073.96	90.65	2.69	36.15	88.37	1.04	35.69	87.91	0.91
Bag10 ASHT R	995.06	91.47	2.95	1016.48	90.61	2.14	33.10	88.52	0.84	33.74	88.07	0.84
Bag10 ASHT W+R	996.52	**91.57**	2.95	1024.02	**90.94**	2.14	33.20	**88.89**	0.84	33.56	88.30	0.84
Bag5 ASHT W+R	551.53	90.75	0.08	562.09	90.57	0.09	19.78	88.55	0.01	20.00	87.99	0.05
OzaBoost	974.69	87.01	130.00	959.14	82.56	123.75	39.40	86.28	4.03	39.97	86.17	4.00
OCBoost	1367.77	84.96	66.12	1332.94	83.43	76.88	59.12	87.21	2.41	60.33	86.97	2.44
FLBoost	976.82	81.24	0.05	986.42	81.34	0.03	30.64	85.04	0.02	30.04	84.75	0.02

Table 6.1: Comparison of algorithms. Accuracy is measured as the final percentage of examples correctly classified over the 1 or 10 million test/train interleaved evaluation. Time is measured in seconds, and memory in MB. The best individual accuracies are indicated in boldface.

6.5. COMPARATIVE EXPERIMENTAL EVALUATION

	RandomRBF No Drift 50 centers			RandomRBF Drift .0001 50 centers			RandomRBF Drift .001 50 centers			RandomRBF Drift .001 10 centers		
	Time	Acc.	Mem.	Time	Acc.	Mem.	Time	Acc.	Mem.	Time	Acc.	Mem.
DecisionStump	74.98	58.60	0.01	79.05	50.54	0.01	81.70	50.46	0.01	61.29	62.99	0.01
NaiveBayes	111.12	72.04	0.01	111.47	53.21	0.01	113.37	53.17	0.01	95.25	75.85	0.01
NB_{ADWIN}	396.01	72.04	0.08	272.58	68.07	0.05	249.1	62.20	0.04	271.76	75.61	0.05
HT	154.67	93.64	6.86	189.25	63.64	9.86	186.47	55.48	8.90	141.63	89.07	6.97
HT DDM	185.15	93.64	13.72	199.95	76.49	0.02	206.41	64.09	0.03	173.31	89.07	13.94
HT EDDM	185.89	93.66	13.81	214.55	75.55	0.09	203.41	64.00	0.02	183.81	89.09	14.17
HAT	794.48	93.63	9.28	413.53	79.09	0.09	294.94	65.29	0.01	438.58	86.36	0.21
HOT5	398.82	94.90	23.67	412.38	67.31	27.04	318.07	56.82	18.49	271.22	89.62	15.80
HOT50	1075.74	95.04	32.04	3472.25	71.48	32.16	1086.89	58.88	32.04	949.94	89.98	32.03
AdaHOT5	400.53	94.29	23.82	415.85	71.82	27.21	319.33	59.74	18.60	270.04	89.71	15.90
AdaHOT50	975.40	94.22	32.04	3515.67	79.26	32.16	1099.77	64.53	32.04	951.88	90.07	32.03
Bag HT	995.46	**95.30**	71.26	1362.66	71.08	106.20	1240.89	58.15	88.52	1020.18	90.26	74.29
Bag_{ADWIN} 10 HT	1238.50	95.29	67.79	1326.12	**85.23**	0.26	1354.03	67.18	0.03	1172.27	**90.29**	44.18
Bag10 ASHT	1009.62	85.47	3.73	1124.40	76.09	3.05	1133.51	66.36	3.10	992.52	84.85	3.28
Bag10 ASHT W	986.90	93.76	3.73	1104.03	76.61	3.05	1106.26	66.94	3.10	983.10	89.58	3.28
Bag10 ASHT R	913.74	91.96	2.65	1069.76	84.28	3.74	1085.99	67.83	2.35	893.55	88.83	2.57
Bag10 ASHT W+R	925.65	93.57	2.65	1068.59	84.71	3.74	1101.10	**69.27**	2.35	901.39	89.53	2.57
Bag5 ASHT W+R	536.61	85.47	0.06	557.20	81.69	0.09	587.46	68.19	0.10	525.83	84.58	0.14
OzaBoost	964.75	94.82	206.60	1312.00	71.64	105.94	1266.75	58.20	88.36	978.44	89.83	172.57
OCBoost	1188.97	92.76	50.88	1501.64	74.69	80.36	1581.96	58.60	87.85	1215.30	89.00	56.82
FLBoost	932.85	71.39	0.02	1171.42	61.85	0.03	1176.33	52.73	0.02	1053.62	74.59	0.03

Table 6.2: Comparison of algorithms. Accuracy is measured as the final percentage of examples correctly classified over the 1 or 10 million test/train interleaved evaluation. Time is measured in seconds, and memory in MB. The best individual accuracies are indicated in boldface.

	Cover Type			Poker			Electricity			CovPokElec		
	Time	Acc.	Mem.	Time	Acc.	Mem.	Time	Acc.	Mem.	Time	Acc.	Mem.
NaiveBayes	31.66	60.52	0.05	13.58	50.01	0.02	0.92	74.15	0.01	91.50	23.52	0.08
NB_{ADWIN}	127.34	72.53	5.61	64.52	50.12	1.97	2.26	81.72	0.04	667.52	53.32	14.51
HT	31.52	77.77	1.31	18.98	72.14	1.15	1.16	78.88	0.06	95.22	74.00	7.42
HT DDM	40.26	84.35	0.33	21.58	61.65	0.21	1.36	84.73	0.04	114.72	71.26	0.42
HT EDDM	34.49	86.02	0.02	22.86	72.20	2.30	1.28	85.44	0.00	114.57	76.66	11.15
HAT	55.00	81.43	0.01	31.68	72.14	1.24	1.76	82.96	0.02	188.65	75.75	0.01
HOT5	65.69	83.19	5.41	31.60	72.14	1.28	2.36	82.80	0.36	138.20	75.93	13.30
HOT50	143.54	85.29	18.62	31.96	72.14	1.28	10.06	83.29	2.30	286.66	82.78	36.74
AdaHOT5	67.01	83.19	5.42	32.08	72.14	1.28	2.44	82.80	0.36	138.20	75.93	13.31
AdaHOT50	148.85	85.29	18.65	32.18	72.14	1.28	10.04	83.29	2.32	296.54	82.78	36.76
Bag HT	138.41	83.62	16.80	121.03	87.36	12.29	3.28	82.16	0.71	624.27	81.62	82.75
Bag_{ADWIN} 10 HT	247.50	84.71	0.23	165.01	84.84	8.79	4.96	84.15	0.07	911.57	**85.95**	0.41
Bag10 ASHT	213.75	83.34	5.23	124.76	86.80	7.19	3.92	82.79	0.37	638.37	78.87	29.30
Bag10 ASHT W	212.17	85.37	5.23	123.72	87.13	7.19	3.96	84.16	0.37	636.42	80.51	29.30
Bag10 ASHT R	229.06	84.20	4.09	122.92	86.21	6.47	3.80	83.31	0.42	776.61	80.01	29.94
Bag10 ASHT W+R	198.04	**86.43**	4.09	123.25	86.76	6.47	3.84	84.83	0.42	757.00	81.05	29.94
Bag5 ASHT W+R	116.83	83.79	0.23	57.09	75.87	0.44	2.54	84.44	0.09	363.09	77.65	0.95
OzaBoost	170.73	85.05	21.22	151.03	**87.85**	14.50	3.66	84.95	1.24	779.99	84.69	105.63
OCBoost	230.94	74.39	9.42	172.29	71.15	11.49	4.70	**86.20**	0.59	1121.49	71.94	73.36
FLBoost	234.56	70.29	0.15	19.92	50.12	0.07	2.66	73.08	0.04	368.89	52.92	0.47

Table 6.3: Comparison of algorithms on real data sets. Time is measured in seconds, and memory in MB. The best individual accuracies are indicated in boldface.

Part III

Closed Frequent Tree Mining

7
Mining Frequent Closed Rooted Trees

This chapter considers the extension to trees of the process of closure-based data mining, well-studied in the itemset framework. We focus mostly on the case where labels on the nodes are nonexistent or unreliable, and discuss algorithms for closure-based mining that only rely on the root of the tree and the link structure. We provide a notion of intersection that leads to a deeper understanding of the notion of support-based closure, in terms of an actual closure operator. We describe combinatorial characterizations and some properties, discuss its applicability to unordered trees, and rely on it to design efficient algorithms for mining frequent closed subtrees both in the ordered and the unordered settings.

7.1 Introduction

Trees, in a number of variants, are basically connected acyclic undirected graphs, with some additional structural notions like a distinguished vertex (root) or labelings on the vertices. They are frequently a great compromise between graphs, which offer richer expressivity, and strings, which offer very efficient algorithmics. From AI to Compilers, through XML dialects, trees are now ubiquitous in Informatics.

One form of data analysis contemplates the search of frequent, or the so-called "closed" substructures in a dataset of structures. In the case of trees, there are two broad kinds of subtrees considered in the literature: subtrees which are just induced subgraphs, called *induced subtrees*, and subtrees where contraction of edges is allowed, called *embedded subtrees*. In these contexts, the process of "mining" usually refers, nowadays, to a process of identifying which common substructures appear particularly often, or particularly correlated with other substructures, with the purpose of inferring new information implicit in a (large) dataset.

Closure-based mining refers to mining closed substructures, in a sense akin to the closure systems of Formal Concept Analysis; although the formal connections are not always explicit. For trees, a closed subtree is one that, if extended in any manner, leads to reducing the set of data trees where it appears as a subtree; and similarly for graphs. Frequent closed trees (or sets, or graphs) give the same information about the dataset as the set of all frequent trees (or sets, or graphs) in less space.

These mining processes can be used for a variety of tasks. Consider web search engines. Already the high polysemy of many terms makes sometimes difficult to find information through them; for instance, a researcher of soil science may have a very literal interpretation in mind when running a web search for "rolling stones", but it is unlikely that the results are very satisfactory; or a computer scientist interested in parallel models of computation has a different expectation from that of parents-to-be when a search for "prams" is launched. A way for distributed, adaptive search engines to proceed may be to distinguish navigation on unsuccessful search results, where the user follows a highly branching, shallow exploration, from successful results, which give rise to deeper, little-branching navigation subtrees.

7.2 Basic Algorithmics and Mathematical Properties

This section discusses, mainly, to what extent the intuitions about trees can be formalized in mathematical and algorithmic terms. As such, it is aimed just at building up intuition and background understanding, and making sure that our later sections on tree mining algorithms rest on solid foundations: they connect with these properties but make little explicit use of them.

Given two trees, a common subtree is a tree that is subtree of both; it is a maximal common subtree if it is not a subtree of any other common subtree; it is a maximum common subtree if there is no common subtree of larger size. Observe the different usage of the adjectives *maximum* and *maximal*.

Two trees have always some maximal common subtree but, as is shown in Figure 7.1, this common subtree does not need to be unique. This figure also serves the purpose of further illustrating the notion of unordered subtree.

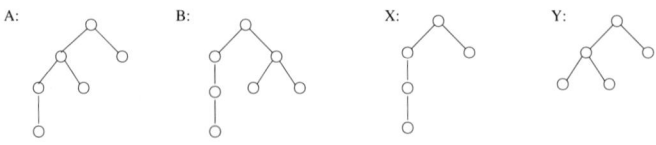

Figure 7.1: Trees X and Y are maximal common subtrees of A and B.

In fact, both trees X and Y in Figure 7.1 have the maximum number of nodes among the common subtrees of A and B. As is shown in Figure 7.2, just a slight modification of A and B gives two maximal common

7.2. BASIC ALGORITHMICS AND MATHEMATICAL PROPERTIES

subtrees of different sizes, showing that the concepts of maximal and maximum common subtree do not coincide in general.

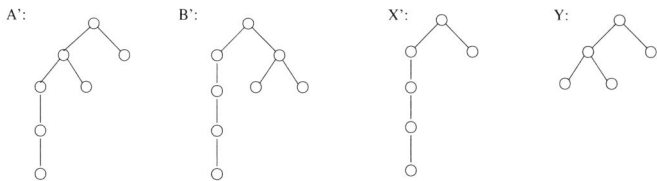

Figure 7.2: Both X' and Y are maximal common subtrees of A' and B', but only X' is maximum.

From here on, the *intersection* of a set of trees is the set of all maximal common subtrees of the trees in the set. Sometimes, the one-node tree will be represented with the symbol •, and the two-node tree by •–•.

7.2.1 Number of subtrees

We can easily observe, using the trees A, B, X, and Y above, that two trees can have an exponential number of maximal common subtrees.

Recall that the aforementioned trees have the property that X and Y are two maximal common subtrees of A and B. Now, consider the pair of trees constructed in the following way using copies of A and B. First, take a path of length $n-1$ (thus having n nodes which include the root and the unique leaf) and "attach" to each node a whole copy of A. Call this tree T_A. Then, do the same with a fresh path of the same length, with copies of B hanging from their nodes, and call this tree T_B. Graphically:

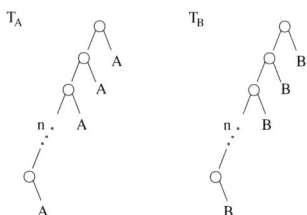

All the trees constructed similarly with copies of X or Y attached to each node of the main path (instead of A or B) are maximal common subtrees of T_A and T_B. As the maximal common subtrees are trees made from all the possible combinations of X an Y attached to the main path, there are 2^n possibilities corresponding to different subtrees. Therefore, the number of different maximal common subtrees of T_A and T_B is at least 2^n (which is exponential in the input since the sum of the sizes of T_A and T_B is $15n$). Any algorithm for computing maximal common subtrees has, therefore, a worst case exponential cost due to the size of the output. We must note, though, that experiments suggest that intersection sets of cardinality beyond 1 hardly ever arise unless looked for (see Section 7.8.2).

7.2.2 Finding the intersection of trees recursively

Computing a potentially large intersection of a set of trees is not a trivial task, given that there is no ordering among the components: a maximal element of the intersection may arise through mapping smaller components of one of the trees into larger ones of the other. Therefore, the degree of branching along the exploration is high. We propose a natural recursive algorithm to compute intersections, shown in Figure 7.3.

The basic idea is to exploit the recursive structure of the problem by considering all the ways to match the components of the two input trees. Suppose we are given the trees t and r, whose components are $t_1, \ldots, t_k$ and $r_1, \ldots, r_n$, respectively. If $k \leq n$, then clearly $(t_1, r_1), \ldots, (t_k, r_k)$ is one of those matchings. Then, we recursively compute the maximal common subtrees of each pair (t_i, r_i) and "cross" them with the subtrees of the previously computed pairs, thus giving a set of maximal common subtrees of t and r for this particular identity matching. The algorithm explores all the (exponentially many) matchings and, finally, eliminates repetitions and trees which are not maximal (by using recursion again).

RECURSIVE INTERSECTION(r, t)
1 **if** (r = •) or (t = •)
2   **then** $S \leftarrow \{\bullet\}$
3 **elseif** (r = ••) or (t = ••)
4   **then** $S \leftarrow \{\bullet\bullet\}$
5 **else** $S \leftarrow \{\}$
6        $n_r \leftarrow$ #COMPONENTS(r)
7        $n_t \leftarrow$ #COMPONENTS(t)
8   **for each** m in MATCHINGS(n_r, n_t)
9   **do** $mTrees \leftarrow \{\bullet\}$
10   **for each** (i, j) in m
11   **do** $c_r \leftarrow$ COMPONENT(r, i)
12                   $c_t \leftarrow$ COMPONENT(t, j)
13                   $cTrees \leftarrow$ RECURSIVE INTERSECTION(c_r, c_t)
14                   $mTrees \leftarrow$ CROSS($mTrees, cTrees$)
15            $S \leftarrow$ MAX SUBTREES($S, mTrees$)
16 **return** S

Figure 7.3: Algorithm RECURSIVE INTERSECTION

We do not specify the data structure used to encode the trees. The only

MAX SUBTREES(S_1, S_2)
1   **for each** r in S_1
2   **do for each** t in S_2
3   **if** r is a subtree of t
4   **then** mark r
5   **elseif** t is a subtree of r
6   **then** mark t
7   **return** sublist of nonmarked trees in $S_1 \cup S_2$

Figure 7.4: Algorithm MAX SUBTREES

condition needed is that every component t' of a tree t can be accessed with an index which indicates the lexicographical position of its encoding $\langle t' \rangle$ with respect to the encodings of the other components; this will be COMPONENT(t, i). The other procedures are as follows:

- #COMPONENTS(t) computes the number of components of t, this is, the arity of the root of t.

- MATCHINGS(n_1, n_2) computes the set of perfect matchings of the graph K_{n_1,n_2}, that is, of the complete bipartite graph with partition classes $\{1, \ldots, n_1\}$ and $\{1, \ldots, n_2\}$ (each class represents the components of one of the trees). For example,

  MATCHINGS$(2, 3) = \{\{(1, 1), (2, 2)\}, \{(1, 1), (2, 3)\}, \{(1, 2), (2, 1)\}, \{(1, 2), (2, 3)\}, \{(1, 3), (2, 1)\}, \{(1, 3), (2, 2)\}\}$.

- CROSS(l_1, l_2) returns a list of trees constructed in the following way: for each tree t_1 in l_1 and for each tree t_2 in l_2 make a copy of t_1 and add t_2 to it as a new component.

- MAX SUBTREES(S_1, S_2) returns the list of trees containing every tree in S_1 that is not a subtree of another tree in S_2 and every tree in S_2 that is not a subtree of another tree in S_1, thus leaving only the maximal subtrees. This procedure is shown in Figure 7.4. There is a further analysis of it in the next subsection.

The fact that, as has been shown, two trees may have an exponential number of maximal common subtrees necessarily makes any algorithm for computing all maximal subtrees inefficient. However, there is still space for some improvement.

7.2.3 Finding the intersection by dynamic programming

In the above algorithm, recursion can be replaced by a table of precomputed answers for the components of the input trees. This way we avoid repeated recursive calls for the same trees, and speed up the computation. Suppose we are given two trees r and t. In the first place, we compute all the trees that can appear in the recursive queries of RECURSIVE INTERSECTION(r, t). This is done in the following procedure:

- SUBCOMPONENTS(t) returns a list containing t if t = •; otherwise, if t has the components $t_1, \ldots, t_k$, then, it returns a list containing t and the trees in SUBCOMPONENTS(t_i) for every t_i, ordered increasingly by number of nodes.

The new algorithm shown in Figure 7.5 constructs a dictionary D accessed by pairs of trees (t_1, t_2) when the input trees are nontrivial (different from • and ••, which are treated separately). Inside the main loops, the trees which are used as keys for accessing the dictionary are taken from the lists SUBCOMPONENTS(r) and SUBCOMPONENTS(t), where r and t are the input trees.

DYNAMIC PROGRAMMING INTERSECTION(r, t)
1   for each s_r in SUBCOMPONENTS(r)
2   do for each s_t in SUBCOMPONENTS(t)
3   do if (s_r = •) or (s_t = •)
4   then $D[s_r, s_t] \leftarrow \{\bullet\}$
5   elseif (s_r = ••) or (s_t = ••)
6   then $D[s_r, s_t] \leftarrow \{\bullet\bullet\}$
7   else $D[s_r, s_t] \leftarrow \{\}$
8                       $ns_r \leftarrow$ #COMPONENTS(s_r)
9                       $ns_t \leftarrow$ #COMPONENTS(s_t)
10   for each m in MATCHINGS(ns_r, ns_t)
11   do $mTrees \leftarrow \{\bullet\}$
12   for each (i, j) in m
13   do $cs_r \leftarrow$ COMPONENT(s_r, i)
14                                      $cs_t \leftarrow$ COMPONENT(s_t, j)
15                                      $cTrees \leftarrow D[cs_r, cs_t]$
16                                      $mTrees \leftarrow$ CROSS($mTrees, cTrees$)
17                              $D[s_r, s_t] \leftarrow$ MAX SUBTREES($D[s_r, s_t], mTrees$)
18 return $D[r, t]$

Figure 7.5: Algorithm DYNAMIC PROGRAMMING INTERSECTION

Note that the fact that the number of trees in SUBCOMPONENTS(t) is linear in the number of nodes of t assures a quadratic size for D. The entries of the dictionary are computed by increasing order of the number of nodes; this way, the information needed to compute an entry has already been computed in previous steps.

The procedure MAX SUBTREES, which appears in the penultimate step of the two intersection algorithms presented, was presented in Section 7.2.2. The key point in the procedure MAX SUBTREES is the identification of subtrees made in steps 3 and 5 of Figure 7.4. This is discussed in depth below, but let us advance that, in the unordered case, it can be decided whether $t_1 \preceq t_2$ in time $O(n_1 n_2^{1.5})$ ([Val02]), where n_1 and n_2 are the number of nodes of t_1 and t_2, respectively.

Finally, Table 7.1 shows an example of the intersections stored in the dictionary by the algorithm DYNAMIC PROGRAMMING INTERSECTION with trees A and B of Figure 7.1 as input.

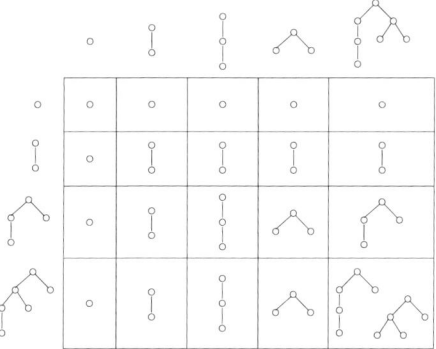

Table 7.1: Table with all partial results computed

7.3 Closure Operator on Trees

Now we attempt at formalizing a closure operator for substantiating the work on closed trees, with no resort to the labelings: we focus on the case where the given dataset consists of unlabeled, rooted trees; thus, our only relevant information is the identity of the root and the link structure. In order to have the same advantages as with frequent closed itemset mining, we want to be able to obtain all frequent subtrees, with their support, from the set of closed frequent subtrees with their supports. We propose a notion of Galois connection with the associated closure operator, in such a way that we can characterize support-based notions of closure with a mathematical operator.

For a notion of closed (sets of) trees to make sense, we expect to be given as data a finite set (actually, a list) of transactions, each of which consisting of its transaction identifier (tid) and a tree. Transaction identifiers are assumed to run sequentially from 1 to N, the size of the dataset. We denote $\mathcal{D} \subset \mathcal{T}$ the dataset, where $\mathcal{T}$ acts as our universe of discourse. General usage would lead to the following notion of closed tree:

Definition 2. *A tree t is closed for $\mathcal{D}$ if no tree t' $\neq$ t exists with the same support such that t $\preceq$ t'.*

We aim at clarifying the properties of closed trees, providing a more detailed justification of the term "closed" through a closure operator obtained from a Galois connection, along the lines of [GW99], [BG07b], [Gar06], or [BB03] for unstructured or otherwise structured datasets. However, given that the intersection of a set of trees is not a single tree but yet another set of trees, we will find that the notion of "closed" is to be applied to subsets of the transaction list, and that the notion of a "closed tree" t is not exactly coincident with the singleton {t} being closed.

To see that the task is not fully trivial, note first that t $\preceq$ t' implies that t is a subtree of all the transactions where t' is a subtree, so that the support of t is, at least, that of t'. Existence of a larger t' with the same support would mean that t does not gather all the possible information about the transactions in which it appears, since t' also appears in the same transactions and gives more information (is more specific). A closed tree is maximally specific for the transactions in which it appears. However, note that the example of the trees A and B given above provides two trees X and Y with the same support, and yet mutually incomparable. This is, in a sense, a problem. Indeed, for itemsets, and several other structures, the closure operator "maximizes the available information" by a process that would correspond to the following: given tree t, find the largest supertree of t which appears in all the transactions where t appears. But doing it that way, in the case of trees, does not maximize the information: there can be different, incomparable trees supported by the same set of transactions. Maximizing the information requires us to find them all.

There is a way forward, that can be casted into two alternative forms, equally simple and essentially equivalent. We can consider each subtree of some tree in the input dataset as an atomic item, and translate each transaction into an itemset on these items (all subtrees of the transaction tree). Then we can apply the standard Galois connection for itemsets, where closed sets would be sets of items, that is, sets of trees. The alternative we describe can be seen also as an implementation of this idea, where the difference is almost cosmetic, and we mention below yet another simple variant that we have chosen for our implementations, and that is easier to describe starting from the tree-based form we give now.

7.3.1 Galois Connection

A Galois connection is provided by two functions, relating two partial orders in a certain way. Here our partial orders are plain power sets of the transactions, on the one hand, and of the corresponding subtrees, in the other. On the basis of the binary relation $t \preceq t'$, the following definition and proposition are rather standard.

Definition 3. *The Galois connection pair:*

- *For finite* $A \subseteq \mathcal{D}$, $\sigma(A) = \{t \in \mathcal{T} \mid \forall t' \in A \, (t \preceq t')\}$
- *For finite* $B \subset \mathcal{T}$, *not necessarily in* $\mathcal{D}$, $\tau_\mathcal{D}(B) = \{t' \in \mathcal{D} \mid \forall t \in B \, (t \preceq t')\}$

Note, that $\sigma(A)$ finds all the subtrees common to all trees of A, and that $\tau_\mathcal{D}(B)$ finds all the trees of the dataset $\mathcal{D}$, that have trees of B as common subtrees.

The use of finite parts of the infinite set $\mathcal{T}$ should not obscure the fact that the image of the second function is empty except for finitely many sets B; in fact, we could use, instead of $\mathcal{T}$, the set of all trees that are subtrees of some tree in $\mathcal{D}$, with exactly the same effect overall. There are many ways to argue that such a pair is a Galois connection. One of the most useful ones is as follows.

Proposition 1. *For all finite* $A \subseteq \mathcal{D}$ *and* $B \subset \mathcal{T}$, *the following holds:*

$$A \subseteq \tau_\mathcal{D}(B) \iff B \subseteq \sigma(A)$$

This fact follows immediately since, by definition, each of the two sides is equivalent to $\forall t \in B \, \forall t' \in A \, (t \preceq t')$.

It is well-known that the compositions (in either order) of the two functions that define a Galois connection constitute closure operators, that is, are monotonic, extensive, and idempotent (with respect, in our case, to set inclusion).

Corollary 2. *The composition* $\tau_\mathcal{D} \circ \sigma$ *is a closure operator on the subsets of* $\mathcal{D}$. *The converse composition* $\Gamma_\mathcal{D} = \sigma \circ \tau_\mathcal{D}$ *is also a closure operator.*

$\Gamma_\mathcal{D}$ operates on subsets of $\mathcal{T}$; more precisely, again, on subsets of the set of all trees that appear as subtrees somewhere in $\mathcal{D}$. Thus, we have now both a concept of "closed set of transactions" of $\mathcal{D}$, and a concept of "closed sets of trees", and they are in bijective correspondence through both sides of the Galois connection. However, the notion of closure based on support, as previously defined, corresponds to single trees, and it is worth clarifying the connection between them, naturally considering the closure of the singleton set containing a given tree, $\Gamma_\mathcal{D}(\{t\})$, assumed nonempty, that is, assuming that t indeed appears as subtree somewhere along the dataset. We point out the following easy-to-check properties:

1. $t \in \Gamma_\mathcal{D}(\{t\})$

2. $t' \in \Gamma_\mathcal{D}(\{t\})$ if and only if $\forall s \in \mathcal{D}(t \preceq s \to t' \preceq s)$

3. t may be, or may not be, maximal in $\Gamma_\mathcal{D}(\{t\})$ (maximality is formalized as: $\forall t' \in \Gamma_\mathcal{D}(\{t\})[t \preceq t' \to t = t'])$). In fact, t is maximal in $\Gamma_\mathcal{D}(\{t\})$ if and only if $\forall t'(\forall s \in \mathcal{D}[t \preceq s \to t' \preceq s] \land t \preceq t' \to t = t')$

The definition of closed tree can be phrased in a similar manner as follows: t is closed for $\mathcal{D}$ if and only if: $\forall t'(t \preceq t' \land \mathrm{supp}(t) = \mathrm{supp}(t') \to t = t')$.

Theorem 8. *A tree t is closed for $\mathcal{D}$ if and only if it is maximal in $\Gamma_\mathcal{D}(\{t\})$.*

Proof. Suppose t is maximal in $\Gamma_\mathcal{D}(\{t\})$, and let $t \preceq t'$ with $\mathrm{supp}(t) = \mathrm{supp}(t')$. The data trees s that count for the support of t' must count as well for the support of t, because $t' \preceq s$ implies $t \preceq t' \preceq s$. The equality of the supports then implies that they are the same set, that is, $\forall s \in \mathcal{D}(t \preceq s \iff t' \preceq s)$, and then, by the third property above, maximality implies $t = t'$. Thus t is closed.

Conversely, suppose t is closed and let $t' \in \Gamma_\mathcal{D}(\{t\})$ with $t \preceq t'$. Again, then $\mathrm{supp}(t') \leq \mathrm{supp}(t)$; but, from $t' \in \Gamma_\mathcal{D}(\{t\})$ we have, as in the second property above, $(t \preceq s \to t' \preceq s)$ for all $s \in \mathcal{D}$, that is, $\mathrm{supp}(t) \leq \mathrm{supp}(t')$. Hence, equality holds, and from the fact that t is closed, with $t \preceq t'$ and $\mathrm{supp}(t) = \mathrm{supp}(t')$, we infer $t = t'$. Thus, t is maximal in $\Gamma_\mathcal{D}(\{t\})$. □

Now we can continue the argument as follows. Suppose t is maximal in some closed set B of trees. From $t \in B$, by monotonicity and idempotency, together with aforementioned properties, we obtain $t \in \Gamma_\mathcal{D}(\{t\}) \subseteq \Gamma_\mathcal{D}(B) = B$; being maximal in the larger set implies being maximal in the smaller one, so that t is maximal in $\Gamma_\mathcal{D}(\{t\})$ as well. Hence, we have argued the following alternative, somewhat simpler, characterization:

Corollary 3. *A tree is closed for $\mathcal{D}$ if and only if it is maximal in some closed set of $\Gamma_\mathcal{D}$.*

A simple observation here is that each closed set is uniquely defined through its maximal elements. In fact, our implementations chose to avoid duplicate calculations and redundant information by just storing the maximal trees of each closed set. We could have defined the Galois connection so that it would provide us "irredundant" sets of trees by keeping only maximal ones; the property of maximality would be then simplified into $t \in \Gamma_\mathcal{D}(\{t\})$, which would not be guaranteed anymore (cf. the notion of stable sequences in [BG07b]). The formal details of the validation of the Galois connection property would differ slightly (in particular, the ordering would not be simply a mere subset relationship) but the essentials would be identical, so that we refrain from developing that approach here. We would obtain a development somewhat closer to [BG07b] than our current development is, but there would be no indisputable advantages.

Now, given any set t, its support is the same as that of $\Gamma_D(\{t\})$; knowing the closed sets of trees and their supports gives us all the supports of all the subtrees. As indicated, this includes all the closed trees, but has more information regarding their joint membership in closed sets of trees. We can compute the support of arbitrary frequent trees in the following manner, that has been suggested to us by an anonymous reviewer: assume that we have the supports of all closed frequent trees, and that we are given a tree t; if it is frequent and closed, we know its support, otherwise we find the smallest closed frequent supertrees of t. Here we depart from the itemset case, because there is no unicity: there may be several noncomparable minimal frequent closed supertrees, but the support of t is the largest support appearing among these supertrees, due to the antimonotonicity of support.

For further illustration, we exhibit here, additionally, a toy example of the closure lattice for a simple dataset consisting of six trees, thus providing additional hints on our notion of intersection; these trees were not made up for the example, but were instead obtained through six different (rather arbitrary) random seeds of the synthetic tree generator of Zaki [Zak02].

The figure depicts the closed sets obtained. It is interesting to note that all the intersections came up to a single tree, a fact that suggests that the exponential blow-up of the intersection sets, which is possible as explained in Section 7.2.1, appears infrequently enough, see Section 7.8.2 for empirical validation.

Of course, the common intersection of the whole dataset is (at least) a "pole" whose length is the minimal height of the data trees.

7.4 Level Representations

The development so far is independent of the way in which the trees are represented. The reduction of a tree representation to a (frequently augmented) sequential representation has always been a source of ideas, already discussed in depth in Knuth [Knu97, Knu05]. We use here a specific data structure [NU03, BH80, AAUN03, NK03] to implement trees that leads to a particularly streamlined implementation of the closure-based mining algorithms.

We will represent each tree as a sequence over a countably infinite alphabet, namely, the set of natural numbers; we will concentrate on a specific language, whose strings exhibit a very constrained growth pattern. Some simple operations on strings of natural numbers are:

Definition 4. *Given two sequences of natural numbers* x, y, *we represent by*

- $|x|$ *the length of* x.

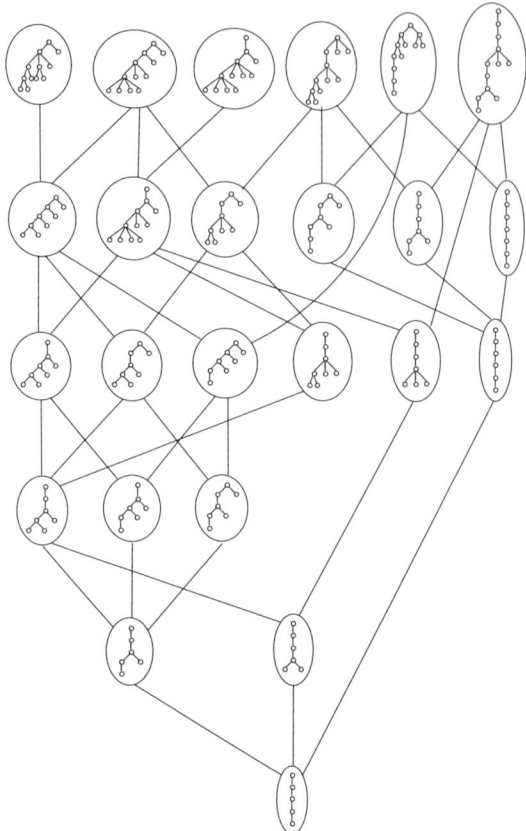

Figure 7.6: Lattice of closed trees for the six input trees in the top row

- $x \cdot y$ *the sequence obtained as concatenation of* x *and* y

- $x + i$ *the sequence obtained adding* i *to each component of* x*; we represent by* x^+ *the sequence* $x + 1$

We will apply to our sequences the common terminology for strings: the term *subsequence* will be used in the same sense as *substring*; in the same way, we will also refer to *prefixes* and *suffixes*. Also, we can apply lexicographical comparisons to our sequences.

The language we are interested in is formed by sequences which never "jump up": each value either decreases with respect to the previous one, or stays equal, or increases by only one unit. This kind of sequences will be used to describe trees.

Definition 5. *A* level sequence *or* depth sequence *is a sequence* $(x_1, \ldots, x_n)$ *of natural numbers such that* $x_1 = 0$ *and each subsequent number* x_{i+1} *belongs to the range* $1 \leq x_{i+1} \leq x_i + 1$.

7.4. LEVEL REPRESENTATIONS

For example, $x = (0, 1, 2, 3, 1, 2)$ is a level sequence that satisfies $|x| = 6$ or $x = (0) \cdot (0, 1, 2)^+ \cdot (0, 1)^+$. Now, we are ready to represent trees by means of level sequences.

Definition 6. *We define a function $\langle \cdot \rangle$ from the set of ordered trees to the set of level sequences as follows. Let t be an ordered tree. If t is a single node, then $\langle t \rangle = (0)$. Otherwise, if t is composed of the trees $t_1, \ldots, t_k$ joined to a common root r (where the ordering $t_1, \ldots, t_k$ is the same of the children of r), then*

$$\langle t \rangle = (0) \cdot \langle t_1 \rangle^+ \cdot \langle t_2 \rangle^+ \cdot \cdots \cdot \langle t_k \rangle^+$$

Here we will say that $\langle t \rangle$ is the level representation of t.

Note the role of the previous definition:

Proposition 2. *Level sequences are exactly the sequences of the form $\langle t \rangle$ for ordered, unranked trees t.*

That is, our encoding is a bijection between the ordered trees and the level sequences. This encoding $\langle t \rangle$ basically corresponds to a preorder traversal of t, where each number of the sequence represents the level of the current node in the traversal. As an example, the level representation of the tree

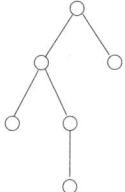

is the level sequence $(0, 1, 2, 2, 3, 1)$. Note that, for example, the subsequence $(1, 2, 2, 3)$ corresponds to the bottom-up subtree rooted at the left son of the root (recall that our subsequences are adjacent). We can state this fact in general.

Proposition 3. *Let $x = \langle t \rangle$, where t is an ordered tree. Then, t has a bottom-up subtree r at level $d > 0$ if and only if $\langle r \rangle + d$ is a subsequence of x.*

Proof. We prove it by induction on d. If $d = 1$, then $\langle r \rangle + d = \langle r \rangle^+$ and the property holds by the recursive definition of level representation.

For the induction step, let $d > 1$. To show one direction, suppose that r is a bottom-up subtree of t at level d. Then, r must be a bottom-up subtree of one of the bottom-up subtrees corresponding to the children of the root of t. Let t' be the bottom-up subtree at level 1 that contains r. Since r is at level $d - 1$ in t', the induction hypothesis states that $\langle r \rangle + d - 1$ is a subsequence of $\langle t' \rangle$. But $\langle t' \rangle^+$ is also, by definition, a subsequence of x. Combining both facts, we get that $\langle r \rangle + d$ is a subsequence of x, as desired. The argument also works in the contrary direction, and we get the equivalence. □

7.4.1 Subtree Testing in Ordered Trees

Top-down subtree testing of two ordered trees can be obtained by performing a simultaneous preorder traversal of the two trees [Val02]. This algorithm is shown in Figure 7.7. There, pos_t traverses sequentially the level representation of tree t and pos_{st} similarly traverses the purported subtree st. The natural number found in the level representation of t at position pos_t is exactly level (t, pos_t).

Suppose we are given the trees st and t, and we would like to know if st is a subtree of t. Our method begins visiting the first node in tree t and the first node in tree st. While we are not visiting the end of any tree,

- If the level of tree t node is greater than the level of tree st node then we visit the next node in tree t

- If the level of tree st node is greater than the level of tree t node then we backtrack to the last node in tree st that has the same level as tree node

- If the level of the two nodes are equal then we visit the next node in tree t and the next node in tree st

If we reach the end of tree st, then st is a subtree of tree t.

ORDERED_SUBTREE(st, t)

    Input: A tree st, a tree t.
    Output: **true** if st is a subtree of t.

```
1   pos_st = 1
2   pos_t = 1
3   while pos_st ≤ SIZE(st) and pos_t ≤ SIZE(t)
4       do if level (st, pos_st) > level (t, pos_t)
5           then while level (st, pos_st) ≠ level (t, pos_t)
6               do pos_st = pos_st − 1
7           if level (st, pos_st) = level (t, pos_t)
8               then pos_st = pos_st + 1
9           pos_t = pos_t + 1
10  return pos_st > SIZE(st)
```

Figure 7.7: The Ordered Subtree test algorithm

The running time of the algorithm is clearly quadratic since for each node of tree t, it may visit all nodes in tree st. An incremental version of this algorithm follows easily, as it is explained in next section.

7.5 Mining Frequent Ordered Trees

In the rest of the chapter, our goal will be to obtain a frequent closed tree mining algorithm for ordered and unordered trees. First, we present in this section a basic method for mining frequent ordered trees. We will extend it to unordered trees and frequent closed trees in the next section.

We begin showing a method for mining frequent ordered trees. Our approach here is similar to gSpan [YH02]: we represent the potential frequent subtrees to be checked on the dataset in such a way that extending them by one single node, in all possible ways, corresponds to a clear and simple operation on the representation. The completeness of the procedure is assured, that is, we argue that all trees can be obtained in this way. This allows us to avoid extending trees that are found to be already nonfrequent.

We show now that our representation allows us to traverse the whole subtree space by an operation of extension by a single node, in a simple way.

Definition 7. *Let x and y be two level sequences. We say that y is a one-step extension of x (in symbols, $x \vdash^1 y$) if x is a prefix of y and $|y| = |x| + 1$. We say that y is an extension of x (in symbols, $x \vdash y$) if x is a prefix of y.*

Note that $x \vdash^1 y$ holds if and only if $y = x \cdot (i)$, where $1 \leq i \leq j + 1$, and j is the last element of x. Note also that a series of one-step extensions from (0) to a level sequence x

$$(0) \vdash^1 x_1 \vdash^1 \cdots \vdash^1 x_{k-1} \vdash^1 x$$

always exists and must be unique, since the x_i's can only be the prefixes of x. Therefore, we have:

Proposition 4. *For every level sequence x, there is a unique way to extend (0) into x.*

For this section we could directly use gSpan, since our structures can be handled by that algorithm. However, our goal is the improved algorithm described in the next section, to be applied when the ordering in the subtrees is irrelevant for the application, that is, mining closed unordered trees.

Indeed, level representations allow us to check only canonical representatives for the unordered case, thus saving the computation of support for all (except one) of the ordered variations of the same unordered tree. Figures 7.8 and 7.9 show the gSpan-based algorithm, which is as follows: beginning with a tree of single node, it calls recursively the FREQUENT_ORDERED_SUBTREE_MINING algorithm doing one-step extensions and checking that they are still frequent. Correctness and completeness follow from Propositions 2 and 4 by standard arguments.

FREQUENT_ORDERED_MINING(D, min_sup)

Input: A tree dataset D, and min_sup.
Output: The frequent tree set T.

1 t ← •
2 T ← ∅
3 T ← FREQUENT_ORDERED_SUBTREE_MINING(t, D, min_sup, T)
4 **return** T

Figure 7.8: The Frequent Ordered Mining algorithm

FREQUENT_ORDERED_SUBTREE_MINING(t, D, min_sup, T)

Input: A tree t, a tree dataset D, min_sup, and the frequent tree set T so far.
Output: The frequent tree set T, updated from t.

1 insert t into T
2 **for** every t' that can be extended from t in one step
3   **do if** support(t') ≥ min_sup
4   **then** T ← FREQUENT_ORDERED_SUBTREE_MINING(t', D, min_sup, T)
5 **return** T

· Figure 7.9: The Frequent Ordered Subtree Mining algorithm

Since we represent trees by level representations, we can speed up these algorithms, using an incremental version of the subtree ordered test algorithm explained in Section 7.4.1, reusing the node positions we reach at the end of the algorithm. If st1 is a tree extended from st in one step adding a node, we can start ORDERED_SUBTREE(st1, t) proceeding from where ORDERED_SUBTREE(st, t) ended. So, we only need to store and reuse the positions pos_t and pos_{st} at the end of the algorithm. This incremental method is shown in Figure 7.10. Note that ORDERED_SUBTREE can be seen as a call to INCREMENTAL_ORDERED_SUBTREE with pos_{st} and pos_t initialized to zero.

7.6 Unordered Subtrees

In unordered trees, the children of a given node form sets of siblings instead of sequences of siblings. Therefore, ordered trees that only differ in permutations of the ordering of siblings are to be considered the same unordered tree.

INCREMENTAL_ORDERED_SUBTREE(st, t, pos_{st}, pos_t)

Input: A tree st, a tree t, and positions pos_{st}, pos_t such that the st prefix of length $pos_{st} - 1$ is a subtree of the t prefix of length pos_t.
Output: **true** if st is a subtree of t.

```
1  while pos_st ≤ SIZE(st) and pos_t ≤ SIZE(t)
2      do if level (st, pos_st) > level (t, pos_t)
3          then while level (st, pos_st) ≠ level (t, pos_t)
4              do pos_st = pos_st − 1
5          if level (st, pos_st) = level (t, pos_t)
6              then pos_st = pos_st + 1
7          pos_t = pos_t + 1
8  return pos_st > SIZE(st)
```

Figure 7.10: The Incremental Ordered Subtree test algorithm

7.6.1 Subtree Testing in Unordered Trees

We can test if an unordered tree r is a subtree of an unordered tree t by reducing the problem to maximum bipartite matching. Figure 7.11 shows this algorithm.

Suppose we are given the trees r and t, whose components are $r_1, \ldots, r_n$ and $t_1, \ldots, t_k$, respectively. If $n > k$ or r has more nodes than t, then r cannot be a subtree of t. We recursively build a bipartite graph where the vertices represent the child trees of the trees and the edges the relationship "is subtree" between vertices. The function BIPARTITEMATCHING returns true if it exists a solution for this maximum bipartite matching problem. It takes time $O(n_r n_t^{1.5})$([Val02]), where n_r and n_t are the number of nodes of r and t, respectively. If BIPARTITEMATCHING returns true then we conclude that r is a subtree of t.

To speed up this algorithm, we store the computation results of the algorithm in a dictionary D, and we try to reuse these computations at the beginning of the algorithm.

7.6.2 Mining frequent closed subtrees in the unordered case

The main result of this subsection is a precise mathematical characterization of the level representations that correspond to canonical variants of unordered trees. Luccio et al. [LERP04, LERP01] showed that a canonical

UNORDERED_SUBTREE(r, t)

　　Input: A tree r, a tree t.
　　Output: **true** if r is a subtree of t.

1　**if** D(r, t) exists
2　　**then** Return D(r, t)
3　**if** (SIZE(r) > SIZE(t) or #COMPONENTS(r) > #COMPONENTS(t))
4　　**then** Return **false**
5　**if** (r = •)
6　　**then** Return **true**
7　$graph \leftarrow \{\}$
8　**for each** s_r in SUBCOMPONENTS(r)
9　　**do for each** s_t in SUBCOMPONENTS(t)
10　　　**do if** (UNORDERED_SUBTREE(s_r, s_t))
11　　　　**then** insert($graph$, edge(s_r, s_t))
12　**if** BIPARTITEMATCHING($graph$)
13　　**then** D(r, t) $\leftarrow$ **true**
14　　**else** D(r, t) $\leftarrow$ **false**
15　**return** D(r, t)

Figure 7.11: The Unordered Subtree test algorithm

representation based on the preorder traversal can be obtained in linear time. Nijssen et al. [NK03], Chi et al. [CYM05] and Asai et al. [AAUN03] defined similar canonical representations.

We select one of the ordered trees corresponding to a given unordered tree to act as a canonical representative: by convention, this canonical representative has larger trees always to the left of smaller ones. More precisely,

Definition 8. *Let* t *be an unordered tree, and let* $t_1, \ldots, t_n$ *be all the ordered trees obtained from* t *by ordering in all possible ways all the sets of siblings of* t. *The canonical representative of* t *is the ordered tree* t_0 *whose level representation is maximal (according to lexicographic ordering) among the level representations of the trees* t_i, *that is, such that*

$$\langle t_0 \rangle = \max\{\langle t_i \rangle \mid 1 \leq i \leq n\}.$$

We can use, actually, the same algorithm as in the previous section to mine unordered trees; however, much work is unnecessarily spent in checking repeatedly ordered trees that correspond to the same unordered tree as one already checked. A naive solution is to compare each tree to

7.6. UNORDERED SUBTREES

be checked with the ones already checked, but in fact this is an inefficient process, since all ways of mapping siblings among them must be tested.

A far superior solution would be obtained if we could count frequency only for canonical representatives. We prove next how this can be done: the use of level representations allows us to decide whether a given (level representation of a) tree is canonical, by using an intrinsic characterization, stated in terms of the level representation itself.

Theorem 9. *A level sequence x corresponds to a canonical representative if and only if for any level sequences y, z and any $d \geq 0$ such that $(y + d) \cdot (z + d)$ is a subsequence of x, it holds that $y \geq z$ in lexicographical order.*

Proof. Suppose that x corresponds to a canonical representative and that $(y+d) \cdot (z+d)$ is a subsequence of x for some level sequences y, z and $d \geq 0$. In this case, both $y+d$ and $z+d$ are subsequences of x and, by Proposition 3, $\langle y \rangle$ and $\langle z \rangle$ are two subtrees of $\langle x \rangle$. Since their respective level representations, y and z, appear consecutively in x, the two subtrees must be siblings. Now, if $y < z$, the reordering of siblings y and z would lead to a bigger level representation of the same unordered tree, and x would not correspond to a canonical representative. Therefore, $y \geq z$ in lexicographical order.

For the other direction, suppose that x does not correspond to a canonical representative. Then, the ordered tree t represented by x would have two sibling subtrees r and s (appearing consecutively in t, say r before s) that, if exchanged, would lead to a lexicographically bigger representation. Let $y = \langle r \rangle$ and $z = \langle s \rangle$. If r and s are at level d in t, then $(y + d) \cdot (z + d)$ would be a subsequence of $x = \langle t \rangle$ (again by Proposition 3). Then, it must hold that $y < z$ in lexicographical order. □

Corollary 4. *Let a level sequence x correspond to a canonical representative. Then its extension $x \cdot \langle i \rangle$ corresponds to a canonical representative if and only if, for any level sequences y, z and any $d \geq 0$ such that $(y + d) \cdot (z + d)$ is a suffix of $x \cdot \langle i \rangle$, it holds that $y \geq z$ in lexicographical order.*

Proof. Suppose that x corresponds to a canonical representative, and let i be such that $x \cdot \langle i \rangle$ is a level sequence. At this point, we can apply Theorem 9 to $x \cdot \langle i \rangle$: it is a canonical representative if and only if all subsequences of the form $(y + d) \cdot (z + d)$ (for appropriate y, z, and d) satisfy that $y \geq z$. But such subsequences $(y + d) \cdot (z + d)$ can now be divided into two kinds: the ones that are subsequences of x and the ones that are suffixes of $x \cdot \langle i \rangle$.

A new application of Theorem 9 to x assures that the required property must hold for subsequences of the first kind. So, we can characterize the property that $x \cdot \langle i \rangle$ corresponds to a canonical representative just using the subsequences of the second kind (that is, suffixes) as said in the statement. □

We build an incremental canonical checking algorithm, using the result of Corollary 4. The algorithm is as follows: each time we add a node of level d to a tree t, we check for all levels less than d that the last two child subtrees are correctly ordered. As it is an incremental algorithm, and the tree that we are extending is canonical, we can assume that child subtrees are ordered, so we only have to check the last two ones.

7.6.3 Closure-based mining

In this section, we propose TREENAT, a new algorithm to mine frequent closed trees. Figure 7.12 illustrates the framework.

Figure 7.13 shows the pseudocode of CLOSED_UNORDERED_SUBTREE_MINING. It is similar to UNORDERED_SUBTREE_MINING, adding a checking of closure in lines 10-13. Correctness and completeness follow from Propositions 2 and 4, and Corollary 4.

The main difference of TREENAT, with CMTreeMiner is that CMTreeMiner needs to store all occurrences of subtrees in the tree dataset to use its pruning methods, whereas our method does not. That means that with a small number of labels, CMTreeMiner will need to store a huge number of occurrences, and it will take much more time and memory than our method, that doesn't need to store all that information. Also, with unlabeled trees, if the tree size is big, CMTreeMiner needs more time and memory to store all possible occurrences. For example, an unlabeled tree of size 2 in a tree of size n has n − 1 occurrences. But when the number of labels is big, or the size of the unlabeled trees is small, CMTreeMiner will be fast because the number of occurrences is small and it can use the power of its pruning methods. Dealing with unordered trees, CMTreeMiner doesn't use bipartite matching as we do for subtree testing. However, it uses canonical forms and the storing of all occurrences.

CLOSED_UNORDERED_MINING(D, min_sup)
    Input: A tree dataset D, and min_sup.
    Output: The closed tree set T.

1   t ← •
2   T ← ∅
3   T ← CLOSED_UNORDERED_SUBTREE_MINING(t, D, min_sup, T)
4 **return** T

Figure 7.12: The Closed Unordered Mining algorithm

CLOSED_UNORDERED_SUBTREE_MINING(t, D, min_sup, T)

Input: A tree t, a tree dataset D, min_sup, and the closed frequent tree set T so far.
Output: The closed frequent tree set T, updated from t.

1   **if** t ≠ CANONICAL_REPRESENTATIVE(t)
2   **then return** T
3   t_is_closed ← TRUE
4   **for** every t' that can be extended from t in one step
5   **do if** support(t') ≥ min_sup
6   **then** T ← CLOSED_UNORDERED_SUBTREE_MINING(t', D, min_sup, T)
7   **do if** support(t') = support(t)
8   **then** t_is_closed ← FALSE
9   **if** t_is_closed = TRUE
10   **then** insert t into T
11 **if** (∃t'' ∈ T | t'' is subtree of t, support(t) =support(t''))
12   **then** delete t'' from T
13 **return** T

Figure 7.13: The Closed Unordered Subtree Mining algorithm

7.7 Induced subtrees and Labeled trees

Our method can be extended easily to deal with induced subtrees and labeled trees in order to compare it with CMTreeMiner in Section 7.8, working with the same kind of trees and subtrees.

7.7.1 Induced subtrees

In order to adapt our algorithms to all induced subtrees, not only rooted, we need to change the subtree testing procedure with a slight variation. We build a new procedure for checking if a tree r is an induced subtree of t using the previous procedure SUBTREE(r, t) (ORDERED_SUBTREE(r, t) for ordered trees or UNORDERED_SUBTREE(r, t) for unordered trees) that checks wether a tree r is a top-down subtree of tree t. It is as follows: for every node n in tree t we consider the top-down subtree t' of tree t rooted at node n. If there is at least one node that SUBTREE(r, t') returns true, then r is an induced subtree of t, otherwise not. Applying this slight variation to both ordered and unordered trees, we are able to mine induced subtrees as CMTreeMiner.

7.7.2 Labeled trees

We need to use a new tree representation to deal with labels in the nodes of the trees. We represent each labeled tree using labeled level sequences [AAUN03, NK03], a labeled extension of the level representations explained earlier.

Definition 9. *A labeled level sequence is a sequence* $((x_1, l_1) \ldots, (x_n, l_n))$ *of pairs of natural numbers and labels such that* $x_1 = 0$ *and each subsequent number* x_{i+1} *belongs to the range* $1 \leq x_{i+1} \leq x_i + 1$.

For example, $x = ((0, A), (1, B), (2, A), (3, B), (1, C))$ is a level sequence that satisfies $|x| = 6$ or $x = ((0, A)) \cdot ((0, B), (1, A), (2, B))^+ \cdot ((0, C))^+$. Now, we are ready to represent trees by means of level sequences (see also [CYM04]).

Definition 10. *We define a function* $\langle \cdot \rangle$ *from the set of ordered trees to the set of labeled level sequences as follows. Let* t *be an ordered tree. If* t *is a single node, then* $\langle t \rangle = ((0, l_0))$. *Otherwise, if* t *is composed of the trees* $t_1, \ldots, t_k$ *joined to a common root* r *(where the ordering* $t_1, \ldots, t_k$ *is the same of the children of* r*), then*

$$\langle t \rangle = ((0, l_0)) \cdot \langle t_1 \rangle^+ \cdot \langle t_2 \rangle^+ \cdot \cdots \cdot \langle t_k \rangle^+$$

Here we will say that $\langle t \rangle$ *is the labeled level representation of* t.

This encoding is a bijection between the ordered trees and the labeled level sequences. This encoding $\langle t \rangle$ basically corresponds to a preorder traversal of t, where each natural number of the node sequence represents the level of the current node in the traversal.

Figure 7.14 shows a finite dataset example using labeled level sequences.

The closed trees for the dataset of Figure 7.14 are shown in the Galois lattice of Figure 7.15.

7.8 Applications

We tested our algorithms on synthetic and real data, and compared the results with CMTreeMiner [CXYM01].

All experiments were performed on a 2.0 GHz Intel Core Duo PC machine with 2 Gigabyte main memory, running Ubuntu 7.10. As far as we know, CMTreeMiner is the state-of-art algorithm for mining induced closed frequent trees in databases of rooted trees.

7.8.1 Datasets for mining closed frequent trees

We present the datasets used in this section for empirical avaluation of our closed frequent tree mining methods. GAZELLE is a new unlabeled tree dataset. The other datasets are the most used ones in frequent tree mining literature.

7.8. APPLICATIONS

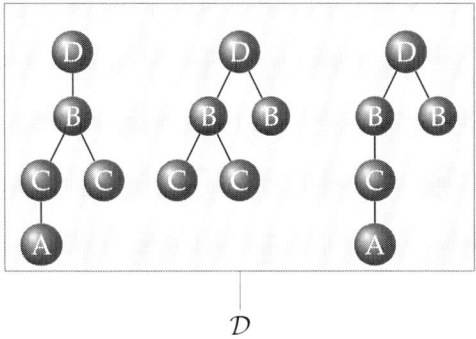

Tid   Trees

1   ((0, D), (1, B), (2, C), (3, A), (2, C))
2   ((0, D), (1, B), (2, C), (2, C), (1, B))
3   ((0, D), (1, B), (2, C), (3, A), (1, B))

Figure 7.14: A dataset example

- ZAKI Synthetic Datasets. Datasets generated by the tree generator of Zaki [Zak02]. This program generates a mother tree that simulates a master website browsing tree. Then it assigns probabilities of following its children nodes, including the option of backtracking to its parent, such that the sum of all the probabilities is 1. Using the master tree, the dataset is generated selecting subtrees according to these probabilities. It was used in CMTreeMiner [CXYM01] empirical avaluation.

- CSLOGS Dataset ([Zak02]). It is available from Zaki's web page. It consists of web logs files collected over one month at the Department of Computer Science of Rensselaer Polytechnic Institute. The logs touched 13,361 unique web pages and CSLOGS dataset contains 59,691 trees. The average tree size is 12.

- NASA multicast data [CA01]. The data was measured during the NASA shuttle launch between 14th and 21st of February, 1999. It has 333 vertices where each vertex takes an IP address as its label. Chi et al. [CXYM01] sampled the data from this NASA data set in 10 minute sampling intervals and got a data set with 1,000 transactions. Therefore, the transactions are the multicast trees for the same NASA event at different times.

- GAZELLE Dataset. It is obtained from KDD Cup 2000 data [KBF+00]. This dataset is a web log file of a real internet shopping mall (gazelle.com). This dataset of size 1.2GB contains 216 attributes. We use the

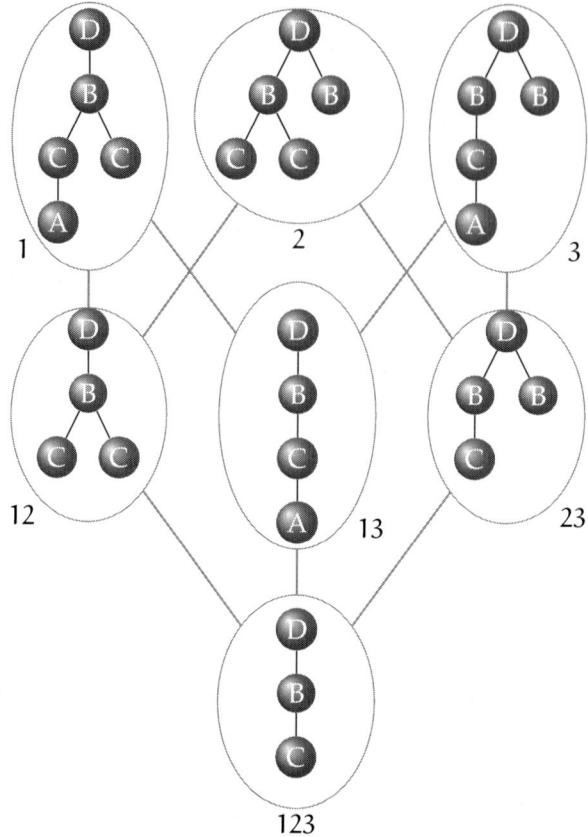

Figure 7.15: Example of Galois Lattice of Closed trees

attribute 'Session ID' to associate to each user session a unique tree. The trees record the sequence of web pages that have been visited in a user session. Each node tree represents a content, assortment and product path. Trees are not built using the structure of the web site, instead they are built following the user streaming. Each time a user visit a page, if he has not visited it before, we take this page as a new deeper node, otherwise, we backtrack to the node this page corresponds to, if it is the last node visited on a concrete level . The resulting dataset consists of 225, 558 trees.

7.8.2 Intersection set cardinality

In order to find how often two trees have intersection sets of cardinality beyond 1, we set up an empirical validation using the tree generation program of Zaki [Zak02] to generate a random set of trees.

Using Zaki's tree generator program we generate sets of 100 random trees of sizes from 5 to 50 and then we run our frequent tree mining algorithm with minimum support 2. Our program doesn't find any two trees with the same transactions list in any run of the algorithm. This fact suggests that, as all the intersections came up to a single tree, the exponential blow-up of the intersection sets is extremely infrequent.

7.8.3 Unlabeled trees

We compare two methods of TREENAT, our algorithm for obtaining closed frequent trees, with CMTreeMiner. The first one is TREENAT TOP-DOWN that obtains top-down subtrees and the second one is TREENAT INDUCED that works with induced subtrees.

On synthetic data, we use the ZAKI Synthetic Datasets for rooted ordered trees restricting the number of distinct node labels to one. We call this dataset T1MN1.

In the T1MN1 dataset, the parameters are the following: the number of distinct node labels is $N = 1$, the total number of nodes in the tree is $M = 10,000$, the maximal level of the tree is $D = 10$, the maximum fanout is $F = 10$ and the number of trees in the dataset is $T = 1,000,0000$.

The results of our experiments on synthetic data are shown in Figures 7.16 and 7.17. We see there that our algorithm TREENAT compares well to CMTreeMiner for top-down subtrees, using less memory in both ordered and unordered cases. Our induced subtree algorithm has similar performance to CMTreeMiner in the ordered case, but it's a bit worse for the unordered case, due to the fact that we take care of avoiding repetitions of structures that are isomorphic under the criterion of unordered trees (which CMTreeMiner would not prune). In these experiments the memory that our method uses depends mainly on the support, not as CMTreeMiner.

In order to understand the behavior of TREENAT and CMTreeMiner respect to the tree structure of input data, we compare the mining performances of TREENAT and CMTreeMiner for two sets of 10,000 identical unlabelled trees, one where all the trees are linear with 10 nodes and another one where all the trees are of level 1 with 10 nodes (1 root and 9 leaves). We notice that

- CMTreeMiner cannot mine the dataset with unordered trees of level 1 and 10 nodes. The maximum number of nodes of unordered trees that CMTreeMiner is capable of mining is 7.

- TREENAT INDUCED has worst performance than CMTreeMiner for linear trees. However, TREENAT TOP-DOWN has similar results to CMTreeMiner.

Figure 7.18 shows the results of these experiments varying the number of nodes. CMTreeMiner outperforms TREENAT with linear trees, and

CHAPTER 7. MINING FREQUENT CLOSED ROOTED TREES

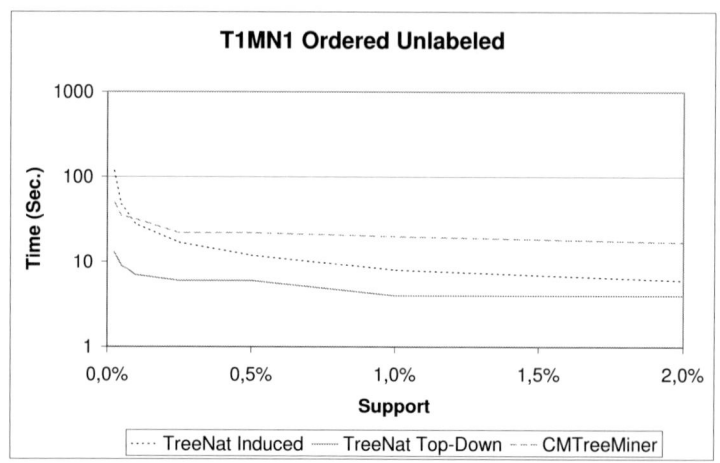

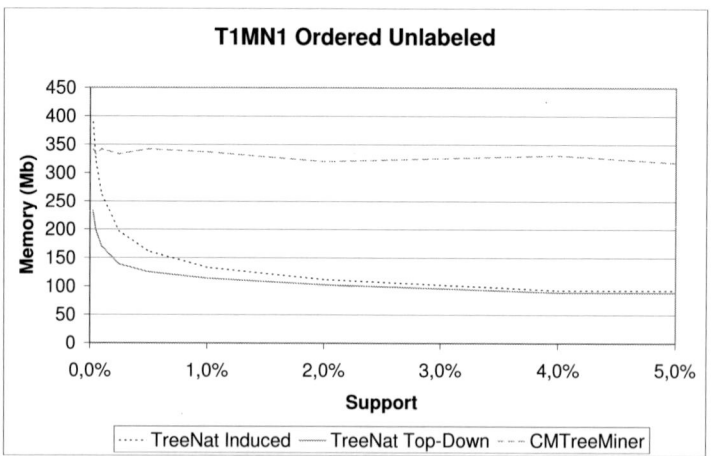

Figure 7.16: Synthetic data experimental results on Ordered Trees: Support versus Running Time and Memory

7.8. APPLICATIONS

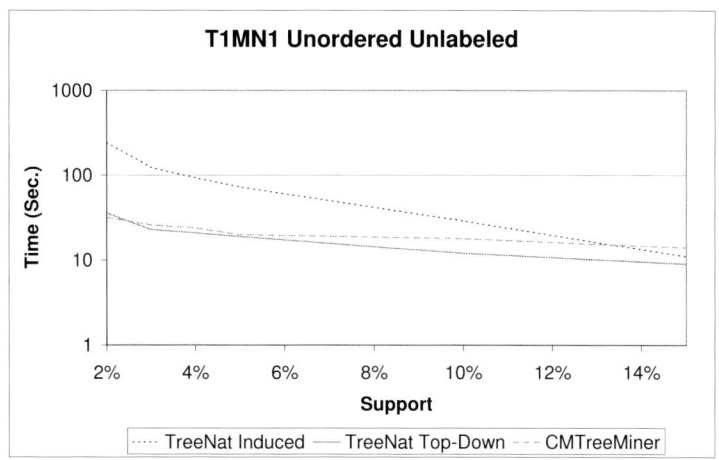

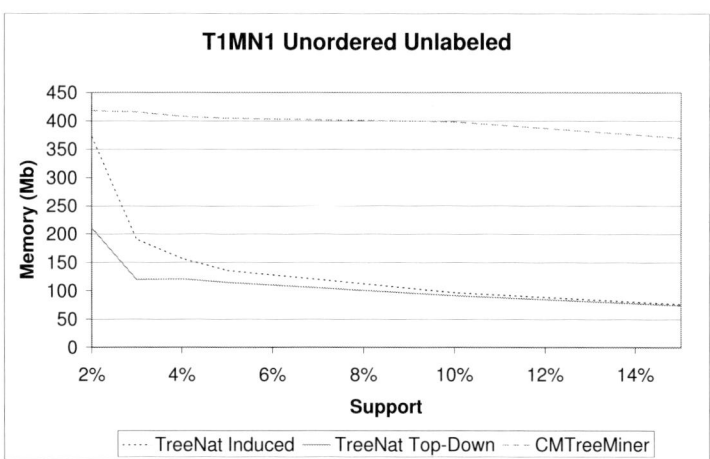

Figure 7.17: Synthetic data experimental results on Unordered Trees: Support versus Running Time and Memory

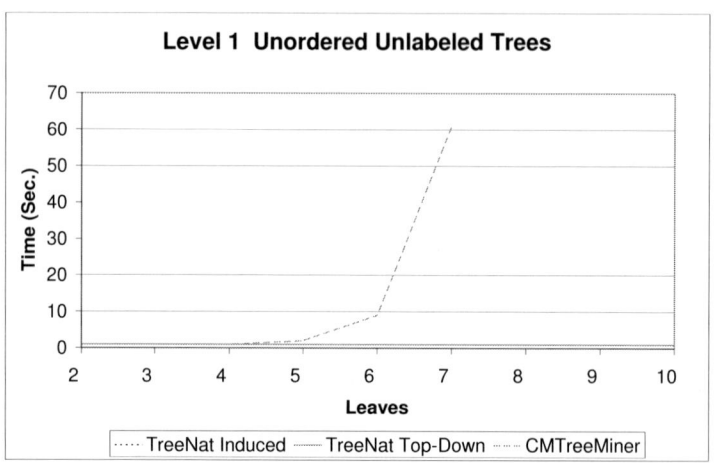

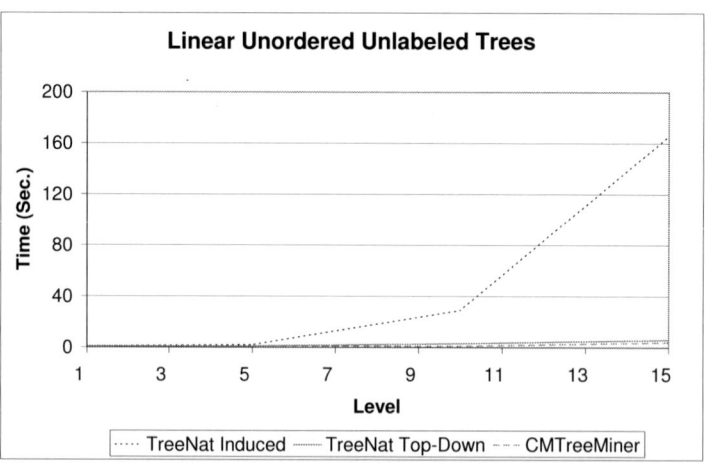

Figure 7.18: Synthetic data experimental results on Unordered Trees varying the number of nodes: Support versus Running Time on level 1 trees and on linear trees

7.8. APPLICATIONS

TREENAT outperforms CMTreeMiner with trees of level 1. CMTreeMiner needs to store all subtree occurrences, but it can use it pruning methods. When the number of leaf nodes is large, the number of occurrences is large and CMTreeMiner has to keep a huge quantity of occurrences. When the trees are linear, CMTreeMiner uses its pruning techniques to outperform TREENAT INDUCED.

We tested our algorithms on two real datasets. The first one is the CSLOGS Dataset. As it is a labeled dataset, we changed it to remove the labels for our experiments with unlabeled trees. Figures 7.19 and 7.20 show the results. We see that CMTreeminer needs more than 1GB of memory to execute for supports lower than 31890 in the ordered case and 50642 for the unordered case. The combinatorial complexity of this dataset seems too hard for CMTreeMiner, since it stores all occurrences of all possible subtrees of one label.

The second real dataset is GAZELLE. Figures 7.21 and 7.22 show the results of our experiments on this real-life data: we see that our method is better than CMTreeMiner at all values of support, both for ordered and unordered approaches. Again CMTreeMiner needs more memory than available to run for small supports.

Finally, we tested our algorithms using the NASA multicast data. The trees of this dataset are very deep trees in average. Neither CMTreeMiner or our method could mine the data considering it unlabeled. The combinatorics are too hard to try to solve it using less than 2 GB of memory. An incremental method could be useful.

7.8.4 Labeled trees

On synthetic data, we use the same dataset as for the unlabeled case. In brief, a mother tree is generated first with the following parameters: the number of distinct node labels from $N = 1$ to $N = 100$, the total number of nodes in the tree $M = 10,000$, the maximal level of the tree $D = 10$ and the maximum fanout $F = 10$. The dataset is then generated by creating subtrees of the mother tree. In our experiments, we set the total number of trees in the dataset to be from $T = 0$ to $T = 8,000,000$.

Figures 7.23 and 7.24 show the results of our experiments on these artificial data: we see that our method outperforms CMTreeMiner if the number of labels is small, but CMTreeMiner wins for large number of labels, both for ordered and unordered approaches. On the size of datasets, we observe that the time and memory needed for our method and CMTreeMiner are linear respect the size of the dataset. Therefore, in order to work with bigger datasets, an incremental method is needed.

The main difference of TREENAT, with CMTreeMiner is that CMTreeMiner needs to store all occurrences of subtrees in the tree dataset to use its pruning methods, whereas our method does not. CMTreeMiner uses oc-

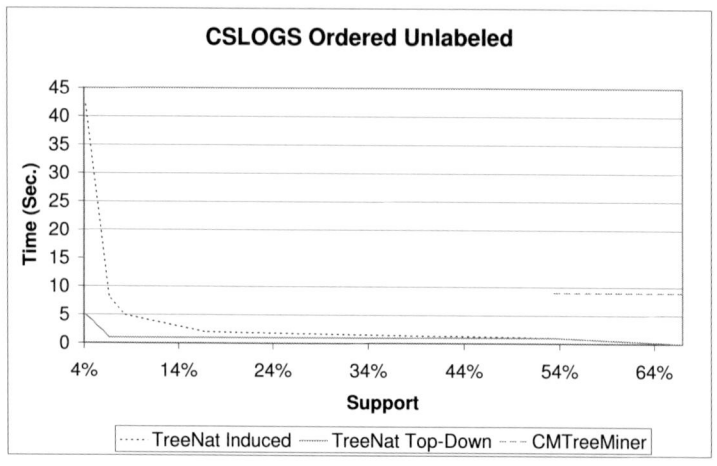

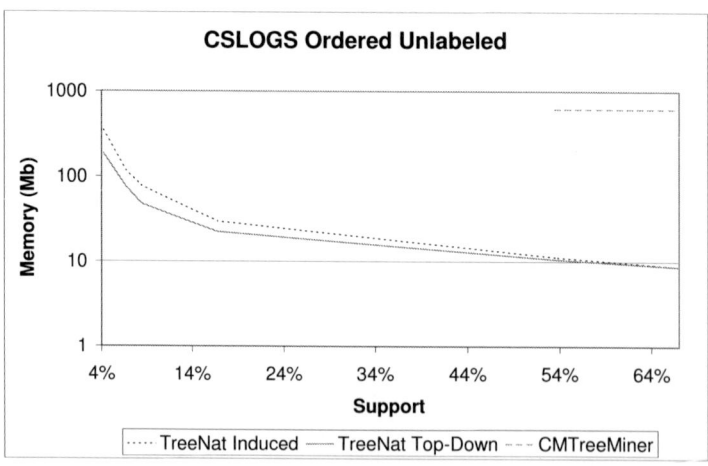

Figure 7.19: CSLOGS real data experimental results on Ordered Trees: Support versus Running Time and Memory

7.8. APPLICATIONS

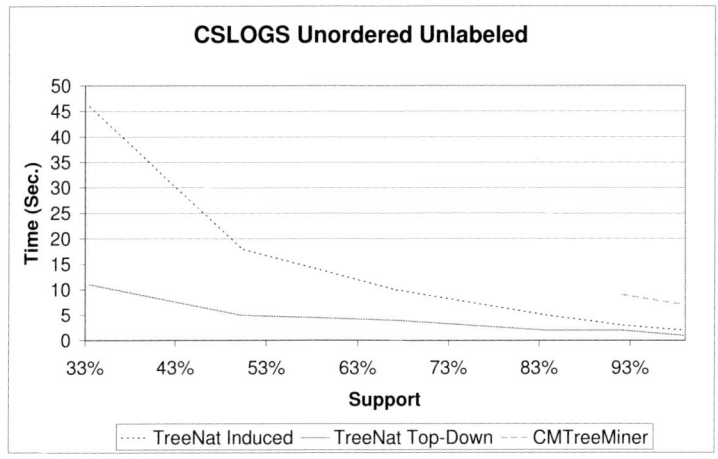

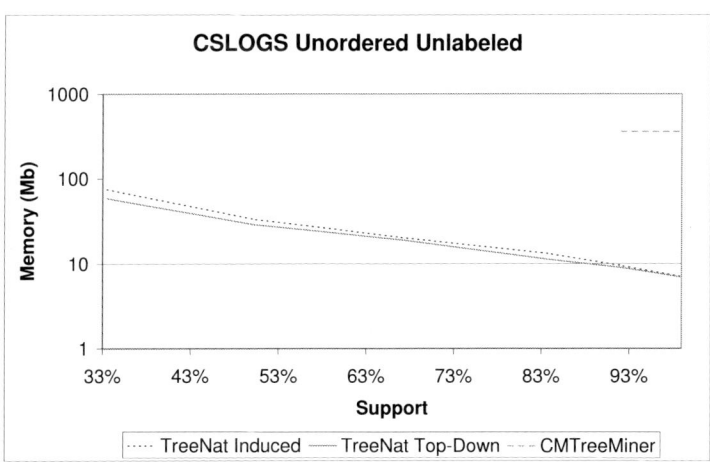

Figure 7.20: CSLOGS real data experimental results on Unordered Trees: Support versus Running Time and Memory

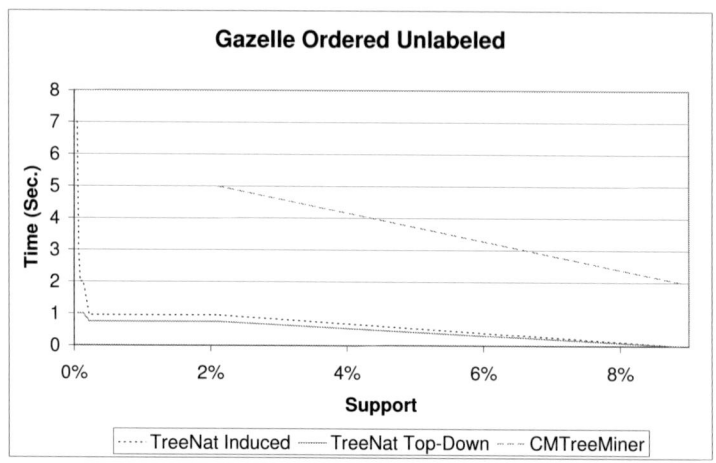

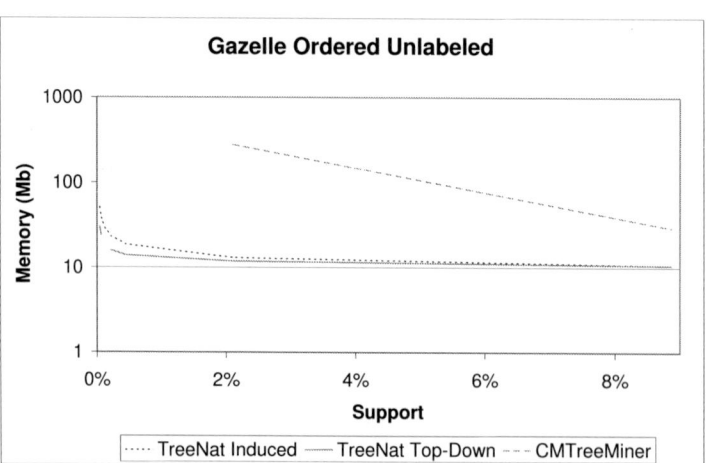

Figure 7.21: Gazelle real data experimental results on Ordered Trees: Support versus Running Time and Memory

7.8. APPLICATIONS

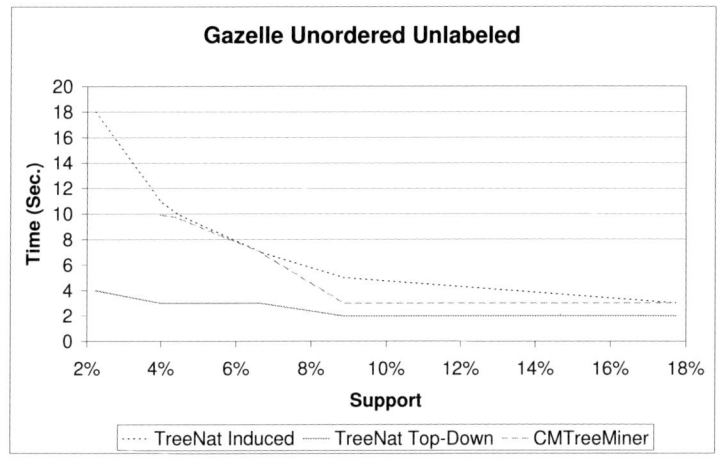

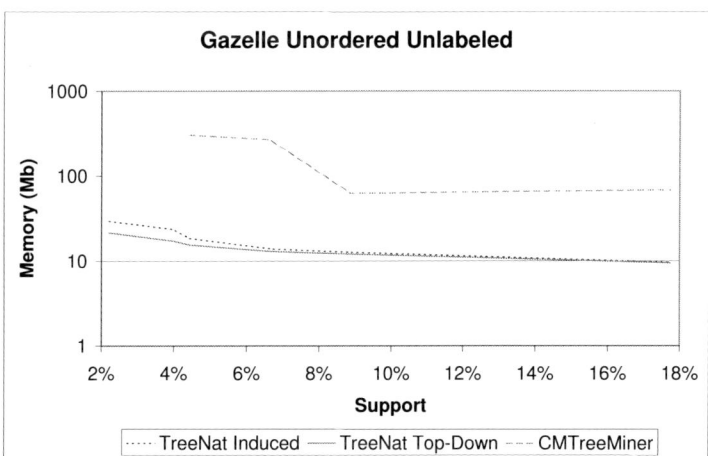

Figure 7.22: Gazelle real data experimental results on Unordered Trees: Support versus Running Time and Memory

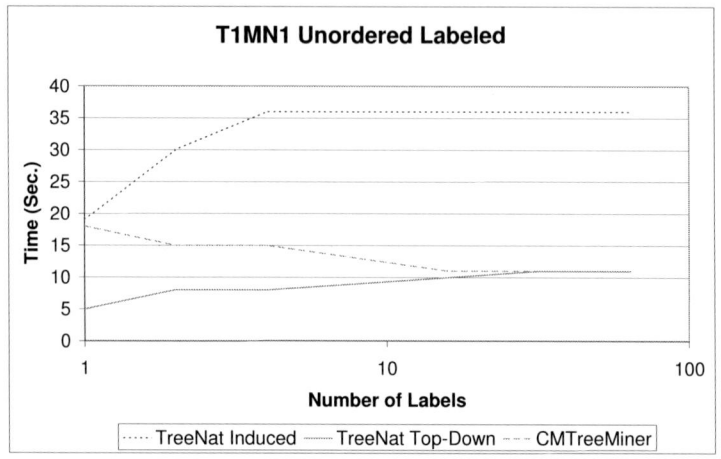

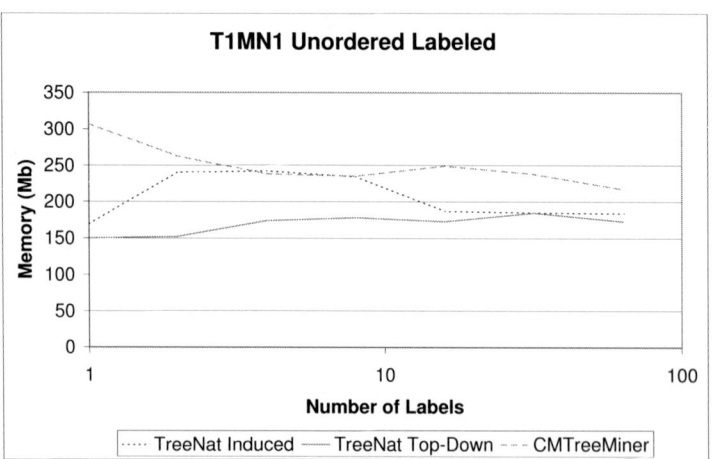

Figure 7.23: Synthetic data experimental results on Labeled Trees: Number of Labels versus Running Time and Memory

7.8. APPLICATIONS

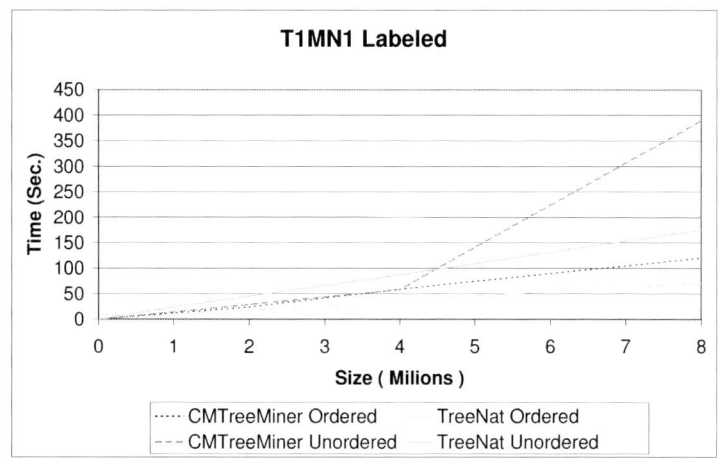

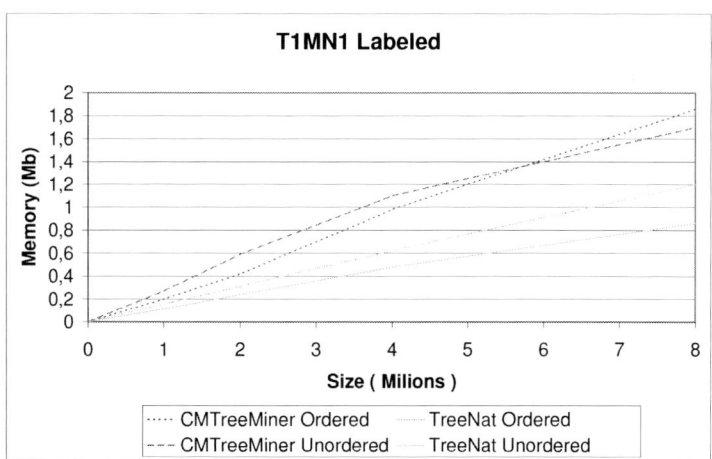

Figure 7.24: Synthetic data experimental results on Labeled Trees: Dataset Size versus Running Time and Memory

currences and pruning techniques based on them. TREENAT doesn't store occurrences. For labeled trees with a small number of labels, CMTreeMiner will need to store a huge number of occurrences, and it will take much more time and memory than TREENAT, that doesn't need to store all that information. Also, with unlabeled trees, if the tree size is big, CMTreeMiner needs more time and memory to store all possible occurrences. But if the number of labels is big, CMTreeMiner will be fast because the number of occurrences is small and it can use the power of its pruning methods.

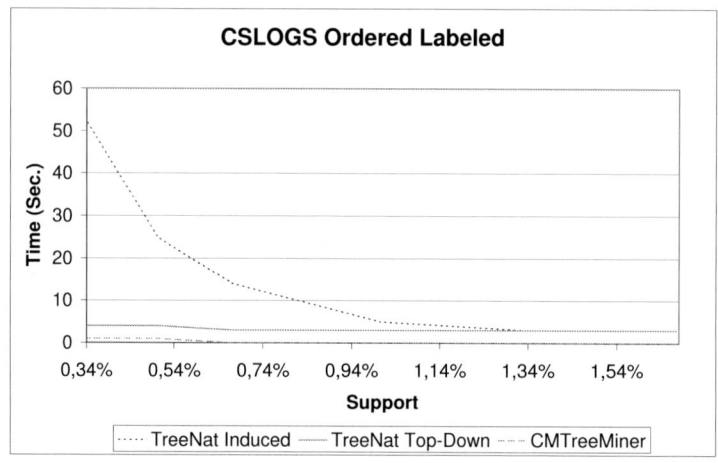

Figure 7.25: CSLOGS real data experimental results on labeled ordered trees: Support versus Running Time

On real dataset CSLOGS, CMTreeMiner outperforms our method as the number of labels is not low as shown in Figure 7.25.

8

Mining Implications from Lattices of Closed Trees

In this chapter we propose a way of extracting high-confidence association rules from datasets consisting of unlabeled trees. The antecedents are obtained through a computation akin to a hypergraph transversal, whereas the consequents follow from an application of the closure operators on unlabeled trees developed in previous chapters. We discuss in more detail the case of rules that always hold, independently of the dataset, since these are more complex than in itemsets due to the fact that we are no longer working on a lattice.

8.1 Introduction

In the field of data mining, one of the major notions contributing to the success of the area has been that of association rules. Many studies of various types have provided a great advance of the human knowledge about these concepts. One particular family of studies is rooted on the previous notions of formal concepts, Galois lattices, and implications, which correspond to association rules of maximum confidence.

These notions have allowed for more efficient works and algorithmics by reducing the computation of frequent sets, a major usual step towards association rules, to the computation of so-called closed frequent sets, a faster computation of much more manageable output size, yet losing no information at all with respect to frequent sets.

It was realized some time ago that the plain single-relational model for the data, as employed by the computation of either closed sets or association rules, whereas useful to a certain extent, was a bit limited in its applicability by the fact that, often, real-life data have some sort of internal structure that is lost in the transactional framework. Thus, studies of data mining in combinatorial structures were undertaken, and considerable progress has been made in recent years. Our work here is framed in that endeavor.

In a previous chapter, we have proposed a mathematical clarification of the closure operator underlying the notion of closed trees in datasets of trees; the closure operator no longer works on single trees but on sets of them. In a sense, made precise there, closed trees do not constitute a lattice. A mathematically precise replacement lattice can be defined, though, as demonstrated in Section 7.3.1, consisting not anymore of trees but of sets of trees, and with the peculiar property that, in all experiments with real-life data we have undertaken, they turn out to be actually lattices of trees, in the sense that every closed set of trees was, in all practical cases, a singleton.

Algorithmics to construct these closed sets have been studied in several references as [CXYM01, TRS04, TRS+08], see the references in the survey [CMNK01]. We continue here this line of research by tackling the most natural next step: the identification of implications out of the lattice of closed sets of trees. We describe a method, along the line of similar works on sequences and partial orders ([BG07b], [BG07a]) to construct implications from the closed sets of trees, and we mathematically characterize, in terms of propositional Horn theories, the implications that we find.

Then, we explain a major difference of our case with previous works: rules that would not be trivial in other cases become redundant, and thus unnecessary, in the case of trees, due to the fact that they are implicit in the combinatorics of the structures. An example will show best our point here. Consider a rule intuitively depicted as follows:

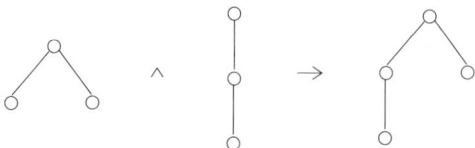

It naturally means that whenever a tree in the dataset under exploration has as (top-down) subtrees the two trees in the antecedent, it also has the one in the consequent. Any tree having a bifurcation at the root, as required by the first antecedent, and a branch of length at least two, as required by the second one, has to have the consequent as a (top-down) subtree. Therefore, the rule says, in fact, nothing at all about the dataset, and is not worthy to appear in the output of a rule mining algorithm on trees.

Our second major contribution is, therefore, a study of some cases where we can detect such implicit rules and remove them from the output, with low computational overhead. Whereas further theoretical work might be useful, our contributions so far already detect most of the implicit rules in real-life datasets, up to quite low support levels, and with a reasonable efficiency. We report some facts on the empirical behavior of our implementations of both the algorithm to find rules and the heuristics to remove implicit rules.

We will construct association rules in a standard form from it, and show that they correspond to a certain Horn theory; also, we will prove the cor-

8.2. ITEMSETS ASSOCIATION RULES

rectness of a construction akin to the iteration-free basis of [Wil94] and [PT02].

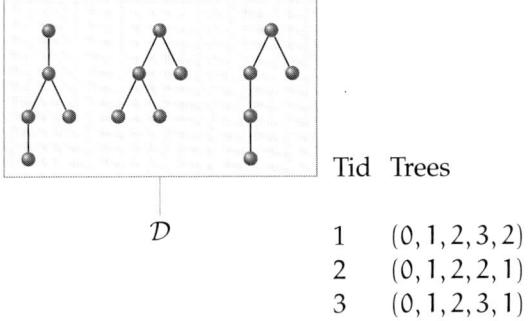

Tid Trees
1   (0,1,2,3,2)
2   (0,1,2,2,1)
3   (0,1,2,3,1)

Figure 8.1: Example of dataset

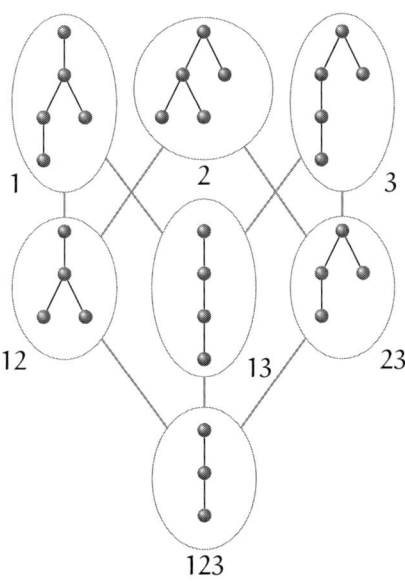

Figure 8.2: Galois lattice of closed trees from the dataset example

8.2 Itemsets association rules

Let $\mathcal{I} = \{i_1, \ldots, i_n\}$ be a fixed set of items. A subset $I \subseteq \mathcal{I}$ is called an itemset. Formally, we deal with a collection of ordered transactions $\mathcal{D} = \{d_1, d_2, \ldots d_n\}$, where each d_i is an itemset. Figure 8.3 shows an example of a dataset of itemsets transactions.

	a	b	c	d
d_1	1	1	0	1
d_2	0	1	1	1
d_3	0	1	0	1

Figure 8.3: Example of a dataset of itemsets transactions

An *association rule* is a pair (G, Z), denoted $G \rightarrow Z$, where $G, Z \subseteq \mathcal{I}$ and $G \subseteq Z$. When $(G) = Z$ for an itemset $G \neq Z$ and G is minimal among all the candidates with closure equal to Z, we say that G is a generator of Z.

We are interested in implications of the form $G \rightarrow Z$, where G is a generator of Z. These turn out to be the particular case of association rules where no support condition is imposed but confidence is 1 (or 100%) Such rules in this context are sometimes called *deterministic association rules*.

For example, from the itemsets dataset in Figure 8.3 we could generate a deterministic association rule $c \rightarrow bcd$, since c is a generator of the closed set bcd as mentioned above.

8.2.1 Classical Propositional Horn Logic

We will review briefly some important notions of classical propositional Horn Logic, following [Gar06]. First, assume a standard propositional logic language with propositional variables. The number of variables is finite and we denote by $\mathcal{V}$ the set of all variables; we could alternatively use an infinite set of variables provided that, the propositional issues corresponding to a fixed dataset, only involve finitely many of them. A literal is either a propositional variable, called a positive literal, or its negation, called a negative literal. A clause is a disjunction of literals and it can be seen simply as the set of the literals it contains. A clause is *Horn* if and only if it contains at most one positive literal. Horn clauses with a positive literal are called *definite*, and can be written as $H \rightarrow v$ where H is a conjunction of positive literals that were negative in the clause, whereas v is the single positive literal in the clause. Horn clauses without positive literals are called *nondefinite*, and can be written similarly as $H \rightarrow \square$, where $\square$ expresses unsatisfiability. A Horn formula is a conjunction of Horn clauses. In Figure 8.4 the set of all variables is $\mathcal{V} = \{a, b, c, d\}$ and $\bar{a} \vee \bar{b} \vee d$ or $a, b \rightarrow d$ is a Horn clause.

A model is a complete truth assignment, i.e. a mapping from the variables to $\{0, 1\}$. We denote by $m(v)$ the value that the model m assigns to the variable v. The intersection of two models is the bitwise conjunction returning another model. A model satisfies a formula if the formula evaluates to true in the model. The universe of all models is denoted by $\mathcal{M}$. For

8.2. ITEMSETS ASSOCIATION RULES

M	a	b	c	d
m_1	1	1	0	1
m_2	0	1	1	1
m_3	0	1	0	1

$$a \to b, d \qquad (\bar{a} \vee b) \wedge (\bar{a} \vee d)$$
$$d \to b \qquad \bar{d} \vee b$$
$$a, b \to d \qquad \bar{a} \vee \bar{b} \vee d$$

Figure 8.4: Example of Horn formulas

example, in Figure 8.4

$$m(a) = 0, m(b) = 1, m(c) = 1, \ldots$$

is a model.

A theory is a set of models. A theory is Horn if there is a Horn formula which axiomatizes it, in the sense that it is satisfied exactly by the models in the theory. When a theory contains another we say that the first is an upper bound for the second; for instance, by removing clauses from a Horn formula we get a larger or equal Horn theory. The following is known, see [DP92], or works such as [KKS95]:

Theorem 10. *Given a propositional theory of models $\mathcal{M}$, there is exactly one minimal Horn theory containing it. Semantically, it contains all the models that are intersections of models of $\mathcal{M}$. Syntactically, it can be described by the conjunction of all Horn clauses satisfied by all models from the theory.*

The theory obtained in this way is called sometimes the *empirical Horn approximation* of the original theory. Clearly, then, a theory is Horn if and only if it is actually *closed under intersection*, so that it coincides with its empirical Horn approximation.

The propositional Horn logic framework allows us to cast our reasoning in terms of closure operators. It turns out that it is possible to exactly characterize the set of deterministic association rules in terms of propositional logic: we can associate a propositional variable to each item, and each association rule becomes a conjunction of Horn clauses. Then:

Theorem 11. *[BB03] Given a set of transactions, the conjunction of all the deterministic association rules defines exactly the empirical Horn approximation of the theory formed by the given tuples.*

So, the theorem determines that the empirical Horn approximation of a set of models can be computed with the method of constructing deterministic association rules, that is, constructing the closed sets of attributes and identifying minimal generators for each closed set.

8.3 Association Rules

The input to our data mining process, now is a given finite dataset $\mathcal{D}$ of transactions, where each transaction $s \in \mathcal{D}$ consists of a transaction identifier, tid, and an unlabeled rooted tree. Tids are supposed to run sequentially from 1 to the size of $\mathcal{D}$. From that dataset, our universe of discourse $\mathcal{U}$ is the set of all trees that appear as subtree of some tree in $\mathcal{D}$. Figure 8.1 shows a finite dataset example and Figure 8.2 shows the Galois lattice.

Following standard usage on Galois lattices, we consider now implications (sometimes called deterministic association rules, see e.g. [PT02]) of the form $A \to B$ for sets of trees A and B from $\mathcal{U}$. Specifically, we consider the following set of rules: $A \to \Gamma_\mathcal{D}(A)$. Alternatively, we can split the consequents into $\{A \to t \mid t \in \Gamma_\mathcal{D}(A)\}$.

It is easy to see that $\mathcal{D}$ obeys all these rules: for each A, any tree of $\mathcal{D}$ that has as subtrees all the trees of A has also as subtrees all the trees of $\Gamma_\mathcal{D}(A)$.

We want to provide a characterization of this set of implications. We operate in a form similar to [BG07a] and [BG07b], translating this set of rules into a specific propositional theory which we can characterize, and for which we can find a "basis": a set of rules that are sufficient to infer all the rules that hold in the dataset $\mathcal{D}$. The technical details depart somewhat from [BG07b] in that we skip a certain maximality condition imposed there, and are even more different from those in [BG07a].

Thus, we start by associating a propositional variable v_t to each tree $t \in \mathcal{U}$. In this way, each implication between sets of trees can be seen also as a propositional conjunction of Horn implications, as follows: the conjunction of all the variables corresponding to the set at the left hand side implies each of the variables corresponding to the closure at the right hand side. We call this propositional Horn implication the propositional translation of the rule.

Also, now a set of trees A corresponds in a natural way to a propositional model m_A: specifically, $m_A(v_t) = 1$ if and only if t is a subtree of some tree in A. We abbreviate $m_{\{t\}}$ as m_t. Note that the models obtained in this way obey the following condition: if $t' \preceq t$ and $v_t = 1$, then $v_{t'} = 1$ too. In fact, this condition identifies the models m_A: if a model m fulfills it, then $m = m_A$ for the set A of trees t for which $v_t = 1$ in m. Alternatively, A can be taken to be the set of maximal trees for which $v_t = 1$.

Note that we can express this condition by a set of Horn clauses: $\mathcal{R}_0 =$

$\{v_t \to v_{t'} \mid t' \preceq t,\ t \in \mathcal{U},\ t' \in \mathcal{U}\}$. It is easy to see that the following holds:

Lemma 2. *Let $t \in \mathcal{D}$. Then m_t satisfies $\mathcal{R}_0$ and also all the propositional translations of the implications of the form $A \to \Gamma_\mathcal{D}(A)$.*

Since $\Gamma_\mathcal{D}(\{t\}) = \{t' \in \mathcal{T} \mid t' \preceq t\}$ by definition, if $m_t \models A$, then $A \preceq t$, hence $\Gamma_\mathcal{D}(A) \preceq \Gamma_\mathcal{D}(\{t\})$, and $m_t \models \Gamma_\mathcal{D}(A)$. For $\mathcal{R}_0$, the very definition of m_t ensures the claim.

We collect all closure-based implications into the following set:

$$\mathcal{R}'_\mathcal{D} = \bigcup_\Delta \{A \to t \mid \Gamma_\mathcal{D}(A) = \Delta,\ t \in \Delta\}$$

For use in our algorithms below, we also specify a concrete set of rules among those that come from the closure operator. For each closed set of trees Δ, consider the set of "immediate predecessors", that is, subsets of Δ that are closed, but where no other intervening closed set exists between them and Δ; and, for each of them, say Δ_i, define:

$$F_i = \{t \mid t \preceq \Delta,\ t \not\preceq \Delta_i\}$$

Then, we define $\mathcal{H}_\Delta$ as a family of sets of trees that fulfill two properties: each $H \in \mathcal{H}_\Delta$ intersects each F_i, and all the $H \in \mathcal{H}_\Delta$ are minimal (with respect to $\preceq$) under that condition.

We pick now the following set of rules $\mathcal{R}_\mathcal{D}$,

$$\mathcal{R}_\mathcal{D} = \bigcup_\Delta \{H \to t \mid H \in \mathcal{H}_\Delta,\ t \in \Delta\}$$

as a subset of the much larger set of rules $\mathcal{R}'_\mathcal{D}$ defined above, and state our main result:

Theorem 12. *Given the dataset $\mathcal{D}$ of trees, the following propositional formulas are logically equivalent:*

i/ the conjunction of all the Horn formulas satisfied by all the models m_t for $t \in \mathcal{D}$;

ii/ the conjunction of $\mathcal{R}_0$ and all the propositional translations of the formulas in $\mathcal{R}'_\mathcal{D}$;

iii/ the conjunction of $\mathcal{R}_0$ and all the propositional translations of the formulas in $\mathcal{R}_\mathcal{D}$.

Proof. Note first that i/ is easily seen to imply ii/, because Lemma 2 means that all the conjuncts in ii/ also belong to i/. Similarly, ii/ trivially implies iii/ because all the conjuncts in iii/ also belong to ii/. It remains to argue that the formula in iii/ implies that of i/. Pick any Horn formula $H \to v$

that is satisfied by all the models m_t for $t \in \mathcal{D}$: that is, whenever $m_t \models H$, then $m_t \models v$. Let $v = v_{t'}$: this means that, for all $t \in \mathcal{D}$, if $H \preceq t$ then $t' \preceq t$, or, equivalently, $t' \in \Gamma_{\mathcal{D}}(H)$. We prove that there is $H' \preceq H$ that minimally intersects all the sets of the form

$$F_i = \{ t \mid t \preceq \Delta, t \npreceq \Delta_i \}$$

for closed $\Delta = \Gamma_{\mathcal{D}}$, and for its set of immediate predecessors Δ_i. Once we have such an H', since $t \in \Delta$, the rule $H' \to t$ is in $\mathcal{R}_{\mathcal{D}}$. Together with $\mathcal{R}_0$, their joint propositional translations entail $H \to t$: an arbitrary model making true H and fulfilling $\mathcal{R}_0$ must make H' true because of $H' \preceq H$ and, if $H' \to t$ holds for it, t is also true in it. Since $\mathcal{R}_0$ and $H' \to t$ are available, $H \to t$ holds.

Therefore, we just need to prove that such $H' \preceq H$ exists. Note that H already intersects all the F_i: $H \preceq \Gamma_{\mathcal{D}}(H) = \Delta$; suppose that for some proper predecessor Δ_i, H does not intersect F_i. This means that $t \preceq \Delta_i$ for all $t \in H$, and thus, the smallest closed set above H, that is, $\Gamma_{\mathcal{D}}(H) = \Delta$, must be below the closed set Δ_i or coincide with it, and neither is possible.

Hence, it suffices to consider all the sets of trees H'', where $H'' \preceq H$, that still intersect all the F_i. This is not an empty family since H itself is in it, and it is a finite family; therefore, it has at least one minimal element (with respect to $\preceq$), and any of them can be picked for our H'. This completes the proof. □

The closed trees for the dataset of Figure 8.1 are shown in the Galois lattice of Figure 8.2 and the association rules obtained are shown in Figure 8.5.

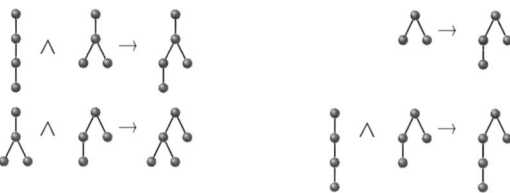

Figure 8.5: Association rules obtained from the Galois lattice of the dataset example

8.4 On Finding Implicit Rules for Subtrees

We formally define inplicit rules as follows:

Definition 11. *Given three trees* t_1, t_2, t_3, *we say that* $t_1 \wedge t_2 \to t_3$ *is an implicit Horn rule (abbreviately, an implicit rule) if for every tree t it holds*

$$t_1 \preceq t \wedge t_2 \preceq t \leftrightarrow t_3 \preceq t.$$

8.4. ON FINDING IMPLICIT RULES FOR SUBTREES

We say that two trees t_1, t_2, have implicit rules if there is some tree t_3 for which $t_1 \wedge t_2 \rightarrow t_3$ is an implicit Horn rule.

A natural generalization having more than two antecedents could be considered; we circumscribe our study to implicit rules of two antecedents.

The aim of the next definitions is to provide formal tools to classify a rule as implicit.

Definition 12. *A tree c is a* minimal common supertree *of two trees a and b if $a \preceq c$, $b \preceq c$, and for every $d \prec c$, either $a \npreceq d$ or $b \npreceq d$.*

In the example of implicit rule given in the introduction, the tree on the right of the implication sign is a minimal common supertree of the trees on the left.

Definition 13. *Given two trees a, b, we define $a \oplus b$ as the minimal common supertree of a and b.*

As there may be more than one minimal common supertree of two trees, we choose the one with smallest level representation, as given in Section 7.6.2 to avoid the ambiguity of the definition.

Definition 14. *A component c_1 of a is* maximum *if any component c_2 of a satisfies $c_2 \preceq c_1$, and it is* maximal *if there is no component c_2 in a such that $c_1 \prec c_2$.*

Note that a tree may not have maximum components but, in case it has more than one, all of them must be equal. The following facts on components will be useful later on.

Lemma 3. *If a tree has no maximum component, it must have at least two maximal incomparable components.*

Proof. Suppose that a is a tree whose maximal components $c_1, \ldots, c_n$ are not maximum. For contradiction, suppose that all c_i's are pairwise comparable. Then, we can proceed inductively as follows. To start, we consider c_1 and c_2 and take the one which contains the other. For the i-th step, suppose we have a component c_j ($1 \leq j \leq i$) which contains the components $c_1, \ldots, c_i$; we now consider c_{i+1} and compare it with c_j: the one which contains the other must be a component containing the first $i+1$ components. Finally, we get a maximum component, contradicting the initial assumption. Therefore, there must be two maximal incomparable components. □

Lemma 4. *Two trees have implicit rules if and only if they have a unique minimal common supertree.*

Proof. Let us consider two trees a and b, and suppose first that they have an implicit rule like $a \wedge b \to c$. We want to show that they have a unique minimal common supertree. Suppose by contradiction that d and e are two different minimal common supertrees of a and b. Then, applying the previous implicit rule, we conclude that $c \preceq d$ and $c \preceq e$. But d and e are minimal common supertrees of a and b, and c is also a supertree of a and b by the definition of implicit rule. Therefore, $c = d = e$, contradicting the assumption.

Suppose, for the other direction, that c is the only minimal common supertree of two trees a and b. Then, to show that $a \wedge b \to c$ is an implicit rule, suppose that, for some tree d, we have $a \preceq d$ and $b \preceq d$. For the sake of contradiction, assume that $c \not\preceq d$. But then, the minimal $d' \preceq d$ which still contains a and b as subtrees, would also satisfy that $c \not\preceq d'$. Then, d' would be a minimal common supertree of a and b different from c, contradicting the uniqueness we assumed for c. Then, it must hold that $c \preceq d$ and, therefore, $a \wedge b \to c$ is an implicit rule. □

Using Lemma 4 we can compute implicit rules in an algorithmically expensive way, obtaining minimal common supertrees, which has quadratic cost. To avoid that, we propose several heuristics to speed up the process.

A simple consequence of these lemmas is:

Corollary 5. *All trees a, b such that $a \preceq b$ have implicit rules.*

Proof. If $a \preceq b$, then $a \wedge b \to b$ is obviously an implicit rule. □

One particularly useful case where we can formally prove implicit rules, and which helps detecting a large amount of them in real-life dataset mining, occurs when one of the trees has a single component.

Theorem 13. *Suppose that a and b are two incomparable trees, and b has only one component. Then they have implicit rules if and only if a has a maximum component which is a subtree of the component of b.*

Proof. Suppose that a and b are two incomparable trees as described in the statement: a has components $a_1, \ldots, a_n$, and b has only the component b_1. We represent their structures graphically as

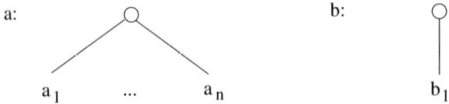

Suppose that a has a maximum component which is a subtree of b_1. Without loss of generality, we can assume that a_n is such a component. Then, we claim that $a \wedge b \to c$ is an implicit rule, where c is a tree with components $a_1, \ldots, a_{n-1}$, and b_1. That is,

8.4. ON FINDING IMPLICIT RULES FOR SUBTREES

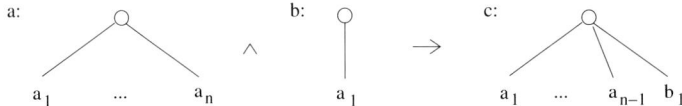

To show that this is actually an implicit rule, suppose that, for some tree x, $a \preceq x$ and $b \preceq x$. From the fact that $a \preceq x$, we gain some insight into the structure of x: it must contain components where a's and b's components can map, and so, there must be at least n components in x. So, let $x_1, \ldots, x_m$ be the components of x, with $m \geq n$, and let us suppose that $a_i \preceq x_i$ for every i such that $1 \leq i \leq n$.

Since b is also a subtree of x, b_1 must be a subtree of some x_i with $1 \leq i \leq m$. We now show that, for every possible value of i, c must be a subtree of x and then, $a \wedge b \to c$ is an implicit rule:

- If $i \geq n$, then $a_k \preceq x_k$ for all $k \leq n-1$, and $b_1 \preceq x_i$.
- If $i < n$, then
    - $a_k \preceq x_k$ for $k \neq i$ and $1 \leq k \leq n-1$
    - $a_i \preceq a_n \preceq x_n$
    - $b_1 \preceq x_i$

In both cases, $c \preceq x$, and we are done.

To show the other direction, let us suppose that a does not have a maximum component which is a subtree of b_1. We will show that, in this case, there are two different minimal common supertrees of a and b. Then, by Lemma 4, we will get the desired conclusion. The previous condition on maximal components can be split into two possibilities:

1. *Tree a does not have a maximum component.* By Lemma 3, there must be two maximal components of a which are incomparable, let us say a_i and a_j. Now we claim that the two trees c and d in the following figure are two different minimal common supertrees of a and b:

In the first place, we show that c and d are different. Suppose they are equal. Then, since b_1 cannot be a subtree of any a_k, $1 \leq k \leq n$ (because a and b are assumed to be incomparable), the components containing b_1 must match. But then, the following multisets (the rest of the components in c and d) must be equal:

$$\{a_l \mid 1 \leq l \leq n \wedge l \neq i\} = \{a_l \mid 1 \leq l \leq n \wedge l \neq j\}.$$

But the equality holds if and only if $a_i = a_j$, which is false. Then $c \neq d$.

Second, we show that c contains a and b minimally. Call $c_1, \ldots, c_n$ to the components of c in the same order they are displayed: $c_k = a_k$ for all $k \leq n$ except for $k = i$, for which $c_k = a_i \oplus b_1$. Suppose now that we delete a leaf from c, getting $c' \prec c$, whose components are $c'_1, \ldots, c'_n$ (which are like the corresponding c_k's except for the one containing the deleted leaf). We will see that c' does not contain a or b by analyzing two possibilities for the location of the deleted leaf, either (a) in the component $c_i = a_i \oplus b_1$ or (b) in any other component:

(a) Suppose that the deleted leaf is from $c_i = a_i \oplus b_1$ (that is, $c'_i \prec c_i$). Then, either $a_i \not\preceq c'_i$ or $b_1 \not\preceq c'_i$. In the case that $b_1 \not\preceq c'_i$, we have that $b \not\preceq c'$ since b_1 is not included in any other component. So, suppose that $a_i \not\preceq c'_i$. In this case, consider the number s of occurrences of a_i in a. Since a_i is a maximal component, the occurrences of a_i in a are the only components that contain a_i as a subtree. Therefore, the number of components of c that contain a_i is exactly s, but it is $s - 1$ in c' due to the deleted leaf in $a_i \oplus b_1$. Then, $a \not\preceq c'$.

(b) Suppose now that the deleted leaf is from c_k for $k \neq i$. In this case, it is clear that $a_k \not\preceq c'_k$, but we must make sure that $a \not\preceq c'$ by means of some mapping that matches a_k with a component of c' different from c'_k. For contradiction, suppose there exists such a mapping, that is, for some permutation π from the symmetric group of n elements, we have $a_m \preceq c'_{\pi(m)}$ for every $m \leq n$. Let l be the length of the cycle containing k in the cycle representation of π (so, we have $\pi^l(k) = k$, and has a value different from k for exponents 1 to $l - 1$). We have that
$$a_k \preceq a_{\pi(k)} \preceq a_{\pi^2(k)} \preceq \cdots \preceq a_{\pi^{l-1}(k)}$$
since for every a_m in the previous chain except the last one, if $\pi(m) \neq i$, then $a_m \preceq c'_{\pi(m)} = a_{\pi(m)}$; while if $\pi(m) = i$, then $a_m \preceq a_{\pi(m)}$ because a_i is a maximum component.

From the previous chain of containments, we conclude that $a_k \preceq a_{\pi^{l-1}(k)}$. But $a_{\pi^{l-1}(k)} \preceq c'_{\pi^l(k)} = c'_k$. Putting it together, we get $a_k \preceq c'_k$, which is a contradiction. Therefore, $a \not\preceq c'$.

Now, from (a) and (b), we can conclude that c is a minimal common supertree of a and b. Obviously, the same property can be argued for d in a symmetric way, and since c and d are different, Lemma 4 implies that a and b cannot have implicit rules.

2. *Tree a has maximum components but they are not subtrees of* b_1. We consider now the following trees:

8.4. ON FINDING IMPLICIT RULES FOR SUBTREES

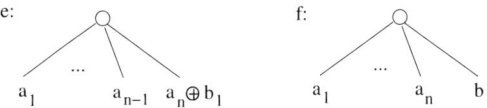

We will show (a) that tree e is a minimal common supertree of a and b, and (b) that tree f is a common supertree of a and b and does not contain e. From (a) and (b), we can conclude that a and b must have two different minimal common subtrees. Take e as one of them. For the other one, let f' be a tree obtained from f by deleting leaves until it is minimal (that is, deleting one more leave would not contain a or b). Since $e \not\preceq f$ (from point (b)), it holds that $e \not\preceq f'$. On the other hand, if we had $f' \preceq e$, since e is minimal, we would have $e = f'$, and then $e \preceq f$, which contradicts point (b). Therefore, e and f' must be two incomparable minimal common supertrees of a and b, and the theorem follows. To complete the proof, it is only left to show:

(a) *Tree e is a minimal common supertree of a and b.* Note that the proof in previous case 1, showing that c is a minimal common supertree of a and b, applies to e as well. The argument for c was based on the maximality of a_i, but a_n is maximum in e, and then it is also maximal, so the proof applies.

(b) *Tree f is a common supertree of a and b, and does not contain e.* Clearly by definition, f is a common supertree of a and b. Now, we will argue that $e \not\preceq f$. For this inclusion to be true, $a_n \oplus b_1$ should be a subtree of some component of f. It cannot be a subtree of one of the a_k's components ($k \leq n$) since then $b_1 \preceq a_k$ and $b \preceq a$, which is false. On the other hand, $a_n \oplus b_1$ cannot be a subtree of b_1 neither, because that would mean that $a_n \preceq b_1$, which is false in this case. Therefore, f does not contain e.

Since we have proved the existence of two minimal common supertrees also for this case, a new application of Lemma 4 completes the proof. □

Corollary 6. *Two trees with one component each have implicit rules if and only if they are comparable.*

Proof. Suppose two 1-trees a and b are incomparable. Since they are 1-trees, their components are maximum, but they are not included in each other. Applying Theorem 13, we conclude that a and b do not have implicit rules.

For the other direction, Proposition 5 shows that if a and b are comparable, they have implicit rules. □

In fact, one fragment of the argumentation of this theorem can be also applied directly as well to some cases that do appear in practice:

Definition 15. *Given two trees* a, b, *we denote by* $a + b$ *the tree built joining the roots of all components of* a *and* b *to a single root node.*

Definition 16. *Given two trees* a *and* b, *tree* a *with components* $a_1, \cdots, a_n$ *and tree* b *with components* $b_1, \cdots, b_k$, *and* $n \geq k$, *we denote by* $a \uplus b$ *the tree built recursively by joining the trees* $a_i \uplus b_i$ *for* $1 \leq i \leq k$, *and* a_i *for* $k < i \leq n$, *to a single root node. If* b *has only a node then* $a \uplus b = a$. *In case that* $n < k$, $a \uplus b$ *is defined as* $b \uplus a$.

Proposition 5. *The rule* $a \wedge b \rightarrow c$ *is not an implicit rule if* $c \not\preceq a + b$ *or* $c \not\preceq a \uplus b$.

Proof. If $c \not\preceq a + b$ or $c \not\preceq a \uplus b$, then $a + b$ or $a \uplus b$ are supertrees of a and b that are not supertrees of c and by the definition of implicit rule, the rule $a \wedge b \rightarrow c$ is not implicit. □

Using Proposition 5, we have implemented an additional recursive heuristic that can be explained as follows: for every rule $a \wedge b \rightarrow c$ we build $a + b$ and $a \uplus b$ and if we realize that one of them is not a supertree of c, then the rule is not implicit.

8.5 Experimental Validation

We tested our algorithms on two real datasets. The first one is CSLOGS Dataset and the second dataset is GAZELLE. These datasets were presented in Section 7.8.1.

On these datasets, we have computed association rules following our method. We have then analyzed a number of issues. First, we have checked how many redundant rules could be avoided by some more sophisticated rule production system along the lines of a Duquenne-Guigues basis; however, the structure of these datasets leads to little or no redundancy for this reason, and we omit further discussion of this consideration.

Then, we have implemented an implicit rule detection step based on all the criteria described in the previous section. Timing considerations are rather irrelevant, in that the time overhead imposed by this implicit rule detection step is reasonably low. We compare the number of rules obtained, the number of implicit and not implicit detected rules, and the number of non implicit rules. Figure 8.6 shows the results for the CSLOGS dataset, and the Gazelle dataset. We observe that when the minimum support of the closed frequent subtrees decreases, the number of rules increases and the number of detected rules decreases. The number of detected rules depends on the dataset and on the minimum support. As an example, our method

8.5. EXPERIMENTAL VALIDATION

detects whether a rule is implicit or not in 91% of the rules obtained from CSLOGS dataset with a support of 7,500, and 32% of the rules obtained from Gazelle Dataset with a support of 500. The number of non implicit rules are more than 75% in the two datasets.

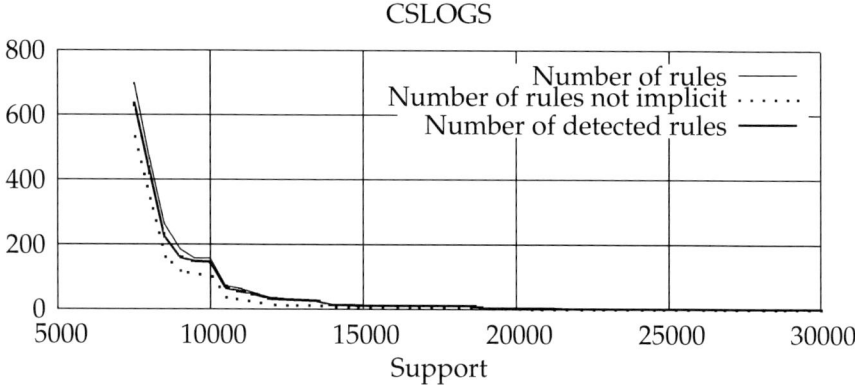

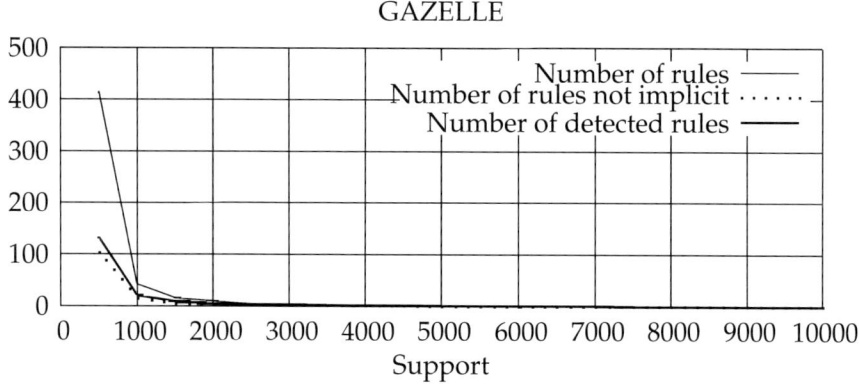

Figure 8.6: Real data experimental results on CSLOGS and Gazelle datasets

Part IV

Evolving Tree Data Stream Mining

9
Mining Adaptively Frequent Closed Rooted Trees

In this chapter we propose a new approach for mining closed rooted trees adaptively from data streams that change over time. We extend the non-incremental methods presented in Chapter 7 to the challenging incremental streaming setting, presented in the first part of this book. Our approach is based on an advantageous representation of trees and a low-complexity notion of relaxed closed trees, as well as ideas from Galois Lattice Theory. We first present three closed tree mining algorithms in sequence: an incremental one, INCTREEMINER, a sliding-window based one, WINTREEMINER, and finally one that mines closed trees adaptively from data streams, ADA-TREEMINER. To the best of our knowledge this is the first work on mining frequent closed trees in streaming data varying with time.

9.1 Relaxed support

Song et al.[SYC+07] introduced the concept of relaxed frequent itemset; we adapt it to general pattern mining. The support space of all subpatterns can be divided into $n = \lceil 1/\epsilon_r \rceil$ intervals, where ϵ_r is a user-specified relaxing factor, and each interval can be denoted by $\mathcal{I}_i = [l_i, u_i)$, where $l_i = (n-i) * \epsilon_r \geq 0$, $u_i = (n-i+1) * \epsilon_r \leq 1$ and $i \leq n$. Then a subpattern t is called a *relaxed closed subpattern* if and only if there exists no proper superpattern t' of t whose support belongs to the same interval $\mathcal{I}_i$.

Mining for relaxed (rather than strict) closed patterns may greatly reduce the number of closed subpatterns in data streams where approximation is acceptable.

We can define *relaxed support* as a mapping from all possible dataset supports to the set of relaxed intervals. We apply it to our mining algorithms replacing the calls to support values with calls to relaxed support values.

We introduce the concept of logarithmic relaxed frequent pattern, by defining $l_i = \lceil c^i \rceil$, $u_i = \lceil c^{i+1} - 1 \rceil$ for the value of c generating n intervals. Now, the mapping from supports to relaxed support intervals is a logarithmic function. It happens often that the number of patterns decreases roughly exponentially as we increase the support threshold. In this case, the notion of logarithmic support may be more appropiate than the linear one, to have roughly equally populated intervals.

9.2 Closure Operator on Patterns

In this section we develop our approach for closed pattern mining based on the use of closure operators. We obtain a notion of closed pattern using intersection and not only support, so antimonotonicity is not the only mathematical property exploited. Our approach relies on much richer mathematics, which, as usual, leads to more powerful algorithmics.

Definition 17. *Let* $B = \{t_1, \ldots, t_n\} \in \mathcal{T}$. *A pattern is a* common *subpattern of the patterns in B if it is subpattern of all the patterns in B. A subpattern is* maximal *in B if it is common, and it is not a subpattern of any other common subpattern of the patterns in B. The* intersection *of a set of patterns B, denoted* $t_1 \cap \ldots \cap t_n$, *is the set of all maximal subpatterns in B.*

Definition 18. *The* closure *of a pattern t for a dataset $\mathcal{D}$ denoted by $\Delta_\mathcal{D}(t)$ is the intersection of all transactions in $\mathcal{D}$ that contain it.*

We can relate the notion of closure to the notion of closed pattern based on support, as previously defined, as follows: a pattern t is closed if it is in its closure $\Delta_\mathcal{D}(t)$.

Proposition 6. *Adding a pattern transaction to a dataset of patterns $\mathcal{D}$ does not decrease the number of closed patterns for $\mathcal{D}$.*

Proof. All previously closed patterns remain closed: A closed pattern would become non-closed if one of its superpatterns reached the same support, but that is not possible because every time the support of a pattern increases, the support of all its subpatterns also increases. □

Proposition 7. *A pattern transaction t added to a dataset of patterns $\mathcal{D}$ will be a closed pattern for $\mathcal{D}$.*

Proof. The supports of superpatterns of pattern t are lower than or equal to the support of pattern t. A pattern transaction t added would be non-closed if one of its superpatterns reach the same support, but that is not possible because only t is added and none of its supperpatterns is added. □

Proposition 8. *Adding a transaction with pattern t to a dataset of patterns $\mathcal{D}$ where t is closed does not modify the number of closed patterns for $\mathcal{D}$.*

9.2. CLOSURE OPERATOR ON PATTERNS

Proof. Let t be the pattern to be added and closed in $\mathcal{D}$, and s a subpattern of t. If s is closed then it will remain closed, as no one of its superpatterns will reach the same support. Suppose s is non-closed and let $t_1, \ldots, t_k$ be the closed superpatterns immediately above s. Since s is non-closed, we know that the support of s equals that of t_i, for some i. For every j, if $t_j \npreceq t$, the support of s must be larger than that of t_j, because every transaction containing t is counted in the support of s but not in that of t_j. So we know that the index i above must correspond to some t_i with $t_i \preceq t$. Then adding t to $\mathcal{D}$ increases, in particular, the supports of t_i and s by exactly 1, their supports remain equal, and s remains non-closed. □

Proposition 9. *Deleting a pattern transaction from a dataset of patterns $\mathcal{D}$ does not increase the number of closed patterns for $\mathcal{D}$.*

Proof. All the previous non-closed patterns remain non-closed: A necessary condition for a non-closed pattern to become closed is that a superpattern with the same support modifies their support, but this is not possible because every time we decrease the support of a superpattern we also decrease the support of this pattern. □

Proposition 10. *Deleting a pattern transaction that is repeated in a dataset of patterns $\mathcal{D}$ does not modify the number of closed patterns for $\mathcal{D}$.*

Proof. By Proposition 7, transactions patterns added to $\mathcal{D}$ are closed. By Proposition 8, adding a transaction with a previously closed pattern to a dataset of patterns $\mathcal{D}$ does not modify the number of closed patterns for $\mathcal{D}$. So deleting from $\mathcal{D}$ a pattern that is closed and repeated cannot change the number of closed patterns either. □

Proposition 11. *Let $\mathcal{D}1$ and $\mathcal{D}2$ be two datasets of patterns. A pattern t is closed for $\mathcal{D}1 \cup \mathcal{D}2$ if and only if it is in the intersection of its closures $\Delta_{\mathcal{D}1}(t)$ and $\Delta_{\mathcal{D}2}(t)$.*

Proof. A pattern t is closed for $\mathcal{D}1 \cup \mathcal{D}2$ only if it is in its closure $\Delta_{\mathcal{D}1 \cup \mathcal{D}2}(t)$, the intersection of all transactions of $\mathcal{D}1$ and $\mathcal{D}2$ that contain it. The closure $\Delta_{\mathcal{D}1 \cup \mathcal{D}2}(t)$ of pattern t is the intersection of all the transactions of $\mathcal{D}1 \cup \mathcal{D}2$ that contain it. Then $\Delta_{\mathcal{D}1 \cup \mathcal{D}2}(t)$ is equal to the intersection of all the transactions of $\mathcal{D}1$ that contains it, and all the transactions of $\mathcal{D}2$ that contains it. Hence, $\Delta_{\mathcal{D}1 \cup \mathcal{D}2}(t)$ is the intersection of the closure of t for $\mathcal{D}1$ and the closure of t for $\mathcal{D}2$.

□

We use Proposition 11 as a closure checking condition when adding a set of transactions to a dataset of patterns.

Corollary 7. *Let $\mathcal{D}1$ and $\mathcal{D}2$ be two datasets of patterns. A pattern t is closed for $\mathcal{D}1 \cup \mathcal{D}2$ if and only if*

- t *is a closed pattern for* $\mathcal{D}1$, *or*

- t *is a closed pattern for* $\mathcal{D}2$, *or*

- t *is a subpattern of a closed pattern in* $\mathcal{D}1$ *and a closed pattern in* $\mathcal{D}2$ *and it is in* $\Delta_{\mathcal{D}_1 \cup \mathcal{D}_2}(\{t\})$.

In summary, the closure-based approach gives us elegant and algorithmically useful conditions that are for checking whether a pattern is closed.

9.3 Closed Pattern Mining

In this section we design an incremental mining method for extracting closed frequent patterns and a sliding window mining algorithm for extraxcting closed frequent patterns.

9.3.1 Incremental Closed Pattern Mining

We propose a new method to do incremental closed pattern mining. Let D_1 be the transaction set seen so far, whose set of closed patterns T1 we have computed already. Suppose that a new batch of patterns D_2 arrives. We compute its set of closed patterns, T2, and then we update the closed pattern set to that of $D_1 \cup D_2$ using procedure CLOSED_SUBPATTERN_ MINING_ADD, shown in Figure 9.1.

In words, let T1 be the existing set of closed patterns, and T2 those coming from the new batch D_2. For each closed pattern in T2, we check whether the pattern is closed in T1. If it is closed, we update its support and that of all its subpatterns, as justified by Proposition 8. If it is not closed, as it is closed for T2, we add it to the closed pattern set, as justified by Corollary 7, and we check for each of its subpatterns whether it is closed or not. In line 18, we use Proposition 11 to do the closure-checking. As we check all the subpatterns of T2 in size-ascending order, we know that all closed subpatterns of t have been checked before.

Note that this is a totally generic algorithm for pattern mining. The best (most efficient) data structure to do this task will depend on the kind of patterns. In general, a lattice is the default option, where each lattice node is a pattern with its support, a list of its closed superpatterns, and a list of its closed subpatterns. When merging the closed patterns, the parameter $\texttt{min\_supp}$ becomes important. If two transaction sets are merged, a pattern that is infrequent in both of them may become frequent in their union. We take care of that using $\texttt{min\_supp}' = \alpha \cdot \texttt{min\_supp} < \texttt{min\_supp}$, so that a pattern can be in the the union of the transaction sets not only if it is closed in only one of them.

CLOSED_SUBPATTERN_MINING_ADD(T_1, T_2, min_supp, T)
    Input: Pattern sets T1 and T2, and min_supp;
        T1 and T2 are the frequent closed patterns of some datasets D1, D2
    Output: The set T of frequent closed patterns of dataset $D1 \cup D2$
1   $T \leftarrow T1$
2   **for** every t in T2 in size-ascending order
3   **do if** t is closed in T1
4   **then** $support_T(t)+ = support_{T2}(t)$
5   **for** every t' that is a subpattern of t
6   **do if** t' is in T1
7   **then if** t' support is not updated
8   **then** insert t' into T
9                            $support_T(t')+ = support_{T2}(t')$
10   **else**
11   skip processing t' and all its subpatterns
12   **else** insert t into T
13   **for** every t' that is a subpattern of t
14   **do if** t' support is not updated
15   **then if** t' is in T1
16   **then** $support_T(t')+ = support_{T2}(t')$
17   **if** t' is closed
18   **then** insert t' into T
19                          $support_T(t')+ = support_{T2}(t')$
20   **else** skip processing t' and all its subpatterns
21   delete from T patterns with support below min_supp
22   **return** T

Figure 9.1: The Closed Subpattern Mining Add algorithm

CLOSED_SUBPATTERN_MINING_DELETE(T1, T2, min_supp, T)

    Input: Pattern sets T1 and T2, and min_supp;
        T1 and T2 are the frequent closed patterns of some datasets D1, D2
    Output: The set T of frequent closed patterns of dataset D1 \ D2

1   T ← T1
2   **for** every t in T2 in size-ascending order
3   **do for** every t' that can be obtained deleting nodes from t
4   **do if** t' support is not updated
5   **then if** t' is in T1
6   **then if** t' is not closed
7   **then** delete t' from T
8   **else** $\text{support}_T(t') -= \text{support}_{T2}(t')$
9   **else** skip processing t' and all its subpatterns
10 delete from T patterns with support below min_supp
11 **return** T

Figure 9.2: The Closed Subpattern Mining Delete algorithm

9.3.2 Closed pattern mining over a sliding window

By adding a method to delete a set of transactions, we can adapt our method to use a sliding window of pattern transactions.

Figure 9.2 shows the pseucodode of CLOSED_SUBPATTERN_MINING_DELETE. We check for every t pattern in T2 in ascending order if its subpatterns are still closed or not after deleting some transactions. We can look for a closed superpattern with the same support. The lattice structure supports this operation well. We can delete a transaction one by one, or delete a batch of transactions of the sliding window. We delete transactions one by one to avoid recomputing the frequent closed patterns of each batch of transactions.

9.4 Adaptive closed pattern mining

In this section we present a new method for dealing with concept drift in pattern mining, using ADWIN, the algorithm for detecting change and dynamically adjusting the length of a data window, presented in Chapter 4.

9.4.1 Closed pattern mining in the presence of distribution change

We propose two strategies to deal with distribution change:

1. Using a sliding window of transactions with an ADWIN estimator de-

ciding the size of the window by monitoring the number of different closed trees. The number of closed trees is a good measure of the distribution change as it will always increase when we add new transactions with different frequent closed patterns, by Proposition 6.

2. Maintaining an `ADWIN` estimator for the support of each closed pattern in the lattice structure.

The second strategy has higher computational cost, but gives us a more precise control, on a one-to-one basis, of which trees are changing their distribution in the data stream and which ones are not. In both strategies we use CLOSED_SUBPATTERN_MINING_ADD to add transactions. In the first strategy we use CLOSED_SUBPATTERN_MINING_DELETE to delete transactions as we maintain a sliding window of transactions.

In the second strategy, we do not delete transactions. Instead, each `ADWIN` monitors the support of a closed pattern. When it detects a change, we can conclude reliably that the support of this pattern seems to be changing in the data stream in recent times. If the support decreases, the number of closed patterns may decrease and we have to delete the non-closed patterns from the lattice. We check whether it and all its subpatterns are still closed by trying to find a superpattern with the same support.

In order to obtain frequent closed patterns with a min_supp support, we will add to our algorithms a min_supp support checking condition, to delete and reduce the number of closed patterns in the lattice.

9.5 Closed Tree Mining Application

In this section we apply the general framework above specifically by considering the tree pattern. The input to our data mining process is a given finite dataset $\mathcal{D}$ of transactions, where each transaction $s \in \mathcal{D}$ consists of a transaction identifier, tid, and an rooted tree. Figure 8.1 shows a finite dataset example.

The closed trees for the dataset of Figure 8.1 are shown in the Galois lattice of Figure 8.2.

9.5.1 Incremental Closed Tree Mining

Following the general framework for patterns presented in Section 9.3, and adapting it to the tree pattern case, it is easy to derive three unlabeled tree mining algorithms:

- INCTREEMINER-U, an incremental closed tree mining algorithm (this algorithm was called INCTREENAT in [BG08]),

- WINTREEMINER-U, a sliding window closed tree mining algorithm (this algorithm was called WINTREENAT in [BG08]),

- ADATREEMINER-U an adaptive closed tree mining algorithm (this algorithm was called ADATREENAT in [BG08])

And for labeled trees, we propose three labeled tree mining algorithms:

- INCTREEMINER-L, an incremental closed tree mining algorithm,
- WINTREEMINER-L, a sliding window closed tree mining algorithm
- ADATREEMINER-L an adaptive closed tree mining algorithm

The batches are processed using the non-incremental algorithm explained in Subsection 7.6.3. We use the relaxed closed tree notion to speed up the mining process.

9.6 Experimental Evaluation

We tested our algorithms on the synthetic and real datasets presented in Section 7.8.1, comparing the results with CMTreeMiner [CXYM01].

All experiments were performed on a 2.0 GHz Intel Core Duo PC machine with 2 Gigabytes of main memory, running Ubuntu 7.10. CMTreeMiner and our algorithms are implemented in C++. The main difference with our approach is that CMTreeMiner is not incremental and only works with induced subtrees, and our method works with both induced and top-down subtrees. In all experiments using ADWIN, its confidence parameter δ is set to 0.01.

9.6.1 Unlabeled Trees

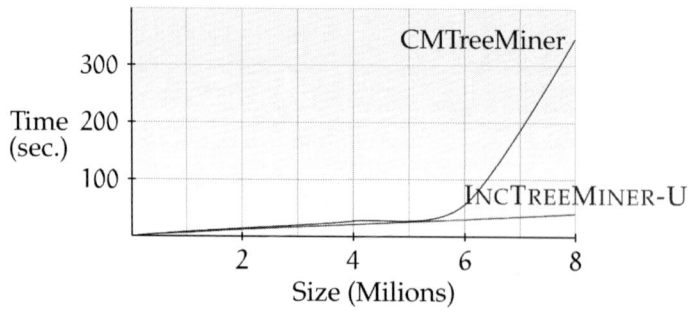

Figure 9.3: Execution time on the ordered unlabeled tree TN1 dataset

On synthetic data, we use the ZAKI Synthetic Datasets for rooted ordered trees restricting the number of distinct node labels to one. We call

9.6. EXPERIMENTAL EVALUATION

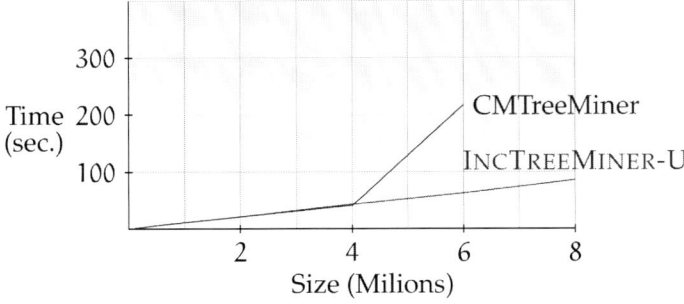

Figure 9.4: Time used on unordered unlabeled trees, TN1 dataset

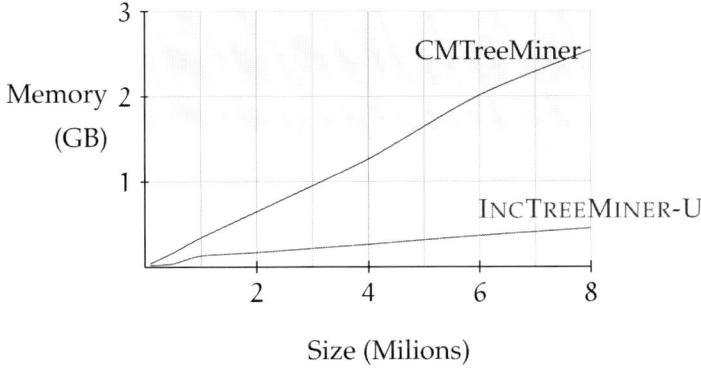

Figure 9.5: Memory used on ordered unlabeled tree TN1 dataset

this dataset TN1. In the TN1 dataset, the parameters are the following: the number of distinct node labels is $N = 1$, the total number of nodes in the tree is $M = 10,000$, the maximal depth of the tree is $D = 10$, the maximum fanout is $F = 10$. The average number of nodes is 3.

The results of our experiments on synthetic data are shown in Figures 9.3, 9.4, 9.5, and 9.6. We used a batch size of $100,000$ for the INCTREEMINER-U method. We varied the dataset size from $100,000$ to 8 milion, and we observed that as the dataset size increases, INCTREEMINER-U time increases linearly, and CMTreeMiner does much worse than INCTREEMINER-U.

At 4 milion samples, in the unordered case, CMTreeMiner needs to use swap memory. After 6 milion samples, CMTreeMiner runs out of main memory and it ends before outputting the closed trees. We observe that as the dataset size increases, CMTreeMiner can not mine datasets bigger than 6 milion trees: not being an incremental method, it must store the whole dataset in memory all the time *in addition* to the lattice structure and the

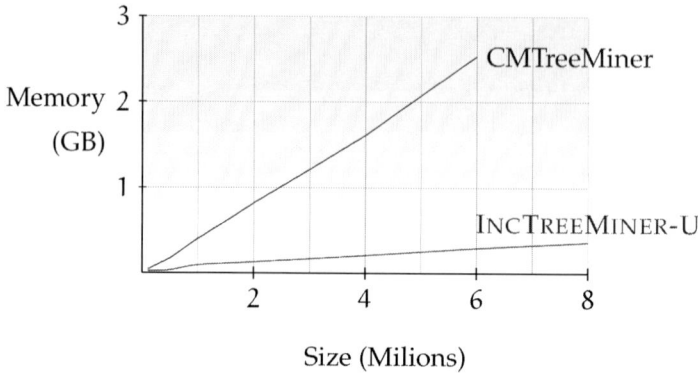

Figure 9.6: Memory used on unordered unlabeled trees, TN1 dataset

occurrences of the trees, in contrast with our algorithms.

Figure 9.7 shows the result of the second experiment: we take a TN1 dataset of 2 milion trees, and we introduce artificial distribution change changing the dataset trees from sample 500,000 to 1,000,000 and from 1,500,000 to 2,000,000, in order to force a small number of closed trees. We compare INCTREEMINER-U, WINTREEMINER-U with a sliding window of $500,000$ and $1,000,000$, and with ADATREEMINER-U using ADWIN to monitor the size of the sliding window. We observe that ADATREEMINER-U detects change faster, and it quickly revises the number of closed trees in its output. On the other hand, the other methods will not really detect change until they have flushed many old trees from their sliding windows, so they take longer to revise the number of closed trees in their output.

To compare the two adaptive methods, we perform a third experiment. We use a data stream of $200,000$ trees, with a static distribution of 20 closed trees on the first $100,000$ trees and 20 different closed trees on the last $100,000$ trees. The number of closed trees remains the same. Figure 9.8 shows the difference between the two methods. The first one, which monitors the number of closed trees, detects change at sample 111,480 and then it reduces the window size immediately. In the second method there are ADWINs monitoring each tree support; they notice the appearance of new closed trees quicker, but overall the number of closed trees decreases more slowly than in the first method.

Finally, we tested our algorithms on the CSLOGS Dataset. Figure 9.9 shows the number of closed trees detected on the CSLOGS dataset, varying the number of relaxed intervals. We see that, in this dataset, support values are distributed in such a way that we find more closed trees using logarithmic relaxed support than using linear relaxed support, but not by a order of magnitude. This higher number of closed trees implies that we

9.6. EXPERIMENTAL EVALUATION

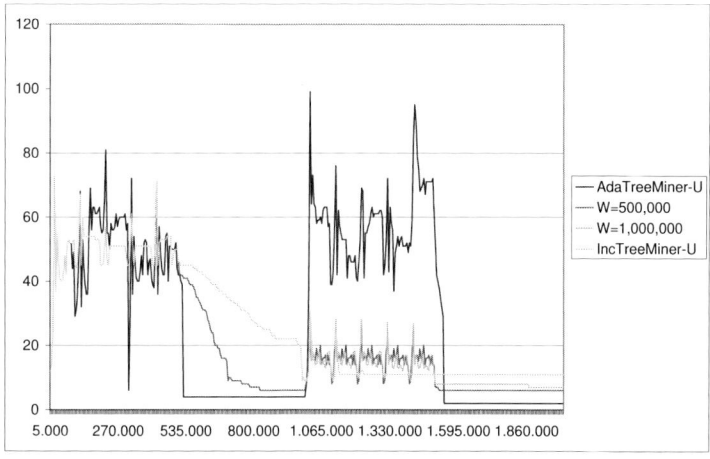

Figure 9.7: Number of closed trees detected with artificial distribution change introduced

obtain more information using the same number of intervals. When the number of intervals is greater than 1,000 the number of intervals is 249, the number obtained using the strict (not relaxed) notion of support.

9.6.2 Labeled Trees

On synthetic labeled data, we use the same dataset as in [CXYM01] and [Zak02] for rooted ordered trees. The synthetic dataset T8M are generated by the tree generation program of Zaki [Zak02]. A mother tree is generated first with the following parameters: the number of distinct node labels $N = 100$, the total number of nodes in the tree $M = 10,000$, the maximal depth of the tree $D = 10$ and the maximum fanout $F = 10$. The dataset is then generated by creating subtrees of the mother tree. In our experiments, we set the total number of trees in the dataset to be from $T = 0$ to $T = 8,000,000$.

The results of our experiments on synthetic data are shown in Figures 9.10, 9.11, 9.12, and 9.13. We observe that as the dataset size increases, INCTREEMINER-L and CMTreeMiner times are similar and that INCTREEMINER-L uses much less memory than CMTreeMiner. CMTreeMiner can not mine datasets bigger than 8 milion trees: not being an incremental method, it must store the whole dataset in memory all the time *in*

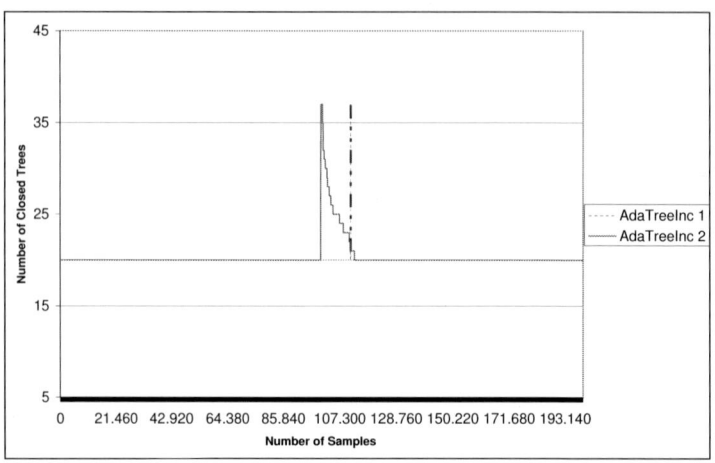

Figure 9.8: Number of closed trees maintaining the same number of closed datasets on input data

addition to the lattice structures, as we already observed for unlabeled trees.

In Figure 9.14 we compare WINTREEMINER-L with different window sizes to ADATREEMINER-L on T8M dataset. We observe that the two versions of ADATREEMINER-L outperforms WINTREEMINER-L for all window sizes.

9.6. EXPERIMENTAL EVALUATION

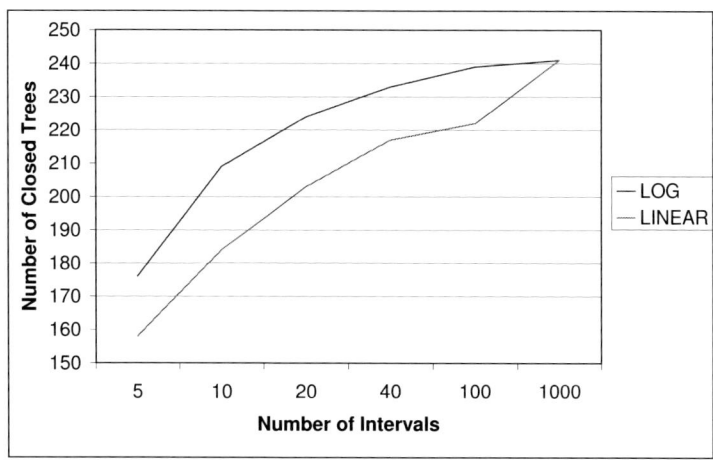

Figure 9.9: Number of closed trees detected on CSLOGS dataset varying Number of relaxed intervals

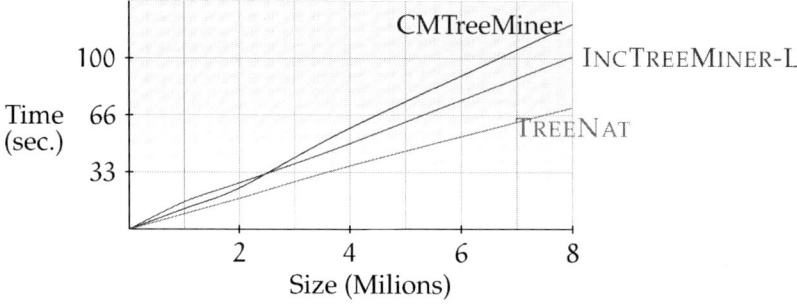

Figure 9.10: Execution time on ordered labeled tree T8M dataset

CHAPTER 9. MINING ADAPTIVELY FREQUENT CLOSED ROOTED TREES

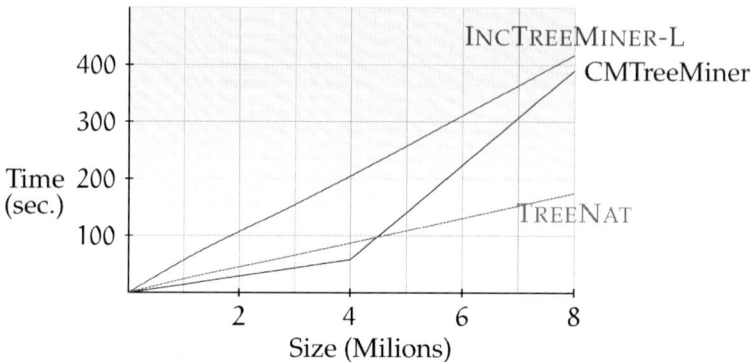

Figure 9.11: Time used on unordered labeled trees, TN1 dataset

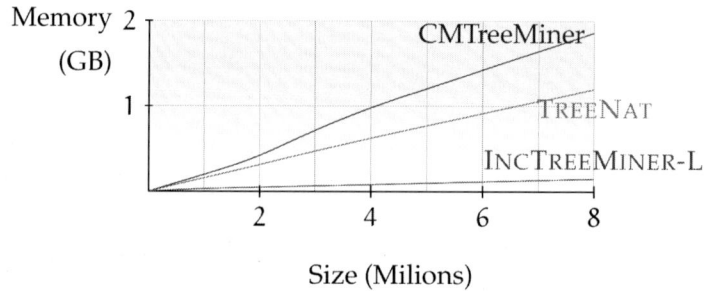

Figure 9.12: Memory used on ordered labeled tree T8M dataset

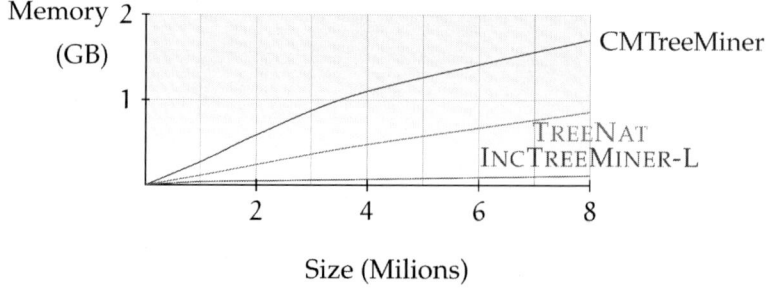

Figure 9.13: Memory used on unordered labeled trees on T8M dataset

9.6. EXPERIMENTAL EVALUATION

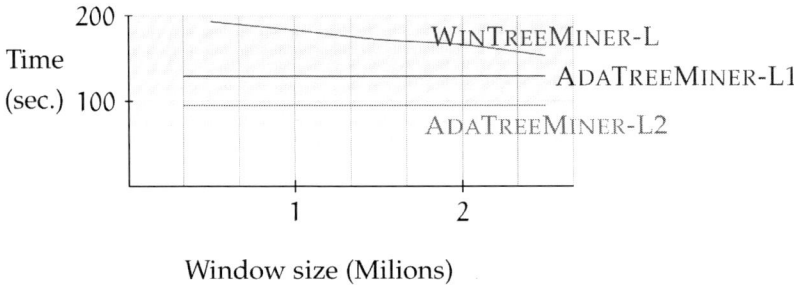

Figure 9.14: Time on ordered labeled trees on T8M dataset, varying window size

10
Adaptive XML Tree Classification

In this chapter, we propose a new method to classify patterns, using closed and maximal frequent patterns. Closed patterns maintain the same information as frequent patterns using less space and maximal patterns maintain approximate information. We use them to reduce the number of classification features. We present a new framework for data stream pattern classification. To the best of our knowledge this is the first work on tree classification in streaming data varying with time.

10.1 Introduction

XML patterns are tree patterns and they are becoming a standard for information representation and exchange over the Internet. XML data is growing and it will soon constitute one of the largest collection of human knowledge. XML tree classification has been done traditionally using information retrieval techniques considering the labels of nodes as bags of words. With the development of frequent tree miners, classification methods using frequent trees appeared [ZA03, KM04, CD01, KK02]. Recently, closed frequent miners were proposed [CXYM01, TRS[+]08, AU05], and using them for classification tasks is the next natural step.

Pattern classification and the frequent pattern discovery task have been important tasks over the last years. Nowadays, they are becoming harder, as the size of the patterns datasets is increasing and we cannot assume that data has been generated from a static distribution.

In this chapter we are going to show how closure-based mining can be used to reduce drastically the number of attributes on tree classification. Moreover, we show how to use maximal frequent trees, to reduce even more the number of attributes needed in tree classification, in many cases without loosing accuracy

XRules is an XML classifier algorithm that Zaki and Aggarwal presented in [ZA03]. Their classification method mines frequent trees in order to create classification rules. They do not use closed frequent trees, only frequent trees. XRules is cost-sensitive and uses Bayesian rule based class decision making. They also proposed methods for effective rule prioritization and testing.

Kudo and Matsumoto presented a boosting method for tree classification in [KM04]. Their proposal consists of decision stumps that uses significant frequent subtrees as features and a Boosting algorithm which employs the subtree-based decision stumps as weak learners. They extended this classification method to graphs in [KMM04], in joint work with Maeda.

Other works use SVMs defining tree Kernels [CD01, KK02]. Tree kernel is one of the convolutions kernels, and maps the example represented in a labeled ordered tree into all subtree spaces. The feature space uses frequent trees and not closed trees.

Garriga et al. [GKL08] showed that when considering labeled itemsets, closed sets can be adapted for classification and discrimination purposes by conveniently contrasting covering properties on positive and negative examples. They formally proved that these sets characterize the space of relevant combinations of features for discriminating the target class.

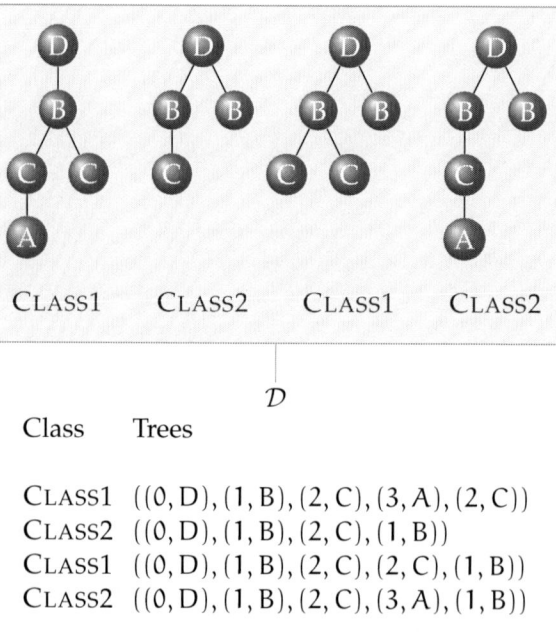

Figure 10.1: A dataset example

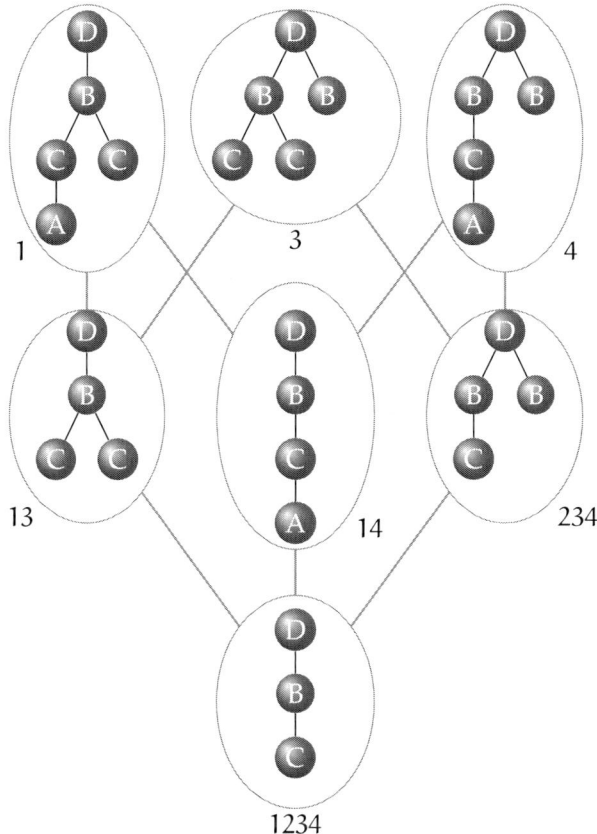

Figure 10.2: Example of Galois Lattice of Closed trees

10.2 Classification using Compressed Frequent Patterns

The pattern classification problem is defined as follows. A finite or infinite dataset $\mathcal{D}$ of transactions is given, where each transaction $s \in \mathcal{D}$ consists of a transaction identifier, tid, a pattern, t, and a discrete class label, y. The goal is to produce from these transactions a model $\hat{y} = f(t)$ that will predict the classes y of future pattern transactions t with high accuracy. Tids are supposed to run sequentially from 1 to the size of $\mathcal{D}$. From that dataset, our universe of discourse $\mathcal{U}$ is the set of all patterns that appear as subpattern of some pattern in $\mathcal{D}$. Figure 10.1 shows a finite dataset example of trees.

We use the following approach: we convert the pattern classification problem into a vector classification learning task, transforming patterns into vectors of attributes. Attributes will be frequent subpatterns, or a sub-

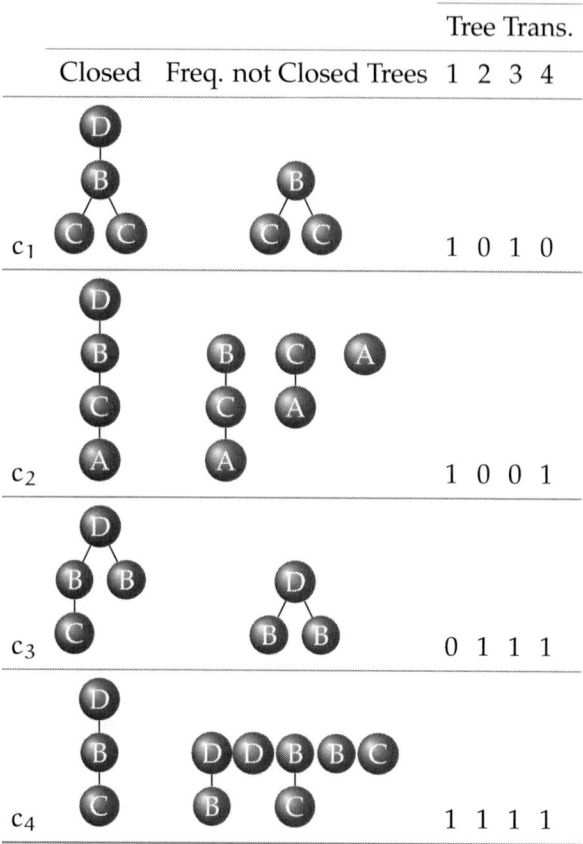

Figure 10.3: Frequent trees from dataset example ($\mathtt{min\_sup} = 30\%$), and their corresponding attribute vectors.

set of these frequent subpatterns.

Suppose $\mathcal{D}$ has d frequent subpatterns denoted by $t_1, t_2, \ldots, t_d$. For each t pattern, we obtain a x vector of d attributes, where $x = (x_1, x_2, \ldots, x_d)$ and for each attribute i, $x_i = 1$ if $t_i \preceq t$ or $x_i = 0$ otherwise.

As the number of frequent subpatterns is very huge, we perform a feature selection process, selecting a subset of these frequent subpatterns, maintaining the same information, or approximate. Figures 10.3 and 10.4 show frequent trees and its conversion to vectors of attributes. Note that closed trees have the same information as frequent trees, and maximal trees only approximate.

10.2. CLASSIFICATION USING COMPRESSED FREQUENT PATTERNS

			Frequent Trees		
	c_1	c_2	c_3		c_4
Id	c_1 f_1^1	c_2 f_2^1 f_2^2 f_2^3	c_3 f_3^1	c_4	f_4^1 f_4^2 f_4^3 f_4^4 f_4^5
1	1 1	1 1 1 1	0 0		1 1 1 1 1 1
2	0 0	0 0 0 0	1 1		1 1 1 1 1 1
3	1 1	0 0 0 0	1 1		1 1 1 1 1 1
4	0 0	1 1 1 1	1 1		1 1 1 1 1 1

	Closed Trees				Maximal Trees			
Id Tree	c_1	c_2	c_3	c_4	c_1	c_2	c_3	Class
1	1	1	0	1	1	1	0	CLASS1
2	0	0	1	1	0	0	1	CLASS2
3	1	0	1	1	1	0	1	CLASS1
4	0	1	1	1	0	1	1	CLASS2

Figure 10.4: Closed and maximal frequent trees from dataset example (min_sup = 30%), and their corresponding attribute vectors.

10.2.1 Closed Frequent Patterns

We consider now implications of the form $A \to B$ for sets of patterns A and B from $\mathcal{U}$. Specifically, we consider the following set of rules: $A \to \Gamma_\mathcal{D}(A)$. Alternatively, we can split the consequents into $\{A \to t \mid t \in \Gamma_\mathcal{D}(A)\}$.

It is easy to see that $\mathcal{D}$ obeys all these rules: for each A, any pattern of $\mathcal{D}$ that has as subpatterns all the patterns of A has also as subpatterns all the patterns of $\Gamma_\mathcal{D}(A)$.

Proposition 12. *Let t_i be a frequent pattern for $\mathcal{D}$. A transaction pattern t satisfies $t_i \preceq t$, if and only if it satisfies $\Delta_\mathcal{D}(t_i) \preceq t$.*

We use Proposition 12 to reduce the number of attributes on our classification task, using only closed frequent patterns, as they keep the same information. The attribute vector of a frequent pattern will be the same as its closed pattern attribute vector. Figure 10.4 shows the attribute vectors for the dataset of Figure 10.1.

10.2.2 Maximal Frequent Patterns

Maximal patterns are patterns that do not have any frequent superpattern. All maximal patterns are closed patterns. If min_sup is zero, then maximal patterns are transaction patterns. We denote by $M_1(t), M_2(t), \ldots, M_m(t)$

the maximal superpatterns of a pattern t. We are interested in the implications of the form $t_c \rightarrow (M_1(t) \vee M_2(t) \vee \ldots \vee M_m(t))$ where t_c is a closed pattern.

Proposition 13. *Let t_c be a closed non-maximal frequent pattern for $\mathcal{D}$. Let $M_1(t_c), M_2(t_c), \ldots, M_m(t_c)$ be the maximal superpatterns of pattern t_c. A transaction pattern t satisfies $t_c \prec t$, if and only if at least one of the maximals superpattern $M_i(t_c)$ of pattern t_c satisfies $M_i(t_c) \preceq t$.*

Proof. Suppose that pattern t_c satisfies $t_c \prec t$ but no maximal superpattern $M_i(t_c)$ satisfies $M_i(t_c) \preceq t$. Then, pattern t_c has no frequent superpattern. Therefore, it is maximal, contradicting the assumption.

Suppose, for the other direction, that a maximal superpattern $M_i(t_c)$ of t_c satisfies $M_i(t_c) \preceq t$. Then, as t_c is a $M_i(t_c)$ subpattern, $t_c \preceq M_i(t_c)$, and it holds that $t_c \preceq M_i(t_c) \preceq t$. □

For non-maximal closed patterns, the following set of rules holds if t_c is not a transaction pattern:

$$t_c \rightarrow \bigvee M_i(t_c)$$

Note that for a transaction pattern t_c that it is closed and non-maximal, there is no maximal superpattern $M_i(t_c)$ of pattern t_c that satisfies $M_i(t_c) \preceq t_c$. If there are no closed non-maximal transaction patterns, we do not need to use all closed patterns as attributes, since non-maximal closed patterns may be derived from maximal patterns.

Using Proposition 13, we may reduce the number of attributes on our classification task, using only maximal frequent patterns, as they keep much of the information as closed frequent patterns.

10.3 XML Tree Classification framework on data streams

Our XML Tree Classification Framework has two components:

- An XML closed frequent tree miner, for which we could use any incremental algorithm that maintains a set of closed frequent trees.

- A Data stream classifier algorithm, which we will feed with tuples to be classified online. Attributes in these tuples represent the occurrence of the current closed trees in the originating tree, although the classifier algorithm need not be aware of this.

In this section, we describe the first component of the framework, the XML closed frequent tree miner. The second component of the framework is based on MOA. **Massive Online Analysis (MOA)** [HKP07] was introduced in Section 3.5.3.

10.3.1 Adaptive Tree Mining on evolving data streams

In this section we review briefly the three closed tree mining algorithms presented in Chapter 9, and how to adapt them to obtain maximal frequent patterns.

The main properties are:

- adding a tree transaction to a dataset of trees $\mathcal{D}$, does not decrease the number of closed trees for $\mathcal{D}$.

- adding a transaction with a closed tree to a dataset of trees $\mathcal{D}$, does not modify the number of closed trees for $\mathcal{D}$.

- deleting a tree transaction from a dataset of trees $\mathcal{D}$, does not increase the number of closed trees for $\mathcal{D}$.

- deleting a tree transaction that is repeated in a dataset of trees $\mathcal{D}$ from it, does not modify the number of closed trees for $\mathcal{D}$.

For maximal frequent trees, the following properties hold:

- adding a tree transaction to a dataset of trees $\mathcal{D}$, may increase or decrease the number of maximal trees for $\mathcal{D}$.

- adding a transaction with a closed tree to a dataset of trees $\mathcal{D}$, may modify the number of maximal trees for $\mathcal{D}$.

- deleting a tree transaction from a dataset of trees $\mathcal{D}$, may increase or decrease the number of maximal trees for $\mathcal{D}$.

- deleting a tree transaction that is repeated in a dataset of trees $\mathcal{D}$ from it, may modify the number of maximal trees for $\mathcal{D}$.

- a non maximal closed tree may become maximal if
   - it was not frequent and now its support increases to a value higher or equal to min_sup
   - all of its maximal supertrees become non-frequent

- a maximal tree may become a non maximal tree if
   - its support decreases below min_sup
   - a non-frequent closed supertree becomes frequent

We could check if a closed tree becomes maximal when

- removing closed trees because they do not have enough support

- adding a new closed tree to the dataset

- deleting a closed tree from the dataset

We use the three tree mining algorithms presented in Chapter 9:

- INCTREEMINER, an incremental closed tree mining algorithm,
- WINTREEMINER, a sliding window closed tree mining algorithm
- ADATREEMINER, an adaptive closed tree mining algorithm

The batches are processed using the non-incremental algorithm explained in Subsection 7.6.3.

We use two strategies to deal with concept drift:

- ADATREEMINER1: Using a sliding window, with an ADWIN estimator deciding the size of the window
- ADATREEMINER2: Maintaining an ADWIN estimator for each closed set in the lattice structure.

In the second strategy, we do not delete transactions. Instead, each ADWIN monitors its support and when a change is detected, then the support may

- increase: the number of closed trees is increasing
- decrease: the number of closed trees may decrease and we have to delete the non-closed trees from the lattice.
    - If the support is lower than min_supp, we delete the closed tree from the lattice
    - If the support is higher than min_supp, we check if it and all its subtrees are still closed finding a supertree with the same support or
    - Using a closure checking property: a tree t is closed if the intersection of all its closed supertrees is t.

10.4 Experimental evaluation

We tested our algorithms on synthetic and real data. All experiments were performed on a 2.0 GHz Intel Core Duo PC machine with 2 Gigabyte main memory, running Ubuntu 8.10.

We evaluate our approach to tree classification on both real and synthetic classification data sets. For synthetic classification, we use the tree generator from Zaki [Zak02] used for the evaluation on mining closed frequent trees. We generate two mother trees, one for each class. The first

Bagging	Time	Acc.	Mem.
ADATREEMINER-L1	161.61	**80.06**	4.93
ADATREEMINER-L2	212.57	65.78	4.42
WINTREEMINER-L W=100,000	192.01	72.61	6.53
WINTREEMINER-L W= 50,000	212.09	66.23	11.68
INCTREEMINER-L	212.75	65.73	4.4

Boosting	Time	Acc.	Mem.
ADATREEMINER-L1	236.31	**79.83**	4.8
ADATREEMINER-L2	326.8	65.43	4.25
WINTREEMINER-L W=100,000	286.02	70.15	5.8
WINTREEMINER-L W= 50,000	318.19	63.94	9.87
INCTREEMINER-L	317.95	65.55	4.25

Table 10.1: Comparison of classification algorithms. Memory is measured in MB. The best individual accuracy is indicated in boldface.

mother tree is generated with the following parameters: the number of distinct node labels $N = 200$, the total number of nodes in the tree $M = 1,000$, the maximal depth of the tree $D = 10$ and the maximum fanout $F = 10$. The second one has the following parameters: the number of distinct node labels $N = 5$, the total number of nodes in the tree $M = 100$, the maximal depth of the tree $D = 10$ and the maximum fanout $F = 10$.

A stream is generated by mixing the subtrees created from these mother trees. In our experiments, we set the total number of trees in the dataset to be from $T = 1,000,000$. We added artificial drift changing labels of the trees every $250,000$ samples, so closed and maximal frequent trees evolve over time. We use bagging of 10 Hoeffding Trees enhanced with adaptive Naive Bayes leaf predictions, as classification method.

Table 10.1 shows classification results. We observe that ADATREEMINER-L1 is the most accurate method, and that the accuracy of WINTREEMINER-L depends on the size of the window.

For real datasets, we use the Log Markup Language (LOGML) dataset from Zaki et al. [PKZ01, ZA03], that describes log reports at their CS department website. LOGML provides a XML vocabulary to structurally express the contents of the log file information in a compact manner. Each user session is expressed in LOGML as a graph, and includes both structure and content.

The real CSLOG data set spans 3 weeks worth of such XML user-sessions. To convert this into a classification data set they chose to categorize each user-session into one of two class labels: edu corresponds to users from an "edu" domain, while other class corresponds to all users visiting the CS department from any other domain. They separate each week's logs into a different data set (CSLOGx, where x stands for the week; CSLOG12 is the combined data for weeks 1 and 2). Notice that the edu class has much lower frequency rate than other.

Table 10.2 shows the results on bagging and boosting using 10 Hoeffding Trees enhanced with adaptive Naive Bayes leaf predictions. The results are very similar for the two ensemble learning methods. Using maximals and closed frequent trees, we obtain results similar to [Zak02]. Comparing maximal trees with closed trees, we see that maximal trees use 1/4 to 1/3rd of attributes, 1/3 of memory, and they perform better.

10.4. EXPERIMENTAL EVALUATION

BAGGING

		Maximal						Closed					
		Unordered			Ordered		Unordered			Ordered			
	# Trees	Att.	Acc.	Mem.	Att.	Acc.	Mem.	Att.	Acc.	Mem.	Att.	Acc.	Mem.
CSLOG12	15483	84	**79.64**	1.2	77	79.63	1.1	228	78.12	2.54	183	78.12	2.03
CSLOG23	15037	88	**79.81**	1.21	80	79.8	1.09	243	78.77	2.75	196	78.89	2.21
CSLOG31	15702	86	**79.94**	1.25	80	79.87	1.17	243	77.6	2.73	196	77.59	2.19
CSLOG123	23111	84	**80.02**	1.7	78	79.97	1.58	228	78.91	4.18	181	78.91	3.31

BOOSTING

		Maximal						Closed					
		Unordered			Ordered		Unordered			Ordered			
	# Trees	Att.	Acc.	Mem.	Att.	Acc.	Mem.	Att.	Acc.	Mem.	Att.	Acc.	Mem.
CSLOG12	15483	84	**79.46**	1.21	77	78.83	1.11	228	75.84	2.97	183	77.28	2.37
CSLOG23	15037	88	79.91	1.23	80	**80.24**	1.14	243	77.24	2.96	196	78.99	2.38
CSLOG31	15702	86	**79.77**	1.25	80	79.69	1.17	243	76.25	3.29	196	77.63	2.62
CSLOG123	23111	84	79.73	1.69	78	**80.03**	1.56	228	76.92	4.25	181	76.43	3.45

Table 10.2: Comparison of tree classification algorithms. Memory is measured in MB. The best individual accuracies are indicated in boldface (one per row).

Bibliography

[AAA+02] Tatsuya Asai, Hiroki Arimura, Kenji Abe, Shinji Kawasoe, and Setsuo Arikawa. Online algorithms for mining semi-structured data stream. In *IEEE International Conference on Data Mining (ICDM'02)*, page 27, 2002.

[AAK+02] Tatsuya Asai, Kenji Abe, Shinji Kawasoe, Hiroki Arimura, Hiroshi Sakamoto, and Setsuo Arikawa. Efficient substructure discovery from large semi-structured data. In *SDM*, 2002.

[AAUN03] Tatsuya Asai, Hiroki Arimura, Takeaki Uno, and Shin-Ichi Nakano. Discovering frequent substructures in large unordered trees. In *Discovery Science*, pages 47–61, 2003.

[Agg06] Charu C. Aggarwal. *Data Streams: Models and Algorithms*. Springer, 2006.

[AGI+92] Rakesh Agrawal, Sakti P. Ghosh, Tomasz Imielinski, Balakrishna R. Iyer, and Arun N. Swami. An interval classifier for database mining applications. In *VLDB '92*, pages 560–573, 1992.

[AIS93] R. Agrawal, T. Imielinski, and A. Swami. Database mining: A performance perspective. *IEEE Trans. on Knowl. and Data Eng.*, 5(6):914–925, 1993.

[AN07] A. Asuncion and D.J. Newman. UCI machine learning repository, 2007.

[AU05] Hiroki Arimura and Takeaki Uno. An output-polynomial time algorithm for mining frequent closed attribute trees. In *ILP*, pages 1–19, 2005.

[B+84] Leo Breiman et al. *Classification and Regression Trees*. Chapman & Hall, New York, 1984.

[BB03] Jaume Baixeries and José L. Balcázar. Discrete deterministic data mining as knowledge compilation. In *Workshop on Discrete Math. and Data Mining at SIAM DM Conference*, 2003.

[BBD+02] B. Babcock, S. Babu, M. Datar, R. Motwani, and J. Widom. Models and issues in data stream systems. In *Proc. 21st ACM Symposium on Principles of Database Systems*, 2002.

[BBDK00]   P.L. Bartlett, S. Ben-David, and S.R. Kulkarni. Learning changing concepts by exploiting the structure of change. *Machine Learning*, 41(2):153–174, 2000.

[BBL06]   José L. Balcázar, Albert Bifet, and Antoni Lozano. Intersection algorithms and a closure operator on unordered trees. In *MLG 2006, 4th International Workshop on Mining and Learning with Graphs*, 2006.

[BBL07a]   José L. Balcázar, Albert Bifet, and Antoni Lozano. Closed and maximal tree mining using natural representations. In *MLG 2007, 5th International Workshop on Mining and Learning with Graphs*, 2007.

[BBL07b]   José L. Balcázar, Albert Bifet, and Antoni Lozano. Mining frequent closed unordered trees through natural representations. In *ICCS 2007, 15th International Conference on Conceptual Structures*, pages 347–359, 2007.

[BBL07c]   José L. Balcázar, Albert Bifet, and Antoni Lozano. Subtree testing and closed tree mining through natural representations. In *DEXA Workshops*, pages 499–503, 2007.

[BBL08]   José L. Balcázar, Albert Bifet, and Antoni Lozano. Mining implications from lattices of closed trees. In *Extraction et gestion des connaissances (EGC'2008)*, pages 373–384, 2008.

[BBL09]   José L. Balcázar, Albert Bifet, and Antoni Lozano. Mining frequent closed rooted trees. In *Machine Learning Journal*, 2009.

[BCCW05]   Albert Bifet, Carlos Castillo, Paul A. Chirita, and Ingmar Weber. An analysis of factors used in a search engine's ranking. In *First International Workshop on Adversarial Information Retrieval on the Web*, 2005.

[BDM02]   B. Babcock, M. Datar, and R. Motwani. Sampling from a moving window over streaming data. In *Proc. 13th Annual ACM-SIAM Symposium on Discrete Algorithms*, 2002.

[BDMO03]   Brain Babcock, Mayur Datar, Rajeev Motwani, and Liadan O'Callaghan. Maintaining variance and k-medians over data stream windows. In *PODS '03: Proceedings of the twenty-second ACM SIGMOD-SIGACT-SIGART symposium on Principles of database systems*, pages 234–243, New York, NY, USA, 2003. ACM Press.

[BFOS94]	L. Breiman, J. Friedman, R. Olshen, and C. Stone. *Classification and Regression Trees*. Wadsworth and Brooks, Monterey, CA, 1994.

[BG06]	Albert Bifet and Ricard Gavaldà. Kalman filters and adaptive windows for learning in data streams. In *Discovery Science*, pages 29–40, 2006.

[BG07a]	José L. Balcázar and Gemma C. Garriga. Characterizing implications of injective partial orders. In *Proceedings of the 15th International Conference on Conceptual Structures (ICCS 2007)*, 2007.

[BG07b]	José L. Balcázar and Gemma C. Garriga. Horn axiomatizations for sequential data. *Theoretical Computer Science*, 371(3):247–264, 2007.

[BG07c]	Albert Bifet and Ricard Gavaldà. Learning from time-changing data with adaptive windowing. In *SIAM International Conference on Data Mining*, 2007.

[BG08]	Albert Bifet and Ricard Gavaldà. Mining adaptively frequent closed unlabeled rooted trees in data streams. In *14th ACM SIGKDD International Conference on Knowledge Discovery and Data Mining*, 2008.

[BG09a]	Albert Bifet and Ricard Gavaldà. Adaptive learning from evolving data streams. In *8th International Symposium on Intelligent Data Analysis*, 2009.

[BG09b]	Albert Bifet and Ricard Gavaldà. Adaptive XML tree classification on evolving data streams. In *Machine Learning and Knowledge Discovery in Databases, European Conference, ECML/PKDD*, 2009.

[BGdCÁF+06]	Manuel Baena-García, José del Campo-Ávila, Raúl Fidalgo, Albert Bifet, Ricard Gavaldá, and Rafael Morales-Bueno. Early drift detection method. In *Fourth International Workshop on Knowledge Discovery from Data Streams*, 2006.

[BH80]	Terry Beyer and Sandra Mitchell Hedetniemi. Constant time generation of rooted trees. *SIAM J. Comput.*, 9(4):706–712, 1980.

[BHP+09]	Albert Bifet, Geoff Holmes, Bernhard Pfahringer, Richard Kirkby, and Ricard Gavaldà. New ensemble methods for evolving data streams. In *15th ACM SIGKDD International Conference on Knowledge Discovery and Data Mining*, 2009.

BIBLIOGRAPHY

[BL99] Michael Berry and Gordon Linoff. *Mastering Data Mining: The Art and Science of Customer Relationship Management.* John Wiley & Sons, Inc., New York, NY, USA, 1999.

[BL04] Michael Berry and Gordon Linoff. *Data Mining Techniques: For Marketing, Sales, and Customer Relationship Management.* John Wiley & Sons, Inc., New York, NY, USA, 2004.

[BLB03] Stéphane Boucheron, Gábor Lugosi, and Olivier Bousquet. Concentration inequalities. In *Advanced Lectures on Machine Learning*, pages 208–240, 2003.

[BN93] Michèle Basseville and Igor V. Nikiforov. *Detection of abrupt changes: theory and application.* Prentice-Hall, Inc., Upper Saddle River, NJ, USA, 1993.

[Bur98] Christopher J. C. Burges. A tutorial on support vector machines for pattern recognition. *Data Mining and Knowledge Discovery*, 2(2):121–167, 1998.

[BW01] Shivnath Babu and Jennifer Widom. Continuous queries over data streams. *SIGMOD Rec.*, 30(3):109–120, 2001.

[BYRN99] Ricardo A. Baeza-Yates and Berthier A. Ribeiro-Neto. *Modern Information Retrieval.* ACM Press / Addison-Wesley, 1999.

[CA01] R. Chalmers and K. Almeroth. Modeling the branching characteristics and efficiency gains of global multicast trees. In *Proceedings of the IEEE INFOCOM'2001*, April 2001.

[CBL06] Nicolo Cesa-Bianchi and Gabor Lugosi. *Prediction, Learning, and Games.* Cambridge University Press, New York, NY, USA, 2006.

[CD01] Michael Collins and Nigel Duffy. New ranking algorithms for parsing and tagging: kernels over discrete structures, and the voted perceptron. In *ACL '02*, pages 263–270, 2001.

[Cha02a] Soumen Chakrabarti. *Mining the Web: Analysis of Hypertext and Semi Structured Data.* Morgan Kaufmann, August 2002.

[Cha02b] Soumen Chakrabarti. *Mining the Web: Analysis of Hypertext and Semi Structured Data.* Morgan Kaufmann, August 2002.

[CMNK01] Yun Chi, Richard Muntz, Siegfried Nijssen, and Joost Kok. Frequent subtree mining – an overview. *Fundamenta Informaticae*, XXI:1001–1038, 2001.

[CS03] E. Cohen and M. Strauss. Maintaining time-decaying stream aggregates. In *Proc. 22nd ACM Symposium on Principles of Database Systems*, 2003.

[CWYM04] Y. Chi, H. Wang, P. S. Yu, and R. R. Muntz. Moment: Maintaining closed frequent itemsets over a stream sliding window. In *Proceedings of the 2004 IEEE International Conference on Data Mining (ICDM'04)*, November 2004.

[CXYM01] Yun Chi, Yi Xia, Yirong Yang, and Richard Muntz. Mining closed and maximal frequent subtrees from databases of labeled rooted trees. *Fundamenta Informaticae*, XXI:1001–1038, 2001.

[CYM04] Y. Chi, Y. Yang, and R. R. Muntz. HybridTreeMiner: An efficient algorithm for mining frequent rooted trees and free trees using canonical forms. In *SSDBM '04: Proceedings of the 16th International Conference on Scientific and Statistical Database Management (SSDBM'04)*, page 11, Washington, DC, USA, 2004. IEEE Computer Society.

[CYM05] Y. Chi, Y. Yang, and R. R. Muntz. Canonical forms for labelled trees and their applications in frequent subtree mining. *Knowledge and Information Systems*, 8(2):203–234, 2005.

[CZ04] Fang Chu and Carlo Zaniolo. Fast and light boosting for adaptive mining of data streams. In *PAKDD*, pages 282–292. Springer Verlag, 2004.

[DGIM02] M. Datar, A. Gionis, P. Indyk, and R. Motwani. Maintaining stream statistics over sliding windows. *SIAM Journal on Computing*, 14(1):27–45, 2002.

[DH00] Pedro Domingos and Geoff Hulten. Mining high-speed data streams. In *Knowledge Discovery and Data Mining*, pages 71–80, 2000.

[DHS00] R. O. Duda, P. E. Hart, and D. G. Stork. *Pattern Classification*. Wiley-Interscience Publication, 2000.

[DKVY06] Tamraparni Dasu, Shankar Krishnan, Suresh Venkatasubramanian, and Ke Yi. An information-theoretic approach to detecting changes in multi-dimensional data streams. In *Proc. Interface*, 2006.

[DP92] Rina Dechter and Judea Pearl. Structure identification in relational data. *Artif. Intell.*, 58(1-3):237–270, 1992.

[Dru92] Peter F. Drucker. *Managing for the Future: The 1990s and Beyond*. Dutton Adult, 1992.

[FQWZ07] Jianhua Feng, Qian Qian, Jianyong Wang, and Li-Zhu Zhou. Efficient mining of frequent closed xml query pattern. *J. Comput. Sci. Technol.*, 22(5):725–735, 2007.

[Gar06] Gemma C. Garriga. *Formal Methods for Mining Structured Objects*. PhD thesis, Universitat Politècnica de Catalunya, June 2006.

[GB04] Gemma C. Garriga and José L. Balcázar. Coproduct transformations on lattices of closed partial orders. In *ICGT*, pages 336–352, 2004.

[GG07] J. Gama and M. Gaber. *Learning from Data Streams – Processing techniques in Sensor Networks*. Springer, 2007.

[GGR02] M. Garofalakis, J. Gehrke, and R. Rastogi. Querying and mining data streams: You only get one look. *Tutorial at 2002 ACM-SIGMOD Int. Conf. on Management of Data (SIGMOD'02) Madison, WI*, June 2002.

[GKL08] Gemma C. Garriga, Petra Kralj, and Nada Lavrač. Closed sets for labeled data. *J. Mach. Learn. Res.*, 9:559–580, 2008.

[GMCR04] J. Gama, P. Medas, G. Castillo, and P. Rodrigues. Learning with drift detection. In *SBIA Brazilian Symposium on Artificial Intelligence*, pages 286–295, 2004.

[GMR04] J. Gama, P. Medas, and R. Rocha. Forest trees for on-line data. In *SAC '04: Proceedings of the 2004 ACM symposium on Applied computing*, pages 632–636, New York, NY, USA, 2004. ACM Press.

[GRC+08] John F. Gantz, David Reinsel, Christopeher Chute, Wolfgang Schlichting, Stephen Minton, Anna Toncheva, and Alex Manfrediz. The expanding digital universe: An updated forecast of worldwide information growth through 2011. March 2008.

[GRG98] Johannes Gehrke, Raghu Ramakrishnan, and Venkatesh Ganti. RainForest - a framework for fast decision tree construction of large datasets. In *VLDB '98*, pages 416–427, 1998.

[GRM03] João Gama, Ricardo Rocha, and Pedro Medas. Accurate decision trees for mining high-speed data streams. In *KDD '03*, pages 523–528, August 2003.

[Gus00] Fredrik Gustafsson. *Adaptive Filtering and Change Detection.* Wiley, 2000.

[GW99] B. Ganter and R. Wille. *Formal Concept Analysis.* Springer-Verlag, 1999.

[GZK05] Mohamed Medhat Gaber, Arkady Zaslavsky, and Shonali Krishnaswamy. Mining data streams: a review. *SIGMOD Rec.*, 34(2):18–26, 2005.

[HAKU+08] Kosuke Hashimoto, Kiyoko Flora Aoki-Kinoshita, Nobuhisa Ueda, Minoru Kanehisa, and Hiroshi Mamitsuka. A new efficient probabilistic model for mining labeled ordered trees applied to glycobiology. *ACM Trans. Knowl. Discov. Data*, 2(1):1–30, 2008.

[Har99] Michael Harries. Splice-2 comparative evaluation: Electricity pricing. Technical report, The University of South Wales, 1999.

[HD03] Geoff Hulten and Pedro Domingos. VFML – a toolkit for mining high-speed time-changing data streams. 2003.

[HJWZ95] J. Hein, T. Jiang, L. Wang, and K. Zhang. On the complexity of comparing evolutionary trees. In Z. Galil and E. Ukkonen, editors, *Proceedings of the 6th Annual Symposium on Combinatorial Pattern Matching*, number 937, pages 177–190, Espoo, Finland, 1995. Springer-Verlag, Berlin.

[HK06] Jiawei Han and Micheline Kamber. *Data Mining: Concepts and Techniques.* Morgan Kaufmann Publishers Inc., San Francisco, CA, USA, 2006.

[HKP05] Geoffrey Holmes, Richard Kirkby, and Bernhard Pfahringer. Stress-testing hoeffding trees. In *PKDD*, pages 495–502, 2005.

[HKP07] Geoffrey Holmes, Richard Kirkby, and Bernhard Pfahringer. MOA: Massive Online Analysis. http://sourceforge.net/projects/moa-datastream. 2007.

[HL94] D.P. Helmbold and P.M. Long. Tracking drifting concepts by minimizing disagreements. *Machine Learning*, 14(1):27–45, 1994.

[HMS01] David J. Hand, Heikki Mannila, and Padhraic Smyth. *Principles of Data Mining (Adaptive Computation and Machine Learning).* The MIT Press, August 2001.

[HSD01] G. Hulten, L. Spencer, and P. Domingos. Mining time-changing data streams. In *7th ACM SIGKDD Intl. Conf. on Knowledge Discovery and Data Mining*, pages 97–106, San Francisco, CA, 2001. ACM Press.

[HTF01] Trevor Hastie, Robert Tibshirani, and Jerome Friedman. *The Elements of Statistical Learning: Data Mining, Inference, and Prediction*. Springer, August 2001.

[HW95] M. Herbster and M. K. Warmuth. Tracking the best expert. In *Intl. Conf. on Machine Learning*, pages 286–294, 1995.

[HWC06] Mark Cheng-Enn Hsieh, Yi-Hung Wu, and Arbee L. P. Chen. Discovering frequent tree patterns over data streams. In *SDM*, 2006.

[JCN07a] Yiping Ke James Cheng and Wilfred Ng. Maintaining frequent closed itemsets over a sliding window. *Journal of Intelligent Information Systems*, 2007.

[JCN07b] Yiping Ke James Cheng and Wilfred Ng. A survey on algorithms for mining frequent itemsets over data streams. *Knowledge and Information Systems*, 2007.

[JG06] Nan Jiang and Le Gruenwald. CFI-Stream: mining closed frequent itemsets in data streams. In *KDD '06: Proceedings of the 12th ACM SIGKDD international conference on Knowledge discovery and data mining*, pages 592–597, 2006.

[JMJH04] K. Jacobsson, N. Möller, K.-H. Johansson, and H. Hjalmarsson. Some modeling and estimation issues in control of heterogeneous networks. In *16th Intl. Symposium on Mathematical Theory of Networks and Systems (MTNS2004)*, 2004.

[Kan06] Gopal K Kanji. *100 Statistical Tests*. Sage Publications Ltd, 2006.

[KBDG04] D. Kifer, S. Ben-David, and J. Gehrke. Detecting change in data streams. In *Proc. 30th VLDB Conf., Toronto, Canada*, 2004.

[KBF+00] Ron Kohavi, Carla Brodley, Brian Frasca, Llew Mason, and Zijian Zheng. KDD-Cup 2000 organizers' report: Peeling the onion. *SIGKDD Explorations*, 2(2):86–98, 2000.

[Kir07] Richard Kirkby. *Improving Hoeffding Trees*. PhD thesis, University of Waikato, November 2007.

[KJ00]   R. Klinkenberg and T. Joachims. Detecting concept drift with support vector machines. In *Proc. 17th Intl. Conf. on Machine Learning*, pages 487 – 494, 2000.

[KK02]   Hisashi Kashima and Teruo Koyanagi. Kernels for semi-structured data. In *ICML*, pages 291–298, 2002.

[KKS95]   H. Kautz, M. Kearns, and B. Selman. Horn approximations of empirical data. *Artificial Intelligence*, 74(1):129–145, 1995.

[KM04]   Taku Kudo and Yuji Matsumoto. A boosting algorithm for classification of semi-structured text. In *EMNLP*, pages 301–308, 2004.

[KMM04]   Taku Kudo, Eisaku Maeda, and Yuji Matsumoto. An application of boosting to graph classification. In *NIPS*, 2004.

[Knu97]   Donald E. Knuth. *The Art of Computer Programming, Volume 1 (3rd ed.): Fundamental Algorithms*. Addison Wesley Longman Publishing Co., Inc., Redwood City, CA, USA, 1997.

[Knu05]   Donald E. Knuth. *The Art of Computer Programming, Volume 4, Fascicle 4: The: Generating All Trees–History of Combinatorial Generation*. Addison-Wesley Professional, 2005.

[KPR90]   Anthony Kuh, Thomas Petsche, and Ronald L. Rivest. Learning time-varying concepts. In *NIPS-3: Proceedings of the 1990 conference on Advances in neural information processing systems 3*, pages 183–189, San Francisco, CA, USA, 1990. Morgan Kaufmann Publishers Inc.

[Lan95]   Pat Langley. *Elements of Machine Learning*. Morgan Kaufmann, September 1995.

[Las02]   M. Last. Online classification of nonstationary data streams. *Intelligent Data Analysis*, 6(2):129–147, 2002.

[LB01]   G.S. Linoff and M.J.A. Berry. *Mining the Web. Transforming Customer Data into Customer Value*. John Wiley & Sons, New York, 2001.

[LERP01]   Fabrizio Luccio, Antonio Mesa Enriquez, Pablo Olivares Rieumont, and Linda Pagli. Exact rooted subtree matching in sublinear time. Technical Report TR-01-14, Università Di Pisa, 2001.

[LERP04]   Fabrizio Luccio, Antonio Mesa Enriquez, Pablo Olivares Rieumont, and Linda Pagli. Bottom-up subtree isomorphism for unordered labeled trees, 2004.

BIBLIOGRAPHY

[LG99] Tyng-Luh Liu and Davi Geiger. Approximate tree matching and shape similarity. In *ICCV*, pages 456–462, 1999.

[LSL06] Hua-Fu Li, Man-Kwan Shan, and Suh-Yin Lee. Online mining of frequent query trees over xml data streams. In *WWW '06: Proceedings of the 15th international conference on World Wide Web*, pages 959–960, 2006.

[Luc08] Claudio Lucchese. *High Performance Closed Frequent Itemsets Mining inspired by Emerging Computer Architectures*. PhD thesis, Università Ca' Foscari di Venezia, February 2008.

[MAR96] Manish Mehta, Rakesh Agrawal, and Jorma Rissanen. SLIQ: A fast scalable classifier for data mining. In *EDBT '96*, pages 18–32, London, UK, 1996. Springer-Verlag.

[MD97] Dragos D. Margineantu and Thomas G. Dietterich. Pruning adaptive boosting. In *ICML '97*, pages 211–218, 1997.

[Mit97] Thomas Mitchell. *Machine Learning*. McGraw-Hill Education (ISE Editions), October 1997.

[MN02] Albert Meyer and Radhika Nagpal. Mathematics for computer science. In *Course Notes*, Cambridge, Massachusetts, 2002. Massachusetts Institute of Technology.

[MR95] Rajeev Motwani and Prabhakar Raghavan. *Randomized Algorithms*. Cambridge University Press, United Kingdom, 1995.

[MR05] Oded Maimon and Lior Rokach, editors. *The Data Mining and Knowledge Discovery Handbook*. Springer, 2005.

[Mut03] S. Muthukrishnan. Data streams: Algorithms and applications. In *Proc. 14th Annual ACM-SIAM Symposium on Discrete Algorithms*, 2003.

[NK03] Siegfried Nijssen and Joost N. Kok. Efficient discovery of frequent unordered trees. In *First International Workshop on Mining Graphs, Trees and Sequences*, pages 55–64, 2003.

[NK07] Anand Narasimhamurthy and Ludmila I. Kuncheva. A framework for generating data to simulate changing environments. In *AIAP'07*, pages 384–389, 2007.

[NU03] Shin-ichi Nakano and Takeaki Uno. Efficient generation of rooted trees. *National Institute for Informatics (Japan), Tech. Rep. NII-2003-005e*, 2003.

[OMM+02] Liadan O'Callaghan, Nina Mishra, Adam Meyerson, Sudipto Guha, and Rajeev Motwani. Streaming-data algorithms for high-quality clustering. In *Proceedings of IEEE International Conference on Data Engineering*, March 2002.

[OR01a] N. Oza and S. Russell. Online bagging and boosting. In *Artificial Intelligence and Statistics 2001*, pages 105–112. Morgan Kaufmann, 2001.

[OR01b] Nikunj C. Oza and Stuart Russell. Experimental comparisons of online and batch versions of bagging and boosting. In *KDD '01*, pages 359–364, August 2001.

[Ord03] C. Ordonez. Clustering binary data streams with k-means. In *ACM SIGMOD Workshop on Research Issues on Data Mining and Knowledge Discovery*, 2003.

[Pag54] E. S. Page. Continuous inspection schemes. *Biometrika*, 41(1/2):100–115, 1954.

[PFB03] S. Papadimitriou, C. Faloutsos, and A. Brockwell. Adaptive, hands-off stream mining. In *29th International Conference on Very Large Data Bases VLDB*, 2003.

[PHK07] Bernhard Pfahringer, Geoffrey Holmes, and Richard Kirkby. New options for hoeffding trees. In *AI*, pages 90–99, 2007.

[PJVR08] Raphael Pelossof, Michael Jones, Ilia Vovsha, and Cynthia Rudin. Online coordinate boosting. 2008.

[PKZ01] J. Punin, M. Krishnamoorthy, and M. Zaki. LOGML: Log markup language for web usage mining. In *WEBKDD Workshop (with SIGKDD)*, 2001.

[PM04] Sankar K. Pal and Pabitra Mitra. *Pattern Recognition Algorithms for Data Mining: Scalability, Knowledge Discovery, and Soft Granular Computing*. Chapman & Hall, Ltd., London, UK, UK, 2004.

[PT02] John L. Pfaltz and Christopher M. Taylor. Scientific knowledge discovery through iterative transformations of concept lattices. In *Workshop on Discrete Math. and Data Mining at SIAM DM Conference*, pages 65–74, 2002.

[Qui93] Ross J. Quinlan. *C4.5: Programs for Machine Learning (Morgan Kaufmann Series in Machine Learning)*. Morgan Kaufmann, January 1993.

[Rey06]   Nima Reyhani. Noise variance estimation for function approximation. Master's thesis, Helsinki University of Technology, March 2006.

[Rob00]   S. W. Roberts. Control chart tests based on geometric moving averages. *Technometrics*, 42(1):97–101, 2000.

[SAM96]   John C. Shafer, Rakesh Agrawal, and Manish Mehta. SPRINT: A scalable parallel classifier for data mining. In *VLDB '96*, pages 544–555, 1996.

[SEG05]   T. Schön, A. Eidehall, and F. Gustafsson. Lane departure detection for improved road geometry estimation. Technical Report LiTH-ISY-R-2714, Dept. of Electrical Engineering, Linköping University, SE-581 83 Linköping, Sweden, Dec 2005.

[SG86]   Jeffrey C. Schlimmer and Richard H. Granger. Incremental learning from noisy data. *Machine Learning*, 1(3):317–354, 1986.

[SK01]   W. Nick Street and YongSeog Kim. A streaming ensemble algorithm (SEA) for large-scale classification. In *KDD '01: Proceedings of the seventh ACM SIGKDD international conference on Knowledge discovery and data mining*, pages 377–382, New York, NY, USA, 2001. ACM Press.

[Sta03]   Kenneth Stanley. Learning concept drift with a committee of decision trees. Technical Report AI Technical Report 03-302, Department of Computer Science, University of Texas at Austin, Trinity College, 2003.

[SWZ04]   Dennis Shasha, Jason T. L. Wang, and Sen Zhang. Unordered tree mining with applications to phylogeny. In *ICDE '04: Proceedings of the 20th International Conference on Data Engineering*, page 708, Washington, DC, USA, 2004. IEEE Computer Society.

[SYC+07]   Guojie Song, Dongqing Yang, Bin Cui, Baihua Zheng, Yunfeng Liu, and Kunqing Xie. CLAIM: An efficient method for relaxed frequent closed itemsets mining over stream data. In *DASFAA*, pages 664–675, 2007.

[TRS04]   Alexandre Termier, Marie-Christine Rousset, and Michèle Sebag. DRYADE: a new approach for discovering closed frequent trees in heterogeneous tree databases. In *ICDM*, pages 543–546, 2004.

[TRS+08] Alexandre Termier, Marie-Christine Rousset, Michèle Sebag, Kouzou Ohara, Takashi Washio, and Hiroshi Motoda. DryadeParent, an efficient and robust closed attribute tree mining algorithm. *IEEE Trans. Knowl. Data Eng.*, 20(3):300–320, 2008.

[Tsy04] Alexey Tsymbal. The problem of concept drift: Definitions and related work. Technical Report TCD-CS-2004-15, Department of Computer Science, University of Dublin, Trinity College, 2004.

[Val02] Gabriel Valiente. *Algorithms on Trees and Graphs*. Springer-Verlag, Berlin, 2002.

[WB95] G. Welch and G. Bishop. An introduction to the Kalman Filter. Technical report, University of North Carolina at Chapel Hill, Chapel Hill, NC, USA, 1995.

[WF05] Ian H. Witten and Eibe Frank. *Data Mining: Practical Machine Learning Tools and Techniques*. Morgan Kaufmann Series in Data Management Systems. Morgan Kaufmann, second edition, June 2005.

[WFYH03] H. Wang, W. Fan, P. Yun, and J. Han. Mining concept-drifting data streams using ensemble classifiers. In *ACM SIGKDD*, 2003.

[Wil94] M. Wild. A theory of finite closure spaces based on implications. *Advances in Mathematics*, 108:118–139(22), September 1994.

[WIZD04] Sholom Weiss, Nitin Indurkhya, Tong Zhang, and Fred Damerau. *Text Mining: Predictive Methods for Analyzing Unstructured Information*. SpringerVerlag, 2004.

[WK96] G. Widmer and M. Kubat. Learning in the presence of concept drift and hidden contexts. *Machine Learning*, 23(1):69–101, 1996.

[XYLD03] Yongqiao Xiao, Jenq-Foung Yao, Zhigang Li, and Margaret H. Dunham. Efficient data mining for maximal frequent subtrees. In *ICDM '03: Proceedings of the Third IEEE International Conference on Data Mining*, page 379, Washington, DC, USA, 2003. IEEE Computer Society.

[YH02] Xifeng Yan and Jiawei Han. gSpan: Graph-based substructure pattern mining. In *ICDM '02: Proceedings of the 2002*

BIBLIOGRAPHY

IEEE International Conference on Data Mining (ICDM'02), page 721, Washington, DC, USA, 2002. IEEE Computer Society.

[YH03] Xifeng Yan and Jiawei Han. CloseGraph: mining closed frequent graph patterns. In *KDD '03: Proceedings of the ninth ACM SIGKDD international conference on Knowledge discovery and data mining*, pages 286–295, New York, NY, USA, 2003. ACM Press.

[YHA03] Xifeng Yan, Jiawei Han, and Ramin Afshar. CloSpan: Mining closed sequential patterns in large databases. In *SDM*, 2003.

[YZH05] Xifeng Yan, X. Jasmine Zhou, and Jiawei Han. Mining closed relational graphs with connectivity constraints. In *KDD '05: Proceedings of the eleventh ACM SIGKDD international conference on Knowledge discovery in data mining*, pages 324–333, New York, NY, USA, 2005. ACM.

[ZA03] Mohammed J. Zaki and Charu C. Aggarwal. Xrules: an effective structural classifier for xml data. In *KDD '03: Proceedings of the ninth ACM SIGKDD international conference on Knowledge discovery and data mining*, pages 316–325, New York, NY, USA, 2003. ACM.

[Zak02] Mohammed J. Zaki. Efficiently mining frequent trees in a forest. In *8th ACM SIGKDD International Conference on Knowledge Discovery and Data Mining*, 2002.

[Zak05] Mohammed Javeed Zaki. Efficiently mining frequent embedded unordered trees. *Fundam. Inform.*, 66(1-2):33–52, 2005.

[ZPD+05] Mohammed Javeed Zaki, Nagender Parimi, Nilanjana De, Feng Gao, Benjarath Phoophakdee, Joe Urban, Vineet Chaoji, Mohammad Al Hasan, and Saeed Salem. Towards generic pattern mining. In *ICFCA*, pages 1–20, 2005.

[ZZS08] Peng Zhang, Xingquan Zhu, and Yong Shi. Categorizing and mining concept drifting data streams. In *KDD '08*, 2008.